The New Idea of a University

The Objects of the College shall be to provide ... all branches of a liberal education ....

University College of Swansea Charter and Statutes as amended June 1993

[Universities] began, as is well known, with their grand aim directed on Theology,—their eye turned earnestly on Heaven. And perhaps, in a sense, it may be still said, the very highest interests of man are virtually intrusted to them. ... what is the nature of this stupendous universe, and what are our relations to it, and to all things knowable by man, or known only to the great Author of man and it. Theology was once the name for all this; all this is still alive for man, however dead the name may grow! In fact, the members of the Church keeping theology in a lively condition—(Laughter)—for the benefit of the whole population, theology was the great object of the Universities. I consider it is the same intrinsically now ....

Thomas Carlyle, *Inaugural Address*, 1866, pp. 11–12

But the religious virtue of knowledge was become a flunkey to the god of material success.

D. H. Lawrence, *The Rainbow*,
ed. Mark Kinkead-Weekes (Penguin edn, 1995, p. 403)

The land was lurching like a galleon steered by a drunken helmsman into the Gothic night of materialism and mailed ballyhoo. The humanities were spat upon; the Arts trampled under foot, the historic sense spurned and ridiculed—in all these haunts of Instruction— those whorehouses of the trades and paid sciences. ... The literary and historic professoriate were all but starved; but they had a specially endowed Window Dressing Faculty with twenty-four branches all of whose professors lived on the scale of Hollywood Stars. It was insupportable.

Ford Madox Ford, unpublished novel *Professor's Progress*, 1939,
quoted in Arthur Mizener, *The Saddest Story*, 1971, p. 458

THE NEW IDEA
OF A UNIVERSITY

Duke Maskell

&

Ian Robinson

Lost was the Nation's Sense, nor could be found,
While the long solemn Unison went round.

IMPRINT
ACADEMIC

Paperback published in 2002 by Imprint Academic
PO Box 1
Thorverton
EX5 5YX
UK

Published in the USA by Imprint Academic
Philosophy Documentation Center
PO Box 7147
Charlottesville, VA
22906-7147

First published in 2001 by Haven Books

ISBN 0-907845-34-7

A full CIP record for this book is available from the British Library
A full CIP record for this book is available from the Library of Congress
Library of Congress number 2002102729

Typeset in Caslon

Contents

Preface

Anecdotes and Judgement

THIRTY YEARS AGO, snootiness about American secondary and higher education was widespread in Britain. The USA was frequently used in British academic circles as a cautionary example. Mass-market culture and television-addiction were thought to have reduced the number of potential American students at the same time as their universities were being swamped by too many students. There, we thought, was the blackboard jungle: the schools had no safeguards like the nationwide standards enforced by our excellent HMIs and visible in our O- and A-level. In the richest nation on earth, students were not properly supported by the state and many had to spend time that should have been given to reading working their way through college. The USA had far too many degree-granting bodies, with the results that there were no common standards and an American first degree often meant nothing: real university work was not started until the postgraduate level, where it could be delayed even longer by things called 'taught masters degrees'. Even research work was probably vitiated by over-specialization and subordination to the department programme of some high-powered professor; but a PhD was necessary because without one work in a university was not obtainable. American academics were often without any security in their posts and were constantly pressured to publish. Our own thorns being different, these were all things we thought we had to be on guard against.

How has it happened then that we have firmly established in Britain exactly the situation we used to attribute (rightly or wrongly) to the USA? Liberal education in England may survive in the twenty-first century, not very conspicuously, at two universities. In Wales (which we know) liberal education has no prospects, and we are not optimistic about its chances in Scotland or Ireland. We think this matters.

*   *   *

Much of this book is what the social scientists sometimes call 'anecdotal': if we can suggest why this is a proper mode of argument part of our work is already done. History is always anecdotal. Statistics, maps, charts come in, but a genuine history is the story of the public experiences of some representative individuals. We think our anecdotes are representative. We write straight out of first-hand experience of a very few institutions and of one subject, the one that used just to be called English. Literature itself consists of anecdotes raised to the level of art. Novelists do not write about life in general, or when they do their readers lose interest, but we are certainly not going to admit that literature is not thinking; our leading example of thought about education is a novel. Literary criticism normally works by comment on well-chosen quotation which by its nature is selective. A critical book rightly practises criticism.

It is also because we are offering criticism that we sometimes write in the first person singular, sometimes in the first person plural. The book is ours, a joint effort for which we are jointly responsible, but different parts arise from different individual experiences, about which we can only speak individually.

I nevertheless had some embarrassment at making detailed public criticisms of colleagues with whom I have worked for many years in reasonable harmony and sometimes friendship, for judgements they made in the reasonable expectation of confidentiality. When, however, they agreed to award high classes for theorizings of a kind I demonstrate below to be intellectually disreputable, the primary university obligation to the pursuit of true judgement had to override ordinary professional reticence. I am grateful, nevertheless, for my participation in university work, and I could not have survived so long had it not been possible for most of my time.

I stuck it out, doing what I could (I say with a clear conscience), but in the end I took 'voluntary redundancy' as the alternative to 'constructive dismissal', a device that would have enabled me to argue to an 'industrial tribunal' that I had been appointed as a lecturer in English Language and Literature, but was now required to acquiesce in the awarding of degrees in nonsense.

Our next step, as people still believing in liberal education, had to be to write this book.

Our hope must be that there are enough survivors of the educated class who have kept their heads down, or joined us in redundancy, to recognize the truth of what we say. We even hope that they can be persuaded to raise their heads, and make a difference. Barefaced power is important, but the educated do have great advantages in forming opinion.

I.R.
October 2000

GENERAL NOTE

Newsletter and *Newyddion* refer to the in-house journal of the University of Wales, Swansea, formerly the University College of Swansea.

Acknowledgements

A version of Chapter 3 appeared in *The Journal of the Philosophy of Education*, July 1999; the article used in Chapter 7 appeared in *The Independent*, 25 October 1990; part of Chapter 9 appeared in *The Spectator*, 6 August 2000. The quotation on the title page is from Pope's *The Dunciad*, Book IV.

I

THE ECONOMIC CASE FOR HIGHER EDUCATION

1   Education as Investment

In general economic success tomorrow will depend on investing in our schools today.

Gordon Brown[1]

Society benefits from higher education to the extent that a graduate pays higher taxes, as well as earning a greater amount post-tax. ... Thirdly, graduates may enhance the productivity of other people in ways not captured in their own incomes (one aspect of so-called externalities).

Dearing Report[2]

LIBERAL EDUCATION is not only not mentioned in either *The Charter for Higher Education*, 1993[3] or the Dearing Report of 1997; both documents are saved from being explicitly enemies of liberal education only by their 'completeness of unconsciousness'[4] that there has ever been any such thing in the world.

Universities are supposed by the *Charter* to 'deliver' a 'service', namely higher education, to 'customers', in two divisions, firstly students, and secondly business, which 'buys' both education and the results of commissioned research. The 'delivery' to students is by way of 'teaching' or 'effective management of... learning', in 'courses', all of which have 'aims and structures' clearly described in advance, and any of which includes 'transferable skills like problem-solving and effective communication'. The standards of these providers of teaching are guaranteed by 'quality assurance systems' which will be 'regularly audited' and will enable applicants to discover 'how well different universities and colleges are performing'.

Each of the phrases within quotation marks, and all of them cumulatively, betray a conception of higher education which is not only not that of the university, but is actively hostile to the university. They will be considered in the necessary detail below.

Education can be thought of in the modernized manner of the *Charter* because of a great discovery, made (like so much of our present civilization) during the 1960s, which has been transforming the whole 'education service' ever since: education is an investment. Education is the same as training; education is useful; education will make us rich.

Historically it has been the other way round: a nation gets rich then uses some of the wealth to endow more universities not as engines of economic growth but as centres of piety, learning and thought. The 'red-brick', 'provincial' universities were founded, as outposts of the spirit of Oxford and Cambridge, *after* the brass had been made out of the muck, and not to make more brass, but because, for instance, 'The rise of modern Universities has accredited an ambassador of poetry to every important capital of industrialism in the country.'[5]

To give just one reminder of the dawn of the new idea in the 1960s, from a source that is a kind of anti-classic:

> First, a simple statement about [education]. There is too little of it. ... Let us be crude. I am not imagining the extreme slowness of our growth in national production. The figures are these: for 1938 let us take the national product as 100 for each case. In the United States it has since gone up to 225; in West Germany to 228; in the OEEC countries on average to 164, and here to under 150 ... [five more lines of figures about GDP]. There is something wrong with us. A good deal of what is wrong, though of course not all, should be put down to our educational deficiencies.[6]

So we needed more education to get our GDP increasing as fast as Germany's. A quarter of a century further on, Snow's policies had still not been fully applied and

> last year, despite the success of a great many British companies, the [average] American produced 20% more.
>
> Now one of the many reasons for that is, a lot of Americans are better trained and educated for their jobs.[7]

Nearly a decade later there was, it seemed, still a long way to go. The incoming Education Minister of the 1997 Labour Government greeted the Dearing Report with, 'Our university system is in crisis. Our competitors in North America and the Far East have more young people going into higher education.' This despite the fact that 'Thirty years ago, one in 20 young [British] people entered higher education. Today the figure is one in three.'[8] One in three is not enough for the economy in the competitive world of the third millennium. Forty years after the great discovery nobody would get a hearing in the Commons on education except by affirming it. If we are still not as rich as we could wish, the reason must still be under-investment and the remedy is, naturally, under the free market as it used to be under socialism, still more education, apparently without limit.

The three establishment parties unanimously turn the great discovery into policy. In the government reshuffle that followed his beating-off of a leadership challenge in 1995, Mr Major reaffirmed his belief in it by amalgamating two ministries and appointing a Minister of *Education and Employment,* an implied cause-and-effect that his Labour successors were happy to keep. Labour outbid Mr Major at its subsequent October conference by announcing its desire for a University *for* Industry, which on assuming power it made haste to found.

So when in 1997 Mr Blair declared his three priorities to be Education, Education, Education, he uttered the wisdom of the age, and was rewarded with the biggest Labour majority in history. 'Invest in Education', as I was exhorted by a Liberal-Democrat poster hoisted in the marginal seat of Hereford the day before the 1997 general election, at which they gained the seat.

The consensus about education only leaves the parties to disagree about which can invest most. The Liberal Democrats, still at a safe distance from office, promised in the same general election campaign to put a penny on income tax to fund more education, and were rewarded by a doubling of their Commons representation; but the parties which have had the chance to Invest in Education have a very good track record that will be hard to beat. According to the latest available figures,[9] education in the UK costs about £38bn a year. This comes nearer to health (£46bn) than to defence, which at £24bn it comfortably exceeds. Education accounts for about 12 per cent of all government spending. Higher education costs about £6bn a year.

The investment is even greater when you take into account contributions by students and parents. In those dark days of minority élites 40 years ago we didn't have to pay a penny for our university fees or living expenses. Students from families rich enough to fail means tests now pay more than £1000 a year to fees and all their living expenses during their university years, and will graduate owing, as a matter of course, £10,000–12,000 or more.

All this could not have been achieved without the wholehearted co-operation of the university bureaucracies, which enthusiastically joined the post-1960s consensus. The 'mission statement' of one university in 1996 expressed the general mood when it declared as one of its principal aims, 'to facilitate regional economic growth and national wealth creation'. Philosophic academics as humane as the authors of *The Universities We Need* are in full accord: 'One of the functions of higher education is to meet the needs of the economy (a point, we should say here and now, that we do not dissent from) ....'[10] The universities' reward has been exponential expansion and the concomitant proliferation of careers and empires.

What a good job, then, that the investment, being so huge, is copper-bottomed and guaranteed by all the parties. They are so confident that none of them even needs to write into its prospectus the kind of warning which all other issuers of prospectuses are forced by law to use: the value of your investments can go down as well as up.

By education—be it in Beauty Science, Philosophy, European Food Studies, Pig Enterprise Management, Sanskrit or Early Childhood Studies with Sports Science—shall ye grow rich. But we are all prone to fears, and some of us to nightmares. What if education were not an investment? What if Mr Blair's election-winning cry of Education, Education, Education really means Money-down-the-drain, Money-down-the-drain, Money-down-the-drain? The facts and figures we need to allay any such fear must surely be abundant and easy to find.

Let us ask about education the questions that are asked about all other investments: what risk is there? and what return on capital? What dividends may education be expected to pay and to quite whom? It is a testimony to the strength of our belief in education as investment that such simple questions are hardly ever asked. They do nevertheless appear, though not in a way that attracts any attention, in the Dearing Report.

The Report doesn't doubt, of course, that higher education is a very good thing but, in its main part, doesn't make it clear quite who it's a good thing for. The individual student, it says, can make it a good thing for himself: we must 'encourage the student to see him/herself as an investor in receipt of a service, and to seek, as an investor, value for money and a good return from the invest-ment.' [11] But whether or not the tax-payer can do the same is something it (with good reason—as we shall see) can't make up its mind about. Although it does call the £6bn of taxes that goes into higher education every year an 'invest-ment', with a 'backlog' which needs to be 'addressed', it also calls it 'costs', 'expenditure' and 'funding', and looks forward to the government's 'delivering' a reduction in it.

Fortunately, the main report has attached to it two sub-reports by professional economists which do make it clear what returns graduates and tax-payers are each likely to get, no. 7 by Colin Sausman and James Steel of the Department of Education and Employment, on the 'Contribution of graduates to the economy: rates of return', and no. 8 by Professor Norman Gemmell of the Department of Economics, University of Nottingham, on 'Externalities to higher education: a review of the new growth literature'. These have the authority of the best economic judgement (in the government's judgement) the government could buy. Whatever economic case these two reports make out for the expansion is officially the economic case for the expansion. And the economic case for expansion is the official case for expansion. What other case, official or unofficial, could there be?

These two reports ought to be well-known—by everyone who pays taxes and especially by those who haven't got degrees. And no-one ought to be put off by the fact that they are technical reports written by economists, for, far from it being the case that only economists can understand them, economists are the last people (the authors included) likely to understand them.

So *is* higher education a good investment? Well, for many graduates, for many years, it has been, and its value as investment is easily understood. The student's investment is what he pays in fees and what he loses in (net) earnings during the period of study; his return is the higher net wages he can expect to earn over a working lifetime as a graduate and then the higher pension.[12] This is what the economists call the 'private rate of return'. If the graduate's costs are low enough, for instance because of generous subsidy by the state from taxes, and if the higher earnings are high enough, for instance in part because some jobs are reserved for graduates, it makes sound financial sense to get a degree. According to Sausman and Steel, the average yield has probably been about 12.5 per cent a year (Table 2.2).

The graduate's investment has some peculiarities. In one way it is rather like the purchase of an annuity. The capital invested in education is not retrievable and vanishes on the retirement or death of the graduate.[13] In another way educational investment is very unlike an annuity, and indeed almost any other kind of investment, in that it only begins to pay dividends when you also in person work hard enough to earn them. It is not so with dividends on shares. The workers work and the shareholders are paid dividends. What allowance should be made for this peculiarity in thinking about the return on educational investment nobody seems to have asked. There are other questions, too, about whether the education causes the graduate's increased income or whether the relation is more problematic. And then Sausman's and Steel's calculations are based on figures ten or more years old. In the intervening years the proportion of the population doing degrees has increased very considerably and grants have been replaced by fees and loans, so the likelihood is that the economic value of a degree is less than it was. Still, let us accept the best current official figures. Given government subsidies, the return is not bad for those who get it. The question is, what about everyone else?

The financial benefit their education confers on those with degrees supplies in itself no clue as to whether or not a large higher education system sustained by subsidies makes good economic sense either for non-graduates or for the economy as a whole. Do non-graduates benefit economically from subsidizing the education of graduates? If they don't, where is the justice of the subsidy and where is the political case for continuing to expand higher education through the tax system? If they don't, can there even be any economic case for the expansion? Professor Gemmell says,

> If the gains from HE (in the form of higher wages) are all reaped by graduates themselves there is no immediate economic case for subsidising the HE system. State-funded education would merely be taxing some individuals (with resulting efficiency losses) in order to enhance the private gains to others. Indeed the

subsidy will encourage some individuals at the margin to undertake a socially wasteful investment [1.3].

So, the semi-official (and wholly unpublicized) view seems to be that if it were only the graduates themselves who benefited from their subsidized education it would be both unjust and bad for the economy. Well, is it?

On the assumptions (which we will have more to say about later) that graduates are more productive than non-graduates, that it is their education that makes them so and that their greater productivity is measured by their higher pay, Sausman and Steel are able to calculate the 'standard social rate of return' —the economic benefit society as a whole gets from graduates, which is analogous to the 'private rate' which the graduates themselves get. The method of calculation is the same as that for the 'private rate' but the measures are somewhat different, and the results are more problematic because some of the costs and benefits cannot be measured directly but have to be inferred from proxies. The costs are the full cost of tuition and the GDP lost to the economy as measured by the students' foregone earnings. The benefit is the supposed higher productivity of graduates as measured by the greater cost of employing them, i.e. higher gross wages plus employers' higher national insurance and pension contributions. The 'standard social rate of return' accounts for the first two ways in which, Dearing says (see the start to the chapter), graduates benefit society as a whole, by earning more after tax and by paying more tax.

But economists also suppose that graduates are not only more productive themselves but make the non-graduates around them, both in their own and other firms, more productive too: in the phraseology of economics, there are beneficial 'externalities' or 'spillovers' to higher education, what a non-economist might think of as 'crumbs' (as in 'from a rich man's table'). Professor Gemmell again:

> If higher education does render educated individuals more productive, the case for subsidising them rests on there being beneficial spillovers (externalities) to others. There may be spillovers both within and between firms so that gains to the economy as a whole exceed those accruing to the educated individuals [1.4].

This is Dearing's third way. These three ways in which graduates, as a class, are supposed to benefit the economy need looking at more closely. Numbered headings might be helpful.

I. WAYS ONE AND TWO—EARNING MORE AFTER TAX AND PAYING HIGHER TAXES—THE 'STANDARD SOCIAL RATE OF RETURN'

From the raw results of Sausman's and Steel's calculations, it might sound to a non-economist as if everyone without a degree does quite well from their compulsory tax-investment in the education of people with them, for they share a return on the investment, apparently, of about 8 per cent (Table 2.1), which, though less than the 12.5 per cent the graduates themselves get, still sounds pretty good. But what non-economists are unlikely to guess is that this supposititious benefit to non-graduates is deduced almost entirely from the higher pay of the graduates. Whether the higher wages and taxes do measure higher productivity is a question we shall raise below but, whether or not, it is surely startling to realize, if we are looking for the economic benefits to non-graduates, that it would make no difference at all to the so-called standard social rate of return calculation if, as Professor Gemmell suggests is possible, 'the gains from HE [were] all reaped by the graduates themselves' (1.3). Even if the non-graduates got not a sniff of any benefits going, by way of taxation or otherwise, they would still be reckoned, according to the—what shall we call them?—counter-intuitive accounting procedures used by economists, to enjoy 'a standard social rate of return' on their subsidy of other people's education of 8 per cent. It's as if someone else could enjoy benefits on your behalf.

It would equally make no difference to the social rate of return, of course, if the Chancellor (like the Sultan in the story below) took all the graduates' higher earnings in tax. It would still make no difference if he handed it over to the non-graduates straight away.

The economist father of a friend of my son's explained the point to me. 'The *distribution* of the benefits,' he said, 'has nothing to do with Economics. The "distribution problem" belongs in Ethics.' He illustrated the point. 'Suppose,' he said, 'there was a very poor country which, because oil was discovered there, became, in a very short time, immensely rich; but all the riches were taken by the Sultan for himself; and not only that, but the Sultan, being a cruel and tyrannical man, used his new riches to increase his own power and to rob and oppress his subjects, making everyone but himself even poorer and more wretched than they had been before. Now, is that country, as a whole, richer or poorer than before? In the eyes of us economists, the country *as a whole*, all its increased poverty and wretchedness notwithstanding, is immensely richer and has come to enjoy a marvellously high "social rate of return" on its oil investment. After all, we mustn't forget that the Sultan himself belongs to the country (even if it does seem rather as if it's the country that belongs to him). All we economists are interested is total GDP. Everything after that is "the distribution problem". Nothing to do with us, old chap. You want someone in Ethics, down the road.'

Even if the greater productivity of graduates were proven, the 'standard social return' would not, then, in itself justify any subsidies to higher education. It does not—as it seems to—answer the question whether it is just or not for non-graduates to subsidize the education of graduates; and it does not—as it seems to—answer the question whether or not those subsidies benefit the economy as a whole. The economic question is whether public subsidy is more efficient than a free market in which all the investment comes from the graduate. Nobody discusses this. The economic case for subsidy must then depend upon:

II. THE THIRD WAY—CRUMBS
A. The theory

First of all, are there any economic theories that posit the existence of crumbs? Well, unfortunately, Professor Gemmell says, 'Traditional human capital theory has ... little to say about externalities', 'neo-classical growth theory [provides] no scope for externalities', 'traditional growth theory [gives] no role for education to play in the creation of "human capital"' (2.1). There have been, however, some 'recent advances in growth theory'. These new theories have (italics added) '*proposed* ... mechanisms whereby education affects productivity levels' but they

> typically incorporate ... *crucial assumptions* [*the*] *empirical basis* [*of which*] *is essentially unknown*. ... Firms are *assumed* not to be able fully to appropriate the gains from the production of knowledge so that spillovers occur.[14]

There are three types of new theory: '"sources of growth" equation models', an 'augmented "Solow" or neo-classical model' and 'endogenous growth models'. Unfortunately, only the third allows for crumbs (2.7, 2.13–14). Moreover, although it does make an 'assumption' that would 'allow' them to be 'inferred' (2.14),

> identifying the existence and extent of education externalities ... is ... fraught with difficulties ... and, until the methodologies and data used in empirical studies are developed further, all results should be treated with caution [3.3].

And that's the sum total of the theoretical justification for subsidizing a large higher education system.

B. The evidence
1. Direct or experimental

There is none.

> To identify HE externalities we ... need to observe the productivity of 'uneducated' workers with and without the presence of their HE-educated colleagues. Unfortunately such controlled experiments are almost never possible [1.7].

2. Indirect

In the absence of direct experimental evidence, we have to rely on inferences made from large-scale statistical comparisons between economies with more and less developed higher education systems. These might be comparisons between the economies of different countries ('cross-country') or between earlier and later stages in the development of the economy of a single country ('time-series'). Both studies belong to 'macro' economics, in contrast to the study of the wages of graduates dealt with earlier, which belongs to 'micro' economics.

(a) Findings

There is some tentative evidence that [there] may [be] indicati[ons of] possible externalities.

OECD countries which expanded their higher education more rapidly … experienced faster growth. The direction of causation however is unclear.

The only specific group of graduates which have been examined for productivity growth effects are 'scientists and engineers'.

There is some evidence that education affects physical capital investment … which … raises income growth rates, though the specific role of higher education is less clear.

There is increasing evidence that research and development activities may be important for productivity growth and … spillover. … The additional link from higher education to research and development (R&D) is yet to be confirmed but some evidence is beginning to suggest that HE may be important.

The most direct evidence on HE externalities comes from comparisons of macro and micro rate of return estimates. There are currently very few of the former, but present evidence suggests, at most, very modest upward revision of standard social rates of return to account for externalities.[15]

(b) Warnings
(i) General (italics original)

data *quality* that is very different … and … proxy variables (of varying degrees of accuracy) [are used] because conceptually more appropriate variables are not available [3.6].

A particular problem concerns human capital measurement. To capture the production externalities of higher education it is clearly necessary to have an accurate measure of the extent to which HE augments the quality of labour input. However, measuring the output of education in general, and HE in particular, is notoriously difficult. As a result input measures tend to be used. … It is very difficult to know how close these proxies are to their conceptual equivalents [3.7].

11

The cross-section regression methodology is a useful means of identifying *correlations* between variables of interest (e.g. HE and income growth). ... It is less good at identifying *causation* from one variable to another, and most regression studies make prior assumptions regarding causality with, at best, limited testing of these assumptions [3.8].

(ii) About 'cross-country' comparisons

One 'strange' finding of 'the most comprehensive evidence from cross-section regressions' is that 'female education (both secondary and tertiary) appears to be inversely related to growth' (3.11); another study throws up the 'puzzle' that although 'the number of scientists and engineers per capita is found to be significant ... similarly strong effects for years of university educational attainment' are not (3.12); and then another couple of studies 'report cross-section regression results in which educational attainment variables appear to be *negatively* related to growth' (3.15). Professor Gemmell sums up this section:

> Cross-section regression studies of growth have numerous methodological drawbacks and much more testing on better quality educational data, particularly for higher education, is required before firm conclusions can be drawn on the direct effect of education on economic growth [3.19].

He does immediately go on to say, 'In my view, the weight of evidence is increasingly that education is positively associated with income growth, and higher education seems to be the most important variable' (3.19). But, as he has already himself pointed out, this does nothing to explain income growth; there is no claim to have established a 'direction of causality'. All it tells us is that when people have a lot of money they also very often have a lot of education (the same goes for wine). It's not a weight of evidence; it's a weight of doubt.

(iii) About 'time-series' comparisons

This kind of study is 'potentially more reliable ... not least because it avoids the questionable assumptions implicit in much cross-country work'. Unfortunately, 'in practice, limited numbers of observations often restricts [*sic*] the use of time-series methods (or their sophistication) and to date there are few studies of this sort' (3.20).

C. Conclusion

> The evidence ... for educational externalities (and especially for those associated with higher education) is still very limited in scope and extent. Any conclusions ... must be regarded as tentative, not least because the quality of both the available data and testing methodologies are [*sic*] ... flawed [4.4].

12

So there you are. *Everything* is tentative and uncertain—data, methods, conclusions. It's all guesswork. And what do you call an investment based on guesswork? A gamble? Well, you might, except that in this case the government goes on betting, year after year, with our money, without having any idea whether we're winning or losing. And calls it an investment. What independent financial advisor would recommend that the Chancellor put his own money where he puts our taxes? An independent financial advisor? A bookie would have scruples.

If no 'externalities' can be reliably identified, then, in Professor Gemmell's words, 'there is no immediate economic case for subsidising the HE system. State-funded education [is] merely taxing some individuals (with resulting efficiency losses) in order to enhance the private gains to others ... a socially wasteful investment'—that is, no investment at all. The entire state-subsidized expansion of higher education, maintained by so many governments over so many years, with no semblance of justification offered for it that isn't economic, has been, it seems, a tremendous error, economically. And if the subsidies were withdrawn, the grotesquely bloated system they have created would shrink back to something that made economic (and educational) sense. The so-called customers would be found simply not to exist and the so-called need for this so-called education would vanish with them. In its present shape and size the whole thing is simply a creation of wastefulness. And that's according to what is in effect the government's own economic advisor, advising a government which, like all its recent predecessors, can't imagine any case for higher education that isn't economic. An investment? It's not even a bet. It's more like throwing money over your shoulder and wishing.

*   *   *

But it isn't just the fact that it has been subsidized through the taxes that makes the fifteen-or-more-fold expansion of the higher education system an error. It would still be an error, we believe, however it were funded. The case for it depends on two assumptions (made as a matter of routine by Sausman and Steel but questioned by Gemmell) which any ordinarily prudent investor would want to query: that people with degrees are more productive than those without and that it is their education that makes them so. Research is supposed to be one of the things that make universities an investment; research into the productivity conferred by the degrees they award is hardly ever undertaken and has never yet produced significant results.

How would you measure how much more productive a graduate was than a non-graduate? As Professor Gemmell says (and as one of us wrote before either had read Professor Gemmell), you'd have to observe the two performing similar tasks and see whether the graduates were more efficient. But, as we saw Professor Gemmell saying, 'Measuring the output of education in general, and HE in particular, is notoriously difficult' (3.7) and 'controlled experiments are almost never possible' (1.7). So the way economists do it is simply by taking the greater income of graduates as a measure of greater productivity: they measure, that is, how much more someone contributes to the economy by measuring how much more he takes from it (his net wages plus whatever else he costs his employer, taxes and national insurance and pension contributions) and treat the one as a proxy for the other. Now this, however scientific a practice, does make for some odd effects of language:

> the economic benefits from graduates ... their higher earnings [Report 7.1]

> the contribution graduates make to the economy ... the high salaries ... they receive [1.1]

These are the wonderland phrases Dearing is echoing when he says, 'Society benefits from higher education to the extent that a graduate [earns] a greater amount post-tax.' If this is how graduates benefit society, it must be more blessed to give than to receive in ways Jesus never dreamt of. Who in his right mind would agree to subsidize someone else's education for the somebody-else to get more pay than himself? What ordinary employer thinks a wage increase in itself evidence of an increase in productivity? It's logic through the looking-glass.

Pay may make, as Sausman and Steel call it, 'a straightforward measure' of productivity, but only in the sense that it is straightforward to make; it's hardly straightforward to think. Do we get what we pay for? Well, perhaps we do, but hardly as surely as we pay for what we get. All an employer can know is whether he is paying the going rate or not; the connection between that rate and the relative productivity of employees of different levels of education is as opaque to him as to any economist, and for the same reason: the experiments that would make it demonstrable can't be performed. The graduate wants more money for his higher qualification and to make up for his lost earnings; the employer is willing to give it him; and they settle, on average, for a certain sum. And that, in the absence of direct comparative evidence, is all that is known; and to know anything more is made all the harder by the fact that a great many jobs that graduates do are not open to non-graduates, so there is no direct competition. Nobody knows what part mere custom plays in setting such differentials.

But even if graduates could be shown to be more productive, it still wouldn't follow that it was their education that made them so. As Professor Gemmell says,

> There is a very credible economics literature which suggests that education (including higher education) may be no more than a screening device which allows employers to identify the more able potential employees from the rest. Thus graduates' wages are higher because they are inherently more productive, for example because they work harder or have more innate ability, but not because they are better educated. If this is the case then the current system of HE may simply be providing employers with a privately cheap, but socially expensive (i.e. wasteful), screening system. If firms know that the most productive individuals will choose

14

to go to (state-subsidised) university, then they will select graduates in preference to non-graduates even if education has no effect on their productivity. Likewise, 18 year olds go to university to signal to employers that they are productive. There may still be a case for governments subsidising this 'screening system' if alternative screening devices are less efficient and if there are adverse social consequences from the mismatches which might result, such as unemployment or high labour turnover. However it is quite possible, if employers and/or employees had to fully fund a screening system privately, that they would be able to devise something more efficient than the current HE system [1.2].

Sausman and Steel acknowledge that it may be difficult to be sure how far it is a graduate's education rather than something else about him that makes him more productive (if he is) but they make their uncertainty a pretext for more calculations which any competent auditor would suspect. They rephrase Professor Gemmell's question, 'How can we know whether it is education that does the trick or not?' as 'How much of the trick does education do?' or, in their own terms, what is the correct value for the *alpha* factor? [16]

So what *is* the *alpha* factor?

Sausman and Steel first of all suppose that the higher productivity of a graduate can be portioned up like the higher wages which are supposed to measure it and each portion attributed to a separate, distinguishable cause: so much to family background, so much to innate ability, so much to education etc. These causes are named 'factors'; 'research' assigns each a numerical value; and education is singled out from them all to be distinguished as *alpha*. Sausman and Steel then talk about 'the *alpha* factor' in the tones of scientists investigating something as ordinarily and verifiably real as the stone Dr Johnson kicked in attempted refutation of Berkeley: 'Given the empirical uncertainties over the value of alpha, we present results for alpha values of 0.6 and 0.8', i.e. we are going to attribute between 60 per cent and 80 per cent of the higher productivity of graduates, which we have inferred from their higher wages, to their education—renamed 'level of human capital' (Annexe A, 11). But this is just verbal magic, mumbo-jumbo, superstition in a modern form. Why do they make this attribution? Where do they get their 0.6 and 0.8 from? These figures are 'suggested by the available research evidence' (Annexe A, 11)—which is no doubt as much to be relied on for any practical purpose as the other 'evidence' presented in these two reports. But wouldn't someone intending to risk his money on a new company with their 60–80 per cent in mind ('We must have graduates because of their much greater productivity') want to know how 'evidence' so scanty and imprecise could support figures so exact, and so large?

So who is right, those who like Sausman and Steel think that the education that graduates receive makes them more productive—'creates human capital'—or those others who think it is merely a 'screening device'? To give the crucial words of Professor Gemmell a little more fully:

So, is it possible to discriminate between 'human capital' and 'screening' arguments in any systematic way ... ? Ideally one would hope to observe workers with different levels of education (but otherwise identical) undertaking similar tasks and see whether the more educated performed these tasks more efficiently. ... Unfortunately such controlled experiments are almost never possible [1.7].

And that is Professor Gemmell's last word on the subject. How can we know whether education makes people more productive or not? We can't. We just don't know in any such way as economists understand knowledge. But we invest billions every year on the assumption that we can and do know, all the same. On that assumption we have already increased the numbers in higher education from 1 in 33 to more than 1 in 3. On that assumption Gordon Brown proposed increasing them to 1 in 2 (*Today* programme, 16 June 2000).

If this is investment, put your money under the mattress.

*   *   *

For the layman—the taxpayer in the enforced role of venture capitalist—to be able to judge for himself whether the Dearing audit is favourable or not, he needs to grasp certain oddities, as they may seem, about the science of economics, and especially about the character of the precise-looking numerical methods it uses. Like other sciences, economics employs a vocabulary and methods which, to understand, you have to be expert in; unlike those of the physical sciences they ride on the back of assumptions that anyone might legitimately have an opinion about but which, as it happens, economists themselves, once they have made them, typically have no interest in whatsoever. When an economist assumes that the higher pay of graduates is proportionate to their higher productivity, he doesn't necessarily *think*, in the ordinary sense, that this is so. Making the assumption is just a technical matter for him, necessary to get him to the point at which he can begin to do what he really wants to do, his calculations. Not being able to measure relative productivity directly, he wouldn't be able to measure it at all if he didn't make some such assumption; therefore he makes it; and there's an end of his interest in the matter. Other economists do likewise; and there, if he needs it, is his justification. As Sausman and Steel say of their rate-of-return calculations, they are 'a long-standing economic technique'.

So it is quite possible for methods which are (at least to a layman's eye) expert and mathematically very sophisticated to depend on assumptions and reasonings which are not only unspecialized but imprecise or even crude. The mathematics can be (it is difficult for an outsider not to conclude) a disguise for guesswork or bluff.[17]

Parts of Gemmell's report a layman might think were mathematics ('Now, this looks something *like* an audit'):

Sources-of-growth equations are typically based on an aggregate Cobb-Douglas production function such as equation (E1) above which, when differentiated gives a relationship between the growth of output and the growth of factor inputs. For example, adapting (E1) to include human capital, H, gives:

$$Y = AK^a l^b H^g \qquad a + b + g = 1 \qquad (E3)$$

(E3) can be written as:

$$y = a + ak + bl + gh \qquad\qquad (E3.1)$$

where, again, lower case letters represent growth rates for their upper case equivalents and a is the growth of total factor productivity (TFP) [2.11].

But the certainty of the part (we presume it is that) is not shared by the whole. Above, below, all around the mathematical certainties are all sorts of uncertainties. The mathematical part—however cogent in itself—is really just uncertainty mathematized.

And on the other side of this seeming precision is real crudeness. The two words that dominate the conception of education in these two sub-reports (as in the main report itself) are, predictably, 'skills' and 'knowledge'. For Sausman and Steel the end result of education is 'appropriate labour skills', of two kinds (the 'specific skills gained from studying for particular degrees' and the 'superior analytical and communication skills' gained from any and all degrees) and many levels. Degree level skills are, of course, of a 'higher level' than A-level level skills, and, of course, correspondingly more valuable.

If 'skills' sums up your idea of education, as it does for Sausman and Steel, you are hardly free to think that higher qualifications mightn't mean 'more productive'. But you won't be any better off if your vocabulary includes, as Gemmell's does, 'knowledge', not if you think of knowledge as a sort of *stuff* that comes in quantities and may be spoken of in phrases like 'knowledge production' and 'the knowledge accumulation process'. If that's your idea of knowledge, then again, how can you think anything but such things as 'an education sector produces human capital for use in the production sector' (like coal mined for steel manufacture) and 'education creates human capital, which directly affects knowledge accumulation and therefore productivity growth' (which is like nothing recognizable at all)?

And if that's the mental world you live in you'd be better off *not* trying to say what education might mean if not jobs and wages. Otherwise you're likely to find yourself, like Sausman and Steel, defying the philistines by asserting that making money is not the only benefit to be had from education: there are 'consumer benefits' too, which may well include not just better health, 'and hence [lower] public health care costs', but also, even though they are very 'very difficult to quantify', the 'objectives that Robbins identified—promoting the general powers of the mind and the advancement of learning'.

Not to mention the spread of cant and accumulation of humbug.

Even if it were established that we do sensibly to invest in scientists and engineers, there are still to be considered the vast majority of graduates, graduates in the arts and in all those new dubiously vocational subjects like Leisure and Tourism. Isn't it *prima facie* likely that, if the philosophy or history or literary graduate has done some genuine work in his subject and acquired a taste for a kind of thought that is disinterested and contemplative, he will be less suited to the instrumental mental activity required in business? The folk-image of the absent-minded professor may after all, like other folk-images, have a core of truth. (We have met some professors like that.) And will it be any better if the graduate has done no genuine work? Isn't the likelihood that someone who has spent three years being trained to make a fake academic study of something practical and down-to-earth will be by so much made less fit for honest and productive work of any kind? It is often supposed that 'third world' economies are held back by large bureaucracies composed of graduates doing little productive work. How do we know that our increasing 'cohorts' of graduates, with their high salary expectations, are different? Education externalities—Gemmell might reflect—can come in the form of costs as well as benefits.

Take the case of economists themselves (perhaps social scientists generally) who have picked up from beneath the tables of the physical scientists any amount of crumbs and, as a result, are better fed than the physical scientists themselves (Report 7, 2.29). How sure can we be that what are, from their private point of view, undeniably crumbs, aren't, from the social, something more like grit? It may be that economists cost their employers an awful lot of money, but surely we can still ask, in our layman's commonsensical sort of a way, whether they are worth it? On the evidence of these two reports, economists themselves over-rate the importance of the mere calculating faculty. Perhaps their employers do too. On this one vexed question of whether or not there is an economic case for an immense, immensely-subsidized Higher Education System—and remembering that there is upwards of £6bn a year of public money risked—isn't it obvious that the way that economists combine rigour of calculation with looseness of thought is absolutely fatal to their pretensions to being socially useful? Perhaps, in calculating the relative worth of different classes of worker, we should make some allowance for the prejudices of a culture that, although faithless in other ways, has a naïve, if not downright superstitious faith in *technik* and numerical method. What value shall we assign to superstition as a factor—the *beta* factor?—to account for the high salaries economists get?

We propose an experiment, though not a numerically rigorous one. Compare the present remarks about the relative productivity of graduates and non-graduates with those of Drs Sausman and Steel and of Professor Gemmell. Which, the highly paid economists, or the two unwaged ex-lecturers in English literature, are actually more productive on what we believe we have demonstrated to be the vexed question of the value of education as an investment?

Financial history is spangled with curious manias and illusions which otherwise hard-headed people have mistaken for investments (black tulips, the South Seas). The 'investment' in graduates may turn out to be one of them.

Investment remains, until the bubble bursts, the magic word that freezes any possibility of protest. It's an investment that makes internet stocks look like gilt-edged securities; it's an investment on which neither of these literary redundants would dream of throwing away their severance payments. The difference from those advertisements (now banned?) for sure-fire can't-fail gambling systems is that the government itself runs this one and it is compulsory for all taxpayers to participate. This is an 'investment' the evasion of which is a crime.

But bubbles do burst—sometimes because they're pricked.

II

THE OLD IDEA
OF A UNIVERSITY

2 Newman

Thought kindling itself at the fire of living Thought

Thomas Carlyle

ABOUT THE MODERN CONSENSUS-VIEW of the good which is the *telos* of education, making money individually and nationally, we shall say little directly. The just and wise societies are not always the richest. The life of classical Athens would seem to us Spartan, and it took the eye of prophecy to see Old-Testament Israel as a land flowing with milk and honey. Even the best-educated modern Western nation, France, has had its periods of comparative poverty. Conversely the richest societies are not always the best educated. (Look across the Atlantic.) The assent to a world in which the only value is indefinite economic 'growth' is just too degraded for serious discussion. D. H. Lawrence imagined the consequent educational arrangements as what would now be called a 'worst case scenario': 'Teach the three Rs, and then proceed with a certain amount of technical instruction, in preparation for the coming job.' This would replace the ideals like 'to strive to produce ... the perfect citizen' and 'disinterested nobility of heart to enable each one to vote properly at a general election' which in Lawrence's time had already become dead ideals.[1] Now that you can't publish anything whatever without a motto or cry, the DfEE[2] puts on the cover of the pamphlet *Financial Support for Students in 1999/2000* the motto 'It pays to aim higher.' That vision is just too low to be criticized.

What is more, this is not a harmless mistake which has benefited the universities by allowing easier access and consequent expansion. We shall show that in practice the changed notion of what universities are expected to do has damaged them, perhaps beyond repair. Before that, we would like to offer some beliefs about what liberal education really is, and what it really is not.

To join the modern consensus we have first to deny a number of traditional distinctions. To begin with we have to believe that education is the same as training; without this belief the doctrine that universities create wealth would be too implausible. Education is not the same as training nor as being instructed. Until recently these were truths generally known.

Philosophy came into being when Socrates went around Athens as one conscious of knowing little, looking for someone who knew more. The men Socrates talked to, those who had a *techne*, that is had been trained in a useful skill, turned out not to know more than he did because they knew *only* their skills. The distinction between liberal education and useful knowledge persisted strongly when the universities developed in the twelfth and thirteenth Christian centuries. The arts faculties' trivium and quadrivium, the three philosophies, the summit in theology, are all pure thought, of no earthly use. Theology of the kind discussed in the medieval universities was quite unnecessary, for instance, to the parish priests. Training was the province of the guilds. Between Chaucer's Clerk (modern English Philosopher) and his guildsmen there is a great gulf.

If education is not after all the same as training for wealth-creation, what is it? and is education a good? for the individual, for the community? and if so in what sort of ways? There has been classical thinking about education, some of it in English. The proper academic instinct is to begin by looking at what has been said, and the obvious place to start is *The Idea of a University*.

We shall have some adverse comments to make on the great J. H. Newman, so it will be good to recognize in the first place that he did some of the essential thinking, for our language and culture, about university education. Newman, moreover, asks precisely our politicians' question, if they were intelligent enough to ask it: 'What is there to show for the expense of a University; what is the real worth in the market of the article called "a Liberal Education"?':[3]

> Now this is what some great men are very slow to allow; they insist that Education should be confined to some particular and narrow end, and should issue in some definite work, which can be weighed and measured. They argue as if every thing, as well as every person, had its price; and that where there has been a great outlay, they have a right to expect a return in kind. This they call making Education and Instruction 'useful', and 'Utility' becomes their watchword. With a fundamental principle of this nature, they very naturally go on to ask, what there is to show for the expense of a University; what is the real worth in the market, of the article called 'a Liberal Education', on the supposition that it does not teach us definitely how to advance our manufactures, or to improve our lands, or to better our civil economy; or again, if it does not at once make this man a lawyer, that an engineer, and that a surgeon; or at least if it does not lead to discoveries in chemistry, astronomy, geology, magnetism, and science of every kind.[4]

The Idea of a University is Newman's attempt to say what the real worth—even in the market—of 'a Liberal Education' is. The attempt was, in practical terms, for a hundred years and more, triumphantly successful. Newman's idea of the university as providing a liberal education, even to those training for the professions—lawyers, engineers, surgeons and scientists of every kind—and thus making them even better lawyers, engineers, surgeons and scientists of every kind—became *the* idea of the university; and even today, though it may be lost sight of, it hasn't been replaced. The university has been remade not in defiance of Newman but in indifference to him. But he says things that, if anybody paid any attention to them, could not fail to kill instantly our new orthodoxy about the universities making us rich.

He describes the difference made by education:

> The Enlargement consists, not merely in the passive reception into the mind of a number of ideas hitherto unknown to it, but in the mind's energetic and simultaneous action upon and towards and among those new ideas, which are rushing in upon it. It is the action of a formative power, reducing to order and meaning the matter of our acquirements; it is a making the objects of our knowledge subjectively our own, or, to use a familiar word, it is a digestion of what we receive, into the substance of our previous state of thought; and without this no enlargement is said to follow. There is no enlargement, unless there be a comparison of ideas one with another, as they come before the mind, and a systematizing of them. We feel our minds to be growing and expanding *then*, when we not only learn, but refer what we learn to what we know already.[5]

Education is of the whole person, not the acquisition of skills:

> Such knowledge is not a mere extrinsic or accidental advantage, which is ours today and another's tomorrow, which may be got up from a book, and easily forgotten again, which we can command or communicate at our pleasure, which we can borrow for the occasion, carry about in our hand, and take into the market; it is an acquired illumination, it is a habit, a personal possession, and an inward endowment. And this is the reason, why it is more correct, as well as more usual, to speak of a University as a place of education, than of instruction, though, when knowledge is concerned, instruction would at first sight have seemed the more appropriate word. We are instructed, for instance, in manual exercises, in the fine and useful arts, in trades, and in ways of business; for these are methods, which have little or no effect upon the mind itself, are contained in rules committed to memory, tradition, use, and bear upon an end external to themselves. But Education is a higher word; it implies an action upon our mental nature, and the formation of a character; it is something individual and permanent, and is commonly spoken of in connexion with religion and virtue. When then we speak of the communication of Knowledge as being Education, we thereby really imply that that Knowledge is a state or condition of mind; and since cultivation of mind is surely worth seeking for its own sake, we are thus brought once more to the conclusion, which the word 'Liberal' and the word 'Philosophy' have already suggested, that there is a Knowledge, which is desirable, though nothing come of it, as being of itself a treasure, and a sufficient remuneration of years of labour.... [6]

Even though Newman does something here which is shockingly contrary to the habits of all recent, respectable thinkers on the subject, that is, to distinguish between education and instruction as if they were opposites, it is still hard to imagine that anyone who understands this passage will dispute it. Here, moreover, Newman was uttering the generally accepted understanding of his time. With Coleridge's view, 'Our gentry must concern themselves in the *education* as well as the *instruction* of their natural clients and dependents....'[7] Matthew Arnold would not have disagreed. We are not so far gone that what Newman says isn't recognizable as self-evidently true. People are instructed in such things as manual exercises, the fine and useful arts, trades and ways of business, methods for which there are rules; yes. The knowledge involved has little or no effect upon the mind itself and is not valued for its own sake; yes. It is an instrument or power bearing upon an end external to itself and aiming at a result beyond itself; yes.

Newman—rightly—doesn't attempt similarly to say that knowledge of some subjects will guarantee education. Anything, he argues, may be studied as a means to an end—not excluding virtue and religion themselves.[8] Instead Newman emphasizes the character of education as an end in itself: it 'dispenses with the necessity of... looking abroad for any end to rest upon external to itself', it is 'excellent in itself', 'a good ... an end', 'desirable, though nothing come of it, as being of itself a treasure, and a sufficient remuneration of years of labour'.

The idea of education as an end in itself is bound up with another: that what educates us forms us: 'not a mere extrinsic or accidental advantage ... it is an acquired illumination, it is a habit, a personal possession, and an inward endowment;' it has an 'effect upon the mind itself... it implies an action upon our mental nature, and the formation of a character; it is something individual and permanent, and is commonly spoken of in connection with religion and virtue.' And here again Newman was speaking for his age. In Mrs Oliphant's novel *The Curate in Charge*, the Newman position comes out as ordinary educated good sense. Mr Mildmay is on the point of declaring his love (as far as anyone ever does that in Mrs Oliphant) but is in no danger of losing his idea of education:

> 'Yes, I should like to be able to pass an examination and get a—what is it called?— *diplôme*, the French say. With that one's chances are so much better,' said Cicely, with a sigh, 'but I have so little time.'
>
> How the young man's heart swelled in the darkness!
>
> 'Self-culture,' he said, with a half laugh, 'must be disinterested, I fear, to be worthy of the name. It must have no motive but the advancement of your mind for your own sake. It is the culture of you for you, not what you may do with it. It is a state, not a profession.'[9]

Newman is absolutely right, isn't he, in connecting what we value as ends with what we essentially are? Our 'ends' are no mere extrinsic or accidental 'objectives' or 'goals', which we choose—the 'we' that does the choosing being thought of as separate from and set over against what it chooses, like someone choosing from a menu. The idea 'a person' and the idea 'ends' go together. A person values things not just for their usefulness, as instruments and means only, but as goods and ends in themselves. Take away 'ends' and the person collapses, becomes a mere sum of mechanical and random 'behaviours', not a person, but matter in motion.

He is also right, isn't he, to talk here as if it is persons not just minds that are educated? Throughout this passage his whole way of talking excludes the possibility that what he means by 'educated' is 'having a trained mind'—as if education developed our mental capacities much as lifting weights our bodily. He doesn't use the words 'intellect' or 'mind' or their cognates without significant qualification.

He describes both education and what he contrasts it with, instruction, as involving (as how could it not?) activity of mind. Plainly no-one can carry out instructions, or even listen to them, without using his mind—for 'manual exercises' as much as 'fine and useful art, trades and ways of business'. Remembering and applying 'rules' and 'methods' obviously involves the mind. With what do we remember if not our minds? Yet Newman treats all these kinds of mental activity as somehow failing fully to engage 'the mind itself'. When engaged in them, the mind falls short of being fully itself. And that's because (isn't this just what distinguishes between education, the 'higher' thing, and anything lower?) these are activities of the mind which have 'little or no effect upon the mind itself', have no 'action upon our mental nature', do nothing towards 'the formation of a character'; they are mental activities, what elsewhere he calls 'exercises of mind', which 'bear upon an end external to themselves'.

In such activities the mind is used, but *only* used—as an instrument, for ends: of comfort, convenience or necessity, supplied to it from elsewhere, ends that aren't its own. What could be more sharply antithetical to that other 'use' of mind in which it is employed better to discern what its own true ends are, what it is and might be? A kind of use in which the mind discovers its own nature and makes and remakes itself continually anew—Arnold's 'free play of mind'?[10] The mind in this latter sense is what else but the person? An educated mind in this sense is not a trained mind but an educated human being.

And that sense is reinforced when Newman describes the value of a liberal education to society: 'If then a practical end must be assigned to a University course, I say it is that of training good members of society. Its art is the art of social life, and its end is fitness for the world.'[11] We shall come back next chapter to the great question here raised, how education may be for the general good, and to this answer of Newman's. Obviously, educated minds in that sense—of anything like good members of society—are nothing like well-trained or healthy bodies.

It is quite possible to attempt to educate people on the assumption that they are their minds. James Mill tried with his own son, though in fact J. S. Mill's education was, to the extent that they can be separated, even more through the influence of his father than his father's programme. Which, the influence or the programme, was more disastrous may be debated. What a ghastly and horrible childhood he had—not an education but, as Dickens shows in his parody of it in *Hard Times*, a kind of crippling, in particular of the emotions, a trauma from which Mill's *Autobiography* shows him to have made only a very incomplete recovery. An 'experiment' is what J. S. Mill himself calls it, but without noticing what he has said, suggesting rather that the 'experiment' wasn't a success but might have been.

But, although such passages make *The Idea* the obvious place to go for an account and a justification of the university as a university and not a training school for dentists,[12] they don't make it the best or, perhaps, even a good place to go, for it isn't a coherent piece of work. There's a lot that's slack in it, and it suffers badly from equivocation. The trouble is that Newman wants to defend liberal education not just to his own satisfaction and on his own terms but also to the satisfaction and on the terms of his opponents, who want education to be above all else practically useful. He wants to convince them without convincing them they are wrong, to win them over to his side without making it necessary for them to give up their own. He finds it too easy to meet the practical-minded on their own ground, and he does not resist sufficiently the tendency of a wonderfully fluent mind to let eloquence substitute for thought. At this decisive moment, of sticking to the essential difference between education and the learning of useful skills, he should have told himself some such thing as Wittgenstein said to Rhees, 'Go the bloody hard way.'[13] But he didn't.

And we are now paying the price. He convinced Victorian England that education as an end in itself was the best means to the end of Utility, and thus paved the way for the defeat of his own party and the success of his opponents', whose descendants, a hundred and more years later, have noticed that they can have their end without his means.

The fault lies not in the bare fact of his claiming that a liberal education is useful as well as good but in his doing so by a sophistry. He is right not to be content to treat 'the good' and 'the useful' as mere alternatives or opposites, not to want to suggest that a liberal education, in being a good and an end in itself, is useless. Disinterestedness is the greatest of the intellectual virtues, but being disinterested doesn't mean 'serving none of my interests'; I have forms of interest which can only be served by my being disinterested. Newman couldn't have made a convincing *Apologia pro Vita Sua*, a project in which in an obvious way he had an interest, without being disinterested. Disinterestedness was in his interest.

It was the purity of his interest in the truth that enabled him to squash Kingsley as flat as he did (or rather: his disinterestedness did the squashing for him).

But Newman fudges this issue. He wants to put Oxford as well as Rome behind the seminarians, to make them more than bog priests, and perhaps also to make Victorian England educate its governing classes, in a university devoted to the pursuit of the good. And how better to do the latter—given the state of mind of the Victorian England which developed the steam age out of the eighteenth-century enlightenment and then gave birth to ours—than by persuading it that pursuing the good is the best way to catch the useful? Newman tries to justify, to a professional and practically-minded people, an education without any obvious professional or practical purpose, on the grounds that it's the best education, from a professional and practical point of view. The 'best aid to professional and scientific study' is not professional and scientific study itself but 'general culture of mind'. The best preparation for 'the successful prosecution of those merely personal objects'[14] means refusing the first place to them, postponing them, seeming to disparage them.

What is the very best means of gaining your professional ends? Having an education which is an end in itself. It doesn't sound honest, and it isn't. Newman was the last person (*pace* Kingsley) who would ever willingly have lied, but he has succeeded here in pulling the wool over his own eyes.

For a lot of *The Idea* Newman seems to be distinguishing between two kinds of education, 'Useful' and 'Liberal', only in order to deny that one of them is an education at all:

> In the one case it is called Useful Knowledge, in the other Liberal. The same person may cultivate it in both ways at once; but this again is a matter foreign to my subject; here I do but say that there are two ways of using Knowledge, and in matter of fact those who use it in one way are not likely to use it in the other, or at least in a very limited measure. You see, then, Gentlemen, here are two methods of Education; the one aspires to be philosophical, the other to be mechanical; the one rises towards ideas, the other is exhausted upon what is particular and external. Let me not be thought to deny the necessity, or to decry the benefit, of such attention to what is particular and practical, the useful or mechanical arts; life could not go on without them; we owe our daily welfare to them; their exercise is the duty of the many, and we owe to the many a debt of gratitude for fulfilling it. I only say that Knowledge, in proportion as it tends more and more to be particular, ceases to be Knowledge ....[15]

And—the implication seems unavoidable—Education, in proportion as it becomes particular, ceases to be Education.

But isn't there something of a fudge there? There are two uses of knowledge but one consists of not putting it to use and the other deprives it of its character as knowledge? You can use the hammer to knock a nail in or you can use it to ... heft about? But what a funny 'use' that is. Surely 'using knowledge' is a phrase that can properly be used of only one of Newman's two 'ways of using' it? The person who uses knowledge as an instrument for some further, external end of necessity or benefit uses it, but the person who 'uses' knowledge as a good and an end in itself doesn't use it at all—any more than he uses any other aspect of his own 'mental nature' or 'character', any more than he uses his 'religion' or his 'virtue'.

And the fudge isn't just a lapse, of the moment. It's part of a sophistry that undermines Newman's whole argument.

> Gentlemen, I will show you how a liberal education is truly and fully a useful, though it be not a professional education. 'Good' indeed means one thing, and 'useful' means another; but I lay it down as a principle, which will save us a great deal of anxiety, that, though the useful is not always good, the good is always useful. Good is not only good, but reproductive of good; this is one of its attributes; nothing is excellent, beautiful, perfect, desirable for its own sake, but it overflows, and spreads the likeness of itself all round itself. Good is prolific; it is not only good to the eye, but to the taste; it not only attracts us, but it communicates itself; it excites first our admiration and love, then our desire and our gratitude, and that, in proportion to its intenseness and fullness in particular instances. A great good will impart great good. If then the intellect is so excellent a portion of us, and its cultivation so excellent, it is not only beautiful, perfect, admirable, and noble in itself, but in a true and high sense it must be useful to the possessor and to all around him; not useful in any low, mechanical, mercantile sense, but as diffusing good, or as a blessing, or a gift, or power, or a treasure, first to the owner, then through him to the world. I say then, if a liberal education be good, it must necessarily be useful too.[16]

Well ... *okay* ... but rather obviously *not* the kind of usefulness 'some great men' are slow to allow the 'liberal' education Newman advocates. It was hardly diffusings of treasure of *that* sort they hoped a 'useful' education to provide. They were more interested in treasure on earth, of the ordinary bankable variety. Had Newman left it there, he couldn't have been convicted of sophistry but his audience might well have gone away feeling cheated.

But he doesn't leave it there. Claiming usefulness in the 'higher' sense for his idea of the university is only a preliminary to claiming it in the low and mercantile sense too.

He draws a specious analogy between a liberal education and a healthy body: as the latter doesn't of itself give you any particular bodily skill but is a prerequisite for all skills, so a liberal education, while it doesn't of itself make you a lawyer or businessman does enable you to become one more easily and more successfully, and so is useful in the lowest sense you could wish:

> Again, as health ought to precede labour of the body, and as a man in health can do what an unhealthy man cannot do, and as of this health the properties are vigour, energy, agility, graceful carriage and action, manual dexterity, and

endurance of fatigue, so in like manner general culture of mind is the best aid to professional and scientific study, and educated men can do what illiterate cannot; and the man who has learned to think and to reason and to compare and to discriminate and to analyse, who has refined his taste, and formed his judgement, and sharpened his mental vision, will not indeed at once be a lawyer, or a pleader, or an orator, or a statesman, or a physician, or a good landlord, or a man of business, or a soldier, or an engineer, or a chemist, or a geologist, or an antiquarian, but he will be placed in that state of intellect in which he can take up any one of the sciences or callings I have referred to or any other, with an ease, a grace, a versatility, and a success, to which another is a stranger. In this sense then, and as yet I have said but a very few words on a large subject, mental culture is emphatically *useful*.[17]

... That philosophical or liberal education, as I have called it, which is the proper function of a University, if it refuses the foremost place to professional interests, does but postpone them to the formation of the citizen, and, while it subserves the larger interests of philanthropy, prepares also for the successful prosecution of those merely personal objects which at first sight it seems to disparage.[18]

Newman evidently felt the need of the latter passage, which he added after the first edition, as the conclusion of his argument on the point. There, stated with all his lucidity, is Newman's fraudulent promise, which the university went on making to practical men (and taxpayers) for almost 150 years: that if it is left free to pursue the good, it will provide them also with the useful, that cultivating disinterestedness is the way to many self-interested ends, that an education which treats knowledge as its own remuneration will be very remunerative.

And how does Newman square the circle? How does he show that the higher mental culture associated with religion and virtue is emphatically useful in a low and mercantile sense? By a sophistry. Now by meaning one thing by 'mental culture', 'culture of the intellect', 'intellectual culture', 'cultivation of mind' and so on, now by meaning another. 'Mind' and its synonyms are, of course, very slippery words. They can be used to mean something very little short of 'the person'—not excluding all sorts of sensations and apprehensions that are just as much bodily as mental—and they can be used to mean 'conscious mind' only or 'intellect', the intellect as 'excellent' perhaps but, nevertheless, as an excellent 'portion' of the person only.

The 'parallel' between mind and body obviously holds for only the second of these senses. But what Newman does is slip and slide between the two, using the former sense when calling a liberal education a good and an end in itself, using the latter when calling it useful. He slides from 'the mind itself... mental nature... character' through 'mind' to 'intellect... faculties... exercises of mind... intellectual powers' and comes to rest finally, fatally, in the idea of the mind as something which can be not just trained but trained scientifically:

We know, not by a direct and simple vision, not at a glance, but, as it were, by piecemeal and accumulation, by a mental process, by going round an object, by the comparison, the combination, the mutual correction, the continual adaptation, of many partial notions, by the joint application and concentration upon it of many faculties and exercises of mind. Such a union and concert of the intellectual powers, such an enlargement and development, such a comprehensiveness, is necessarily a matter of training. And again, such a training is a matter of rule; it is not mere application, however exemplary, which introduces the mind to truth, nor the reading many books, nor the getting up many subjects, nor the witnessing many experiments, nor the attending many lectures. All this is short of enough; a man may have done it all, yet be lingering in the vestibule of knowledge ... he may have no power at all of advancing one step forward of himself, in consequence of what he has already acquired, no power of discriminating between truth and falsehood, of sifting out the grains of truth from the mass, of arranging things according to their real value, and, if I may use the phrase, of building up ideas. Such a power is the result of a scientific formation of mind ... .[19]

Although he only means by that last phrase something like, 'doing things systematically or methodically' or perhaps even just, as he says a couple of lines later, according to 'discipline and habit', he means something by 'mind' here very different from what he meant by 'the mind itself'.[20] It's true that he says that the proper object of the intellect is truth, and that cultivating the intellect is fitting it to apprehend and contemplate truth, but what he means by 'truth' here is certainly nothing like any truth that might belong with a way and a life; it is more like the modern philosopher's 'truth value' or 'correspondence', more like mere accuracy. As Newman speaks of it here, truth is an 'object'; truth, whatever and however it is, is so independently of our seeing it; we come to discern it by the conscientious employment of 'many faculties and exercises of mind'; learning to employ our minds in this way is 'necessarily' a matter of training; such training is a matter of 'rule', the result of a 'scientific' formation of mind.

Newman is now talking as if what gets educated is not us but mental skills and competencies which we can be trained to develop like muscles. We learn to contemplate truth by exercising the muscles of our mental eye in the same way a 'Bates practitioner' corrects short-sightedness by training the muscles of the bodily eye. This isn't even the analogy he started out with: mental culture as the equivalent of all-round bodily health. The activities of the mind described here are pretty much of the same sort as those which he elsewhere thinks of as not amounting to 'the mind itself'. This takes Newman to the top of a slippery slope at the bottom of which we meet, next century, something we shall mention in due course, 'personal transferable skills'.

The slide is present incipiently even in that phrase 'cultivation of mind'[21] which comes shortly after 'the mind itself'. The idea of the mind as something to be 'cultivated'—by a self or a will which is distinct from it—stands in marked contrast to the idea of the mind as something which is acted upon and formed by its own activity. Whether it's mind or potatoes we cultivate, we know in advance what end we seek, and all we have to do is find the means of obtaining it. We might be pleased by success but we aren't formed by either success or failure. The 'we' that did the cultivating remains as it was.

The other case couldn't be more different. For the mind's activity to have an effect upon the mind itself, act upon its own nature, form its character, that activity can't be a mere adapting of means to ends which are already known; it is the ends of its own activity themselves which the mind is learning to see more clearly. We are learning what to think *for*. We are learning not how to get what we want but what *to* want. It isn't powers that are being developed but the good that is being pursued. 'Truth' now is not accuracy but an aspect of the good; it isn't so much an 'object'—to walk around, scrutinizing—as a virtue, and capable of being lost, and found, but not necessarily in the same place.

Whatever else 'truth' is, it is certainly something that matters. And what could be more common than for thinking and feeling man to discover that what once mattered to him does so no longer—has become not so much false as dead? Hazlitt, for instance, discovering under Coleridge's influence that his own thoughts (in *An Essay on the Principles of Human Action*) had become to him not just untrue but *unthinkable*:

> I sat down to the task shortly afterwards for the twentieth time, got new pens and paper, determined to make clear work of it, wrote a few meagre sentences in the skeleton-style of a mathematical demonstration, stopped half-way down the second page; and after trying in vain to pump up any words, images, notions, apprehensions, facts, or observations, from that gulph of abstraction in which I had plunged myself for four or five years preceding, gave up the attempt as labour in vain, and shed tears of helpless despondency on the blank, unfinished paper. [22]

Now, *that's* what it is for thought to have an effect upon the mind itself. *There's* an instance of education: the differences between the Hazlitt-that-was who wrote the *Essay*, the Hazlitt-in-the-making who could write nothing and *Hazlitt*—who wrote the paragraph just quoted. Hazlitt, educated into the Scottish enlightenment by his father, had to be educated out of it by his new friends: not by their arguments or their opinions but *by them*. With the result that such truth as he was capable of, he discovered, had migrated or changed its form. It was no longer to be found in abstractions and analysis, it had passed into mere anecdote and description; truth not an object to be conscientiously observed but a virtue found in the 'observer' himself. Hazlitt describes there a moment in which truth had ceased to exist for him at all. One sort of truth had gone dead for him and another not yet come to life, that is, he had ceased to be one person but had not yet become another.

This is a way of talking about the matter that makes 'education' and 'society' practically the same thing, as it is for Shakespeare's Orlando, whose complaint at the beginning of *As You Like It* is just that by depriving him of education his eldest brother has deprived him of a gentleman's place in the world. He has been made to feed with hinds. Dickens's equivalent was the blacking factory and Chapter 11 of *David Copperfield*. It's the truth contained in Newman's remarks about the university's art being 'the art of social life' divested of Newman's fallacy of its 'training the mind'. As Hazlitt found, education for good and for ill belongs to the influence that people have on one another. It isn't courses that educate, it's persons, and not always the persons running the courses. If the education is genuine this influence is not of the form 'You must do it this way because I in authority say so' but because the lecturer's authority, that of the whole man or the whole woman, is shown in a mode of judgement the student can recognize as genuine, even when the recognition takes the form of dissent. And '... Successful collaborations often arise fortuitously and spontaneously. They share with friendship a resistance to planning.'[23]

It would be a mistake to think that this view of education, if true at all, is true only of 'the arts'. The force of personal example is what educates (if anything does) in the sciences too. Science, when it has the character of education, is a sociable and co-operative venture in which men and women have a direct personal influence on one another every bit as much as they do in the arts. You can see this in a book like James Watson's *Double Helix*—not because Watson gives it as his opinion that it is so; but because he just can't help showing it to be so. That Watson is plainly, outside science, a foolish man, whose opinions, whether of science or anything else, are of absolutely no interest whatsoever, makes his testimony to the sociability of the scientist's world all the more telling: he shows it like this not because (like Michael Polanyi) he has thought about it but because it can't be shown otherwise.

The 'course'—when it isn't simply a charade—is only a contrivance for providing opportunities for personal influence. In itself the course is inert. On the 'arts' side at least, the 'course' is most what it ought to be when it is least in evidence, when the classroom loses its character as a classroom and when the relations of teacher and taught are subsumed in those of partners in a particularly vivid and engaging conversation. As a friend, made during university days, said with aphoristic complacency—an older man (at thirty-six he seemed very old at the time)—'Seminars aspire to reproduce the talk in the pub the night before.' And as he said to a similar effect on another occasion—only with more emphatic self-congratulation as well as in extenuation of freedoms taken—'But *we* don't stop being students when we step out of the lecture theatre.' He might as easily have said (and perhaps did), 'Nor start when we step into it.'

(It follows that no genuine university can practise 'franchising', by which a university, instead of running a course itself, will let the staff of a college of further education [or whatever] run 'the same' course. 'The college delivers the whole or part of courses, units or programmes that are developed and validated by the HE institution.'[24] This is the effort to apply the sometimes lucrative though risky formula whereby a commercial operation is carried out not by the firm that originated it but by licensees, quality guaranteed by the originator. 'Although the course is delivered outside, our quality procedures still apply.'[25] So the core activity of the new university is courses, whose quality depends on no-one in particular. By definition the franchised course is freed from the influence of those who devised it, and removed from the unpredictable discussions, questions and snags one actually meets in university work. The next step is franchising to computer.)

If 'truth' has a character anything remotely like the development Hazlitt discovered in himself, there can be no question of training the intellect by method and rule, scientifically, to get hold of such truth. All such mental exercises performed on the walkabout round the object are distractions, falsifications, impediments. What lays hold of truth is not exercise but a character allowing itself to be modified by thinking.

Newman was right, we believe, to say that it is a fallacy of Locke and his disciples that 'no education is useful which does not teach us some temporal calling, or some mechanical art, or some physical secret,'[26] but what he calls his own 'solution' is just another fallacy. If education is a good it is neither because it trains dentists nor because it trains intellects which help dentists become dentists more easily, gracefully, versatilely and successfully than they otherwise would.

*   *   *

So who *will* show us what education is, how it may be both a good in itself and, without being training, in some sense useful too? Hazlitt will, when he puts his education to use in 'On My First Acquaintance with Poets'. Wordsworth will in his great poem about the growth of the poet's mind. Coleridge will. Newman himself actually tells us more about education in his *Apologia pro Vita Sua* than in *The Idea of a University*, though not by argument. Carlyle will. Matthew Arnold will. F. R. Leavis will. (What a scandal that *Education and the University* is out of print.) But more even than our distinguished tradition of thinkers on the subject—who from Carlyle to Collingwood and Leavis have understood the necessary connection between the intellectual disciplines and the pursuit of the good, in the formation of character and of an educated class—the great English novelists will. Education isn't just a particular subject a novelist may choose to deal with or not, like the poor law or madhouses, but something that must be part of any serious attempt to represent life. Dickens shows what education is. Lawrence does, especially in *The Rainbow*. But no-one does so more clearly or more convincingly than Jane Austen in *Pride and Prejudice*.

3   Jane Austen,
Leading Authority
on Liberal Education

The thing *I*'m afraid of is ... am I Mary Bennet too?

Brian Crick

A SCENE that often used to be found in the English departments of universities: seven people are sitting around a table, one man and six women, five young, one 'mature'. The man has a text, a letter, which he is familiar with but which none of the women has seen before. The man invites the women to say what they think of it but without—except in hints that take as much reading as the text itself—saying what he himself thinks. The man takes it for granted that what's called for is a judgement and that judging the letter is judging its writer.

Three of the six women aren't capable of thinking disinterestedly about anything because they judge things only by their bearing on themselves. Two of these don't think anything about the letter because all they can think about is men. The third takes to the writer because he seems to think as she does.

Of the other three women, one is a paradigm of academic disinterestedness, but only if that means 'personally, not involved at all'. She is keen to have a say but without, apparently, having anything to say. She has learned from the Biblical injunction, 'Judge not, that ye be not judged,' only as far as not to want to risk a real judgement, one that would lay her open to being judged in her turn. She won't hold the writer to account for his words and won't let herself be held to account for her own. She is perfectly objective and non-judgemental; in some eyes, a model student.

Both remaining women spot something in the letter—the same thing— which if they only follow it up will lead them to a definite judgement: that the writer apologizes for something he isn't responsible for and couldn't be supposed to regret. But where one woman lapses into 'candour' and gives nonsense the credit of sense—'Though it is difficult to guess in what way he can mean to make us the atonement he thinks our due, the wish is certainly to his credit'—the other, alerted by something in the style, follows up the clue she has given herself and, adding it to others, comes by steps, and in doubt, to a firm conclusion:

> Elizabeth was chiefly struck with his extraordinary deference for Lady Catherine, and his kind intention of christening, marrying, and burying his parishioners whenever it were required.
>
> 'He must be an oddity, I think,' said she. 'I cannot make him out.—There is something very pompous in his stile.—And what can he mean by apologising for being next in the entail?—We cannot suppose he would help it, if he could.—Can he be a sensible man, sir?'

And her conclusion is, of course, the man's own, the one he has been looking for and hoping to elicit all along. He is satisfied. He replies, 'No, my dear; I think not. I have great hopes of finding him quite the reverse.'

What could be more like a seminar in an English department (in a way that, on the whole, is to the credit of both seminars and breakfasts) than this family breakfast in Chapter 13 of *Pride and Prejudice*? This is exactly what we used to do under the name of 'practical criticism' until we abandoned it in favour of 'theory'. Such fathers and daughters—or teachers and students—are necessary to one another. It's easy to see why Elizabeth is Mr Bennet's favourite daughter, and why she would make anyone's favourite student. Jane Austen gives us a glimpse of what education is and of how it takes place—not by instruction, but by invitation, accepted or refused or just not noticed in the talk over the table— or in the pub—that seminars aspire to reproduce.

What a peculiar thing that the English should be in so hopeless a state of muddle and confusion about education when their favourite book—most read, best loved—is one of the best and most illuminating things on the subject in their own or any other language. It must mean that they read, and love, *Pride and Prejudice*, without understanding it. There is a piece of educating to be done, to teach them that what they read as a good and an end in itself is also immensely useful and capable of rescuing them from their state of confusion.

For no book has more to say to us about education than *Pride and Prejudice*; and it says it in the way we all most like things to be said, scenically and in art-speech, not discursively by consecutive reasoning and argument but by instances and patterns, showing us what education is and is not (but may be mistaken for) in pictures whose truth our own common sense and everyday experience can confirm.

Now *Pride and Prejudice* isn't about education in the way that *Hard Times* or *Educating Rita* is. *Pride and Prejudice* has plenty of breakfast and dinner scenes but no classrooms. But *Educating Rita* has so little to teach us about education, and *Pride and Prejudice* so much, that (if the respective authors had been anything like equals) one thing the contrast would suggest is that the best place to see education at work is not establishments specially set aside and dedicated to it but in the accidents of daily life. *Educating Rita* is supposed to be about ... well ... educating her, but though we repeatedly see her with her tutor in his room carrying folders which are supposed to contain essays, we don't really see the work that goes on there. We don't learn what work he sets her, how he wants her to go about doing it, what she writes, what criticism he makes of it or how she responds to his criticism. The change in the way she thinks and judges—from 'before' to 'after'—and the means by which it is brought about, are entirely hidden from view. We have to take them on trust. Whereas Jane Austen shows us changes in Elizabeth and Darcy which, however surprisingly, must be seen as education.

It isn't in question whether or not Jane Austen values education as ordinarily understood. For instance, when Elizabeth hears her uncle Mr Gardiner talking to Darcy, she

> could not but be pleased, could not but triumph. It was consoling, that he should know she had some relations for whom there was no need to blush. She listened most attentively to all that passed between them, and gloried in every expression, every sentence of her uncle, which marked his intelligence, his taste, or his good manners.[1]

And the book is full of a kind of disgust with those of its characters who are so variously uneducated: Kitty and Lydia—'silly and ignorant'; Mrs Bennet—'mean understanding, little information'; Mr Collins—'not a sensible man'; Lady Catherine de Bourgh, whose lack of 'breeding' makes Darcy feel ashamed of her, his aunt, just as Elizabeth feels proud of her uncle.

But what is in question, everywhere you look in the book, is what education *is*. Of course, *we* have no difficulty with this question. We know exactly what education is: unproblematic *instruction*; lifelong learning—of facts and skills. And yet those of Jane Austen's characters who share our view are all monsters. 'It shall ever be my earnest endeavour to demean myself with grateful respect towards her Ladyship,' says Mr Collins, obviously a monster of sycophancy with whom we have nothing in common. But Mr Collins is absolutely at one with us in his view of education: 'There can be nothing so advantageous to [young ladies] as instruction.'[2]

And Lady Catherine de Bourgh—'her Ladyship' herself—is another monster, therefore not a bit like us (not even those of us who are Ladies): 'I take no leave of you, Miss Bennet: I send no compliments to your mother. You deserve no such attention. I am most seriously displeased.'[3] But Lady Catherine is *just* like us in her view of education: 'I always say that nothing is to be done in education without steady and regular instruction, and nobody but a governess can give it.'[4]

Mary Bennet we all recognize to be a monster. But she is wonderfully instructed, as though for a circus, a kind of reverse Caliban, a person without a mind made to act as if she had one: not at all like us. And yet Elizabeth Bennet, everybody's favourite character, and intelligent and educable, contradicts us and Mary at once: 'We all love to instruct, though we can teach only what is not worth knowing.'[5]

What are we to make of the fact that it is the monsters who talk like us— saying things that we cannot, at the moment of reading, find to be anything but what Carlyle called jargon, falsity, hearsay and chimera? And that the one who is a pattern of loveable and intelligent womanhood says the exact opposite, with the full authority of her author?

Jane Austen consistently, systematically, presents the instructed mentality as the opposite of the educated, and the reception of instruction as one way of not being educated at all. And not just in *Pride and Prejudice*. Another set of Jane Austen's monsters is the Bertrams, in *Mansfield Park*. When cousin Fanny comes to live with them they express the same sort of shock at her ignorance as Tony Blair's at news of the nation's position in the international skills league table (see p. 74):

> 'I cannot remember the time when I did not know a great deal that she has not the least notion of yet. How long ago it is, aunt, since we used to repeat the chronological order of the kings of England, with the dates of their accession, and most of the principal events of their reigns!'
>
> 'Yes,' added the other: 'and of the Roman emperors as low as Severus; besides a great deal of the Heathen Mythology, and all the Metals, Semi-Metals, Planets and distinguished philosophers.'[6]

Fanny 'does not know the difference between water-colours and crayons' and 'does not want to learn either music or drawing.' But the Bertrams, like Lady Catherine, and Tony Blair, know what remedial measure to take. Fanny is to have what all modern British schoolchildren have, 'a regular instructress' and 'proper masters', professionals. And by this means—the magic wand of professional instruction—she is to be turned into the sort of young lady who can, as Bingley, in *Pride and Prejudice*, mockingly says, 'paint tables, cover skreens, net purses,' someone like the Bertram girls themselves, who 'exercise their memories, practise their duets, and grow tall and womanly,'[7] someone like George Eliot's Rosamond Vincy in *Middlemarch*, who 'was admitted to be the flower of Mrs Lemon's school, the chief school in the county, where the teaching included all that was demanded of the accomplished female—even to extras, such as the getting in and out of a carriage.'[8]

What those nineteenth-century girls were expected to know is, naturally, very different from what our own twenty-first-century girls are. Whereas Lady Catherine de Bourgh and Sir Thomas Bertram want girls to be taught ladylike accomplishments, playing the piano, singing and drawing, modern government spokespersons want them, like boys, to be taught the unisex and economically valuable skills of numeracy, literacy and information technology. And these two could scarcely be further apart, could they: the practically, the commercially useful versus the ornamental?

But in a world in which, for a girl, there are no jobs to be had, only husbands —and men want what George Eliot not very forgivingly calls 'a paradise with sweet laughs for bird-notes, and blue eyes for a heaven'... where everything is given to you and nothing claimed'[10]—what is more commercially useful than ornamental femininity? A girl wasn't expected to earn her living by her accomplishments directly. She didn't play for a paying audience or sell screens to tourists. But she was expected to earn her living by them indirectly—and perhaps the livings of other members of her family too, as Miss Maria Ward does in *Mansfield Park*. There was a point of view—the Bertram or de Bourgh point of view—from which her accomplishments gave her added value as a wife. The common alternative was the awful fate (as the Brontës show it to be) of becoming a governess: and what, after all, was a governess but a woman who had a job instead of a husband? And what governess wouldn't rather have had the husband even if he wasn't quite a Mr Rochester or a M. Paul Emmanuel? In Charlotte Lucas's case any husband is better, even Mr Collins. Marriage can even be seen as the reward of training and skill of the kind Charlotte Lucas recommends to Elizabeth Bennet for her sister Jane, the skill of 'fixing' a man by 'shew[ing] *more* affection than she feels'.[11] Playing the piano proves just such a useful skill for Rosamond Vincy. It's one of the things that fixes Lydgate.

Nowadays we don't want our daughters to be accomplished, we want them educated. We want them to read and to think, to know. But this view too has a spokesman in *Pride and Prejudice*—and a less monstrous one than Lady Catherine de Bourgh. When Caroline Bingley says that, to deserve to be called accomplished, a woman 'must have a thorough knowledge of music, singing, drawing, dancing, and the modern languages... and besides all this, she must possess a certain something in her air and manner of walking, the tone of her voice, her address and expressions,' Darcy adds, 'All this she must possess, and to all this she must yet add something more substantial, in the improvement of her mind by extensive reading.' (Elizabeth Bennet replies, 'I am no longer surprised at your knowing *only* six accomplished women. I rather wonder now at your knowing *any*.')[12]

And the novel has, too, an example of a woman who reads very extensively just in order to improve her mind. She 'worked hard for knowledge and accomplishments'[13] and, even without professional help, is the best-instructed person in the Bennet household. She would make—according to a very common idea of what a student should be—a model, one who would certainly go on to do research (perhaps in Gender Studies or The Invention of the Idea of 'Englishness',

1790–1820), with which 'project' she would enter the broad, well-trodden path of an academic career: Mary Bennet—'who piqued herself upon the solidity of her reflections', such as

> 'Pride is a very common failing I believe. By all that I have ever read, I am convinced that it is very common indeed, that human nature is particularly prone to it, and that there are very few of us who do not cherish a feeling of self-complacency on the score of some quality or other, real or imaginary. Vanity and pride are different things, though the words are often used synonimously. A person may be proud without being vain. Pride relates more to our opinion of ourselves, vanity to what we would have others think of us.'[14]

Like the ideal examination candidate she has learned not only the lesson but the style. Allowing for the distance of time and phraseology, her style—when she can find nothing from a text-book to quote—is just like that of the modern career academic: cagey to the point of self-extinction. Mary has as a gift what in real life is only obtained at the cost of many pains and great sacrifice; she has expelled all trace of herself—of any living, breathing woman—from her own words. Who that has ever worked in an English department could fail to recognize her comment on Mr Collins's letter? 'In point of composition his letter does not seem defective. The idea of the olive branch is perhaps not wholly new, yet I think it is well expressed.'[15] Here's prophecy for you. What modernization does it need beyond a few conditionals, in place of indicatives? —a 'would seem' or two? In spirit what modernization does it need at all? Her first sentence gets the question on to the safe ground of the technical, made safer still by a caveat. Her second parodies academic 'balance'.

When Mary speaks, no-one replies; there is no-one there to reply to. Is her sister Elizabeth to walk three muddy miles from Longbourn to Netherfield—and back—to see Jane who is unwell? Mary's advice is: first do a cost-benefit analysis: '"I admire the activity of your benevolence," observed Mary, "but every impulse of feeling should be guided by reason; and, in my opinion, exertion should always be in proportion to what is required."'[16] But no-one can hear: 'We will go as far as Meryton with you,' say Catherine and Lydia as if Mary weren't there (as she isn't). Mary doesn't talk, she makes observations.

When the Bennets learn that Lydia has ruined not just her own but the reputation of the whole family by running off with Wickham, it's true that the one thing they can give one another in the dreadful circumstances is consolation. But the very last thing any normal person could find consoling is Mary's way of stating the fact:

> 'This is a most unfortunate affair; and will probably be much talked of. But we must stem the tide of malice, and pour into the wounded bosoms of each other, the balm of sisterly consolation.'[17]

When she unsurprisingly gets no reply, she adds:

'Unhappy as the event must be for Lydia, we may draw from it this useful lesson; that loss of virtue in a female is irretrievable—that one false step involves her in endless ruin—that her reputation is no less brittle than it is beautiful,—and that she cannot be too much guarded in her behaviour towards the undeserving of the other sex.'[18]

The necessary judgement comes—silently—from Elizabeth, who 'lifted up her eyes in amazement, but was too much oppressed to make any reply.'

Mary Bennet is the deconstructionists' ideal. Her speech hasn't just been invaded by others', it is over-run, authorless. The things she says can't be replied to, only ignored—or deconstructed. Her father sometimes forestalls them by deconstructing them in advance:

'What say you, Mary? for you are a young lady of deep reflection I know, and read books, and make extracts.'
Mary wished to say something very sensible, but knew not how.
'While Mary is adjusting her ideas,' he continued, 'let us return to Mr Bingley.'[19]

And who in the novel most resembles Mary Bennet, the ideal student? Wickedly, Jane Austen makes it Mr Collins, who isn't educated at all. The sense Jane Austen gives to 'uneducated' is worth some attention:

Mr Collins was not a sensible man, and the deficiency of nature had been but little assisted by education or society; the greatest part of his life having been spent under the guidance of an illiterate and miserly father; and though he belonged to one of the universities, he had merely kept the necessary terms, without forming at it any useful acquaintance.[20]

She talks as if formal 'education' and 'society' serve the same purpose. What confirmed the deficiencies of nature in Mr Collins was not any want of schooling, either as a child or young man, but, firstly, the influence upon his own character of his father's (his father's illiteracy being thought of not as a want of skills but a quality of character on a par with miserliness) and then his own independent failure to take advantage of university—his failure there lying not in his not studying hard enough but in his not forming 'any useful acquaintance', people, that is, who might have been useful to him by acquainting him with an educated standard to think, talk and behave by.

The uneducated in this sense and the studious have a natural affinity for one another, it seems. None of the other Bennet girls can bear him but Mary would have him: 'She rated his abilities much higher than any of the others; there was a solidity in his reflections which often struck her ....'[21] Though she thinks he needs encouraging to read and improve himself by her example, he doesn't in fact need her example at all. His own talk about and to Lady Catherine is every bit as premeditated as her own. Just like her, he doesn't talk but makes speeches and gives lectures.

Although the deficiencies of his nature haven't been much assisted by education, his mental habits conform so perfectly to those recommended in a not at all uncommon kind of teaching that, when he proposes to Elizabeth Bennet, he does so in the form of a well-structured essay, much on the model recommended by cribs to A-level candidates. He is going to propose, to ask a young woman to marry him, be his wife etc etc. And 'he set about it in a very orderly manner, with all the observances which he supposed a regular part of the business.'[22] He does use to Elizabeth the words 'marrying', 'marriage', 'wife', 'happiness', 'feelings', 'affection', 'love'—and not in ways that any computer programme or teacher of EFL could rule to be ungrammatical—but he does so without ever managing to say or, apparently, even realizing that he is called on to say, that he loves and wants her. He doesn't lie, like Pierre Bezuhov in *War and Peace* proposing to his first wife: he can't get that close to speaking the truth. He has, of course, reasons—quite good ones—for marrying, reasons—quite good ones—for coming to Longbourn for the purpose of arranging a marriage and reasons—quite good ones—for selecting Elizabeth from the girls he finds there. He does not neglect to 'state'[23] them, general and particular, sub-divided and numbered, and—with an emphasis here and a repetition there—as clearly as if he were obeying an A-level rubric: 'Candidates are reminded that the assessment criteria include the ability to organize and present information, ideas, descriptions and arguments clearly and logically, with correct use of grammar ... .' Unfortunately, all this is to a proposal of marriage what, in Bingley's words, conversation is to dancing: 'Much more rational ... but ... not ... near so much like a ball.'[24] The first, last, best reason Elizabeth could have for refusing him is his proposal itself.

> 'My reasons for marrying are, first, that I think it a right thing for every clergyman in easy circumstances (like myself) to set the example of matrimony in his parish. Secondly, that I am convinced it will add very greatly to my happiness; and thirdly —which perhaps I ought to have mentioned earlier, that it is the particular advice and recommendation of the very noble lady whom I have the honour of calling patroness.'[25]

He then appropriately expands—unpacks—this last point, before moving on (but not without glancing back):

> 'Thus much for my general intention in favour of matrimony; it remains to be told why my views were directed to Longbourn instead of my own neighbourhood, where I assure you there are many amiable young women. But the fact is, that being, as I am, to inherit this estate after the death of your honoured father, (who, however, may live many years longer), I could not satisfy myself without resolving to chuse a wife from among his daughters, that the loss to them might be as little as possible, when the melancholy event takes place—which, however, as I have already said, may not be for several years. This has been my motive, my fair cousin,

and I flatter myself it will not sink me in your esteem. And now nothing remains for me but to assure you in the most animated language of the violence of my affection.'[26]

And having said so—and therefore having done so too—all that does remain is to add the footnotes:

> 'To fortune I am perfectly indifferent, and shall make no demand of that nature on your father, since I am well aware it could not be complied with; and that one thousand pounds in the 4 per cents which will not be yours until after your mother's decease, is all that you may ever be entitled to. On that head, therefore, I shall be uniformly silent; and you may assure yourself that no ungenerous reproach shall ever pass my lips when we are married.'[27]

Pursuing this line of thought (and it is that, thought, as well as the most marvellously entertaining art) of the studious as a form of the miseducated, Jane Austen (Terry Eagleton thinks he's an iconoclast?) yet more wickedly gives Darcy a style that has recognizable affinities with Mary's and Mr Collins's. Darcy is, of course, a genuinely educated man with a kind of seriousness derived from being so which, when the novel opens, Elizabeth Bennet stands more in need of than she knows. Bingley has 'of his judgement the highest opinion'; and he is right: 'In understanding Darcy was the superior. Bingley was by no means deficient, but Darcy was clever.'[28] But, until he comes under Elizabeth's influence, he makes being educated seem like a personal disadvantage (like Richardson's Mr Walden in *Sir Charles Grandison*). It has allied itself with social pride to make his conversation rather wooden, pompous, theoretic. We shouldn't mistake it for Mary Bennet's or Mr Collins's. It is all the same a bit would-be Johnsonian—Johnsonian without also being conversational, too bookish, and too proud of it. It is a style of talking which bears out what Bingley says about his writing: 'he does *not* write with ease. He studies too much for words of four syllables:'[29]

> 'Your list of the common extent of accomplishments has too much truth. The word is applied to many a woman who deserves it no otherwise than by netting a purse, or covering a skreen. But I am very far from agreeing with you in your estimation of ladies in general. I cannot boast of knowing more than half a dozen, in the whole range of my acquaintance, that are really accomplished.'[30]

> 'Undoubtedly there is meanness in all the arts which ladies sometimes condescend to employ for captivation. Whatever bears affinity to cunning is despicable.'[31]

> 'The country can in general supply but few subjects for such a study [of intricate characters]. In a country neighbourhood you move in a very confined and unvarying society.'[32]

(No wonder Mrs Bennet is provoked to reply, 'I assure you there is quite as much of *that* going on in the country as in town.' One can sympathize.)

'Nothing is more deceitful than the appearance of humility. It is often only care-lessness of opinion, and sometimes an indirect boast.'[33]

'Will it not be advisable, before we proceed on this subject, to arrange with rather more precision the degree of importance which is to appertain to this request, as well as the degree of intimacy subsisting between the parties?'[34]

And so on; too much like T. S. Eliot remembering he is serious; and when he is trying to be light, heavy. In this character Mr Darcy makes his own first proposal to Elizabeth.

In the most important respect of all, nothing could be more different from Mr Collins's. Darcy does propose, not just carry out the regular observances: '…how ardently I admire and love you.'[35] But all the same there are curious, modified, reminders of Mr Collins in him, a not unlike emphasis on the history of his own reasons, motives, considerations, for and against—as if what were wanted here were explanations. He 'spoke well' and is 'eloquent' when, again, perhaps something other than excellence of performance is what is wanted.[36] And what the character of his eloquence is we can gather from the indirect speech Jane Austen summarizes his conclusion with:

He concluded with representing to her the strength of that attachment which, in spite of all his endeavours, he had found impossible to conquer; and with expressing his hope that it would now be rewarded by her acceptance of his hand.[37]

We again recognize these well-formed eighteenth-century periods as (without its being implied that there is some other particular style that is called for) not quite the thing called for. He is too much master of his words, and his words are too much those of a species—the educated eighteenth-century gentleman. They are too familiar a part of 'the regular business'. At any rate, that, more or less, is how Elizabeth sees them—and in this there is another passing resemblance to Mr Collins, to the difference between saying things and meaning them: 'He *spoke* of apprehension and anxiety, but his countenance expressed real security.'[38] So here, again, is a proposal which supplies the grounds on which it is to be rejected; and, again, we see Elizabeth as a true judge and critic.

The changes that take place in Elizabeth and Darcy as a result of this proposal and its refusal—the changes they bring about in one another—show us how (in modification of Elizabeth's dictum) we can teach what is worth knowing, even if we can't do it by instructing. As Mr Bennet, without aiming to, just in the ordinary course of domestic life, educates his daughter Elizabeth, so Elizabeth re-educates the formally educated Darcy, and is educated by him in turn.

What Darcy might have to learn from Elizabeth that he did not learn at university is beautifully suggested in the conversation between them that con-cludes Chapter 12. The conversation is something like an eighteenth-century version of the wit combats of Beatrice and Benedick—except that, it being the turn of the eighteenth not sixteenth century and the participants being a kind of lady and gentleman that Beatrice and Benedick are not, the conversation *is* a conversation as well as a game. There's more stating, and no puns. It's 'polite'. But this combat differs in another, more particular way too. All the playfulness (until the very end) is on one side. It's not so much a combat of wit as a combat between wit and what evidently takes itself for wisdom. Elizabeth is playful, ironic, jokey—without being frivolous. Darcy is literal-minded and discursive—as if anything else were beneath him. The subject of the conversation, unfortunately for him, is whether he's a fit subject for laughter or not (the poor man having to suffer not just Elizabeth Bennet's jokes but Jane Austen's too). It's Caroline Bingley who has let him in for it by saying—but not as a joke—that he's no subject for laughter. Elizabeth takes it up; and, as the ball is batted back and forth, quickly, neatly, tellingly from one side, ponderously from the other, it seems as if she has not just all the humour but all the intelligence too:

'Mr Darcy is not to be laughed at!' cried Elizabeth. 'That is an uncommon advantage, and uncommon I hope it will continue, for it would be a great loss to *me* to have many such acquaintance. I dearly love a laugh.'

'Miss Bingley,' said he, 'has given me credit for more than can be. The wisest and the best of men, nay, the wisest and best of their actions, may be rendered ridiculous by a person whose first object in life is a joke.'

'Certainly,' replied Elizabeth—'there are such people, but I hope I am not one of *them*. I hope I never ridicule what is wise or good. Follies and nonsense, whims and inconsistencies *do* divert me, I own, and I laugh at them whenever I can.—But these, I suppose, are precisely what you are without.'

'Perhaps that is not possible for any one. But it has been the study of my life to avoid those weaknesses which often expose a strong understanding to ridicule.'

'Such as vanity and pride.'

'Yes, vanity is a weakness indeed. But pride—where there is a real superiority of mind, pride will always be under good regulation.'

Elizabeth turned away to hide a smile.

'Your examination of Mr Darcy is over, I presume,' said Miss Bingley;—'and pray what is the result?'

'I am perfectly convinced by it that Mr Darcy has no defect. He owns it himself without disguise.'

'No'—said Darcy. 'I have made no such pretension. I have faults enough, but they are not, I hope, of understanding. My temper I dare not vouch for.—It is, I believe, too little yielding—certainly too little for the convenience of the world. I cannot forget the follies and vices of others so soon as I ought, nor their offences against myself. My feelings are not puffed about with every attempt to move them. My temper would perhaps be called resentful.—My good opinion once lost is lost for ever.'

'*That* is a failing indeed!'—cried Elizabeth. 'Implacable resentment *is* a shade in a character. But you have chosen your fault well.—I really cannot *laugh* at it. You are safe from me.'

'There is, I believe, in every disposition a tendency to some particular evil, a natural defect, which not even the best education can overcome.'

'And *your* defect is a propensity to hate every body.'

'And yours,' he replied with a smile, 'is wilfully to misunderstand them.'[39]

And there he at last relaxes under the warmth of her teasing, and replies, with a smile, in kind; and we glimpse a side of him that is both more educable and more likeable than we had perhaps seen before. Until then it has seemed to be precisely his understanding, not his temper, which is deficient; until then superiority of mind has looked to be the last quality he could justifiably claim. But with that last remark and the smile that accompanies it, we can see that he is capable of learning, not from instruction but from—again—the invitation implicit in example, the invitation he shows himself ready to accept. (This is process and progress, not instant conversion. Their education is still incomplete at the end of the novel when Elizabeth holds back from mocking the now-accepted lover: 'She remembered that he had yet to learn to be laught at, and it was rather too early to begin.'[40]) Not quite by the way we also notice that this passage tells us much more about vanity and pride than the academic authority Mary, quoted above.

Short as it is, this conversation makes it clear why Elizabeth is so irresistibly attractive to Darcy. It's not just that she has qualities that might attract any man; it's also that he is peculiarly in need of them. As he says later, he 'admires her for the liveliness of her mind';[41] he can't help himself; her sort of liveliness is the very thing he lacks; he's incomplete without it.

And if learning from her example, in whatever measure he can, isn't being educated ... nothing is. (It's a lesson the modern academy is as far from learning as Mary Bennet is: that intelligence and seriousness belong as much with play-fulness as with propositions possessing truth-value.)

The book is the story of Elizabeth's education out of prejudice as well as Darcy's out of pride, and prejudice of a more interesting kind than her initial dislike of Darcy. These glimpses of what it is to be educated are opened out in the story of her changing relations with him and Wickham. It proves to be one thing for a clever young woman to see what Mr Collins is made of, another thing altogether to see through Wickham—not because, as Jane Austen shows it, he is intrinsically any harder to fathom, but because he is so for a marriageable young woman, however clever. Elizabeth Bennet isn't, like her sisters Kitty and Lydia, just any (in the Johnsonian phrase) 'unidea-ed' girl but she is, like Kitty and Lydia, a girl, as much at the mercy of good looks and a charming manner as any other. And that she is, is part of the marvellous truthfulness of Jane Austen's art.

The two crucial tests for Elizabeth (and the reader) are what Wickham says about Darcy in the conversation in Chapter 16 in which he blames Darcy for the bad relations between them, and what Darcy says about Wickham in the letter in Chapter 35 in which he defends himself and puts the blame on Wickham.

When Elizabeth, with her sisters, meets Wickham in the street, in Chapter 15, Jane Austen conveys with a beautifully light touch the character both of Wickham's appeal and Elizabeth's response to it, which, for all her superiority to her sisters, is no less automatic and undifferentiated than theirs:

> This was exactly as it should be; for the young man wanted only regimentals to make him completely charming. His appearance was greatly in his favour; he had all the best part of beauty, a fine countenance, a good figure, and very pleasing address. The introduction was followed up on his side with a happy readiness of conversation—a readiness at the same time perfectly correct and unassuming.[42]

There, irony doesn't, quite, precipitate from description but it does in the next chapter; and it leaves the reader with no-one to blame but himself if, by the chapter's end, he hasn't seen how thorough a charlatan Wickham is and how thoroughly Elizabeth is taken in.

Not that Elizabeth is satisfied just to admire him. She both admires him and finds her admiration to be justified: She 'felt, she had neither been seeing him before, nor thinking *that* of him since, with the smallest degree of unreasonable admiration.'[43] What makes her admiration reasonable? His superiority of 'person, countenance, air' and (beautifully) 'walk': 'He was the happy man towards whom almost every female eye was turned, and Elizabeth was the happy woman by whom he finally seated himself.'[44] And it is her happiness, in the conversation that follows, to be shown every last twist and turn of his—as Mr Bennet later calls it—impudence and hypocrisy, without being able to recognize it. It is true that he is very adroit at sounding her out and seeing how far he can go in blackening Darcy's character without risking his own; but his adroitness, his calculation and caution, are, after all, themselves there to be seen—if Elizabeth had her eyes as well open as when she is looking at Mr Collins. As entirely convincing as it is that she should be taken in, the means by which she is taken in are, by any account, pretty crude. What else—being means—could they be? Wickham may be adroit but that doesn't make him any less transparent.

He begins not with Darcy at all but the distance Netherfield is from Meryton. He brings Darcy in only 'in an hesitating manner'[45] and as no more than what might be taken for an indifferent conversation piece, asking how long he had been staying there. Then, on Elizabeth's frankly owning her interest in Darcy, he ventures as far as his estate, and—without venturing off it—invites her to invite him to approach the man himself: it is an estate about which he can give 'certain information' because of the 'particular manner' in which 'I have been connected with his family ... from my infancy'.[46] To make quite sure of his ground: is Elizabeth much acquainted with the man? As much as she ever wants to be? Perfect. The way is clear.

But that doesn't stop it being devious. Elizabeth may frankly avow her dislike of Darcy, Wickham is too good a man to do any such thing. He has no right to give his opinion, he is not qualified to form one—for, after all, he has known Darcy too long and too well... to be a fair judge or impartial. If Darcy is generally disliked, he can't pretend to be sorry, but only from a love of justice: he wouldn't want any man to be thought better of than he deserved. It's true that Darcy has used him very badly—scandalously badly—but he regrets that not for his own but for Darcy's sake... and Darcy's father's. He could forgive Darcy for what he has done to him. The disgrace and disappointment he has brought to his own father—'one of the best men that ever breathed... the truest friend I ever had... a thousand tender recollections... excessively attached to me'—he never can forgive.[47]

And so it goes—wonderfully—on, even to Wickham's claiming to have (like Mr Collins speaking of the 'violence' of his affections) a 'warm, unguarded temper'.[48] Wickham is not a bit less impossible a prospect as a husband than Mr Collins, and his impossibility is not (for someone with eyes to see) a bit less visible. The clever man who calculates the impression he makes can no more disguise what he is and what he is doing than the man who is too stupid to know he is making any particular impression at all. Language is such, the conditions of life are such, that the one as helplessly reveals what he is as the other ('Each mortal thing does one thing and the same;/Deals out that being indoors each one dwells'[49])—but not to Elizabeth. She and Wickham talk 'with mutual satisfaction'. His account of Darcy seems a 'very rational' one, and she goes away 'with her head full of him'.[50] Later, of course, under the influence of Darcy's repudiation of what Wickham tells her, she sees 'the impropriety of such communications to a stranger' and 'the indelicacy of putting himself forward as he had', and she sees also that she ought to have seen it at the time: she 'wondered it had escaped her.'[51]

She might well wonder. For, in a way, she does at the time recognize the impropriety and indelicacy, sufficiently so at least to feel scruples on her own account. At the start of the conversation she knows that, much as she would like to, she 'could not hope' to hear about Darcy from Wickham, and 'dared not even mention that gentleman';[52] and part way through, as keen as she is to hear more, 'the delicacy of it prevented farther inquiry.'[53] So 'all' she has to do is to apply to Wickham a standard which she applies to herself: if it would be indelicate of her to ask, what is it for him to volunteer? Similarly, she is perfectly capable of reading Caroline Bingley's 'high flown expressions' with 'all the insensibility of distrust'[54]—so why not Wickham's? In a way, she does already know what Wickham is and, from that, what Darcy cannot be. She just (as if it were so easy) needs to recognize it.

The first and last thing to be insisted on is that whatever else is effectual in education, it isn't 'facts'. Facts are necessary but they won't do the job for Elizabeth. She has to agonize before she even decides what the facts are, but only because of what the facts might mean to her. The fact that Wickham, having said he would never avoid Darcy, does avoid him at the Netherfield ball, is no help to Elizabeth—she blames Darcy. The fact that Wickham drops her to go after Miss King because the latter has come into £10,000 is no help either—she excuses him on the grounds of his need. She discounts Bingley's testimony because it must rest on Darcy's. She discounts Bingley's sister's because it is tainted by snobbery (even though, if she thought, she'd recognize that it must be disinterested). Charlotte Lucas's advice not to risk offending a rich man for the sake of a poor one condemns itself. And Mrs Gardiner's caution is scarcely distinguishable from Charlotte Lucas's: if only Wickham were rich, Elizabeth could scarcely do better; as it is .... Jane is no use, of course: she speaks up for Darcy ... and Wickham. And in this case Mr Bennet is no help either: like everyone else, at this stage, he is 'partial' to Wickham.[55]

Darcy is not just the one who happens to open Elizabeth's eyes. He seems to be the only one capable of opening them. But that isn't *only* because he has information other people don't have. It isn't the information that opens her eyes. It's true that Darcy does give her 'another side of the story', which makes it 'impossible not to feel that there was gross duplicity on one side or the other,'[56] but the question remains for her ... which?

> She ... weighed every circumstance with what she meant to be impartiality—deliberated on the probability of each statement—but with little success. On both sides it was only assertion.[57]

The most that the new information can do is show her that the affair was 'capable of' a turn she hadn't expected.[58] The question still remains: but which man is honest, which the liar? It's not facts she needs, to vouch for character, but a judgement of character to vouch for 'facts'.

Now, Darcy's letter has a definite character. To begin with it's long—not so far short of 3000 words, longer than some of Jane Austen's own chapters, longer than a broadsheet review or a mid-length learned article—and it's well-organized. It has things in common with Mr Collins's proposal. It has a beginning, middle and end; and its middle divides into sections and sub-sections, which we should have no difficulty in numbering. It's the letter of a man accustomed not merely to write at length but at the same time to develop a train of thought, to analyse, to use evidence, to blend argument and narrative. It's the letter of an educated man, a university man who has done more than keep the necessary terms.

But whereas the degree of organization Mr Collins gives his proposal is part of what stops it being a proposal, the organization of Darcy's letter is part of what makes it a self-vindication, and, in its own, odd way, a real love letter too—made so just by avoiding any hint of love. Its organization is part of what justifies his saying, 'I demand your attention ... I demand it of your justice.'[59] He has to earn the right to make such a demand, and he does: the length, thoroughness, connectedness of part with part—and distinctness of part from part—of his letter, all help him to. These things are not just signs of the strenuous sincerity of his effort to make himself clear to her, they are a form that that sincerity takes. He is seeking earnestly to come to a disinterested judgement of himself which she can concur in. So he has to distinguish— between topic and topic, the more from the less grave, where he has been in the right from where he has been in error, error that is innocent from error that isn't quite so innocent, the effects of his actions from their motives, cases where his judgement is certain from cases where—though definite—it may be corrigible. What else can the letter be but long and highly organized? Who but an educated man could write it? 'I believed it on impartial conviction, as truly as I wished it in reason.'[60] Who but an educated man could say such a thing? Here is education not as a training in mental gymnastics or form of social advantage but as character, something individual and permanent, desirable, though nothing come of it, as being of itself a treasure, and a sufficient remuneration of years of labour. To Darcy, of course, it proves something else Newman calls it, not only a good but productive of good, useful, emphatically useful, the means of his winning his wife, 'dearest, loveliest Elizabeth!' (not only 'worthy of being pleased' but by his letter made more worthy to please[61]). Darcy vindicates himself to his future wife and in doing so does something to vindicate a liberal education too.

He would never have written such a letter, of course—one so free of complacency—except under the influence of Elizabeth herself. Without some such shock to his opinion of himself as the terms of her refusal give him, any account he gives of himself would be likely to be very different. We have his own word for it:

> a selfish being all my life ... taught what was *right*, but ... not taught to correct my good principles, but left to follow them in pride and conceit ... spoilt ... allowed, encouraged, almost taught ... to be selfish and overbearing, to care for none beyond my own family circle, to think meanly of all the rest of the world ... Such I was, from eight to eight and twenty; and such I might still have been but for you, dearest, loveliest Elizabeth! What do I not owe you! You taught me a lesson, hard indeed at first, but most advantageous. By you, I was properly humbled. I came to you without a doubt of my reception. You shewed me how insufficient were all my pretensions to please a woman worthy of being pleased.[62]

And we can see for ourselves the change in him in the difference between the way he describes his objections to her family when he proposes and the way he describes them when he writes. It's not, though, that he softens them in the letter. Actually, they are more severe there, but disentangled from any taint of social pride.

But just as the effect on him of Elizabeth's rejection depended on what he should make of it, so the effect of his letter on her—no matter how good it is—is out of his hands. That depends on her and what she makes of it. His letter may vouch for his honesty as plainly as Wickham's conversation does for his dishonesty, but there's nothing to guarantee that Elizabeth will see the one any more than the other. His letter is only an invitation, after all, which she can always refuse. And at first, on the subject of her family, to refuse to see him or Wickham in any light but the one she is accustomed to seems the thing she is likeliest to do: she's amazed that he thinks he can make any apology, steadfast in the belief that he can have no explanation, strongly prejudiced against everything he might say, instantly resolved that he's untruthful, too angry to wish to do him justice, convinced his letter is all pride and insolence. And even though she reads the part about Wickham 'with somewhat clearer attention', she nevertheless 'wished to discredit it entirely', repeatedly calling it 'false' and putting it away 'protesting that she would not regard it, that she would never look at it again.'[63]

But that, in her honesty, she acknowledges, 'would not do'. She gets out the letter again and 'commanded herself so far as to examine the meaning of every sentence ... she read, and re-read with the closest attention'—not to learn anything new but to learn whether or not she must look at what she already knows in a new light. She goes back over Wickham's behaviour and conversation—just as she does over Darcy's letter—and finds that the parts that compose it, all familiar, each no different from what it was before, take up a new pattern contradictory of the old. She now sees what had previously escaped her: that all her good opinion of Wickham derived from his 'social powers' alone, his 'countenance, voice, and manner ... charm of air and address' but no 'instance of goodness ... trait of integrity or benevolence', no more 'substantial good than the general approbation'. And then, going back over that first conversation, from which 'many of his expressions were still fresh in her memory', she sees everything she ought to have seen at the time.[64] But to do so she has had not just to be shown it but to look for herself: the truth of Darcy's letter can't be communicated to her without herself laying hold of it. And when she does, it is not just Wickham that she comes to judge differently, or even Darcy along with him. Everything changes for her. She sees her family in a new, harsher light, and herself too:

> She grew absolutely ashamed of herself.—Of neither Darcy nor Wickham could she think, without feeling that she had been blind, partial, prejudiced, absurd.
>
> 'How despicably have I acted!' she cried.—'I, who have prided myself on my discernment!—I, who have valued myself on my abilities! who have often disdained the generous candour of my sister, and gratified my vanity, in useless or blameable distrust.—How humiliating is this discovery!—Yet, how just a humiliation!—Had

I been in love, I could not have been more wretchedly blind. But vanity, not love, has been my folly.—Pleased with the preference of one, and offended by the neglect of the other, on the very beginning of our acquaintance, I have courted prepossession and ignorance, and driven reason away, where either were concerned. Till this moment, I never knew myself.' [65]

The echo of the Delphic oracle is unusually grave for Jane Austen, but fully justified. Know thyself—and realize that it's difficult. Darcy's letter, having, in one section, effected that change in her, also makes it possible for her to read its other section, on her family, quite differently. Her first reading ('all pride and insolence' [66]), she comes to see, is a misreading. But, it must be said, misreading or not, it is a real reading, even in its lapses, and in itself illustrates what it is about her that attracts Darcy and makes her new understanding possible. She has a kind of hunger for meaning (which is the basis of all knowledge, all understanding, all real education—Jane Austen has put a lot of herself into her):

how eagerly she went through [its contents], and what a contrariety of emotion they excited. Her feelings as she read were scarcely to be defined. ... She read, with an eagerness which hardly left her power of comprehension, and from impatience of knowing what the next sentence might bring, was incapable of attending to the sense of the one before her eyes. [67]

And although her second reading is 'widely different', because her judgement of the writer has become so ('How could she deny that credit to his assertions, in one instance, which she had been obliged to give in the other?' [68]), it has in common with her first a fallible but passionate sincerity in her

giving way to every variety of thought; re-considering events, determining probabilities, and reconciling herself as well as she could, to a change so sudden and so important ....

Mr Darcy's letter, she was in a fair way of soon knowing by heart. She studied every sentence: and her feelings towards its writer were at times widely different ....' [69]

This is what 'studying' is—when it is what it ought to be—the antithesis of Mary's studiousness. This is what it is to be disinterested: to follow a sense passionately even if it is the one one wants most to deny. This is education, the opposite of instruction. Darcy's letter does educate Elizabeth but it couldn't do so without her co-operation, any more than her refusal of him could have taught him the lesson it did without his. Each is changed by the truths the other teaches, but they wouldn't be without actively reaching for and laying hold of those truths themselves. Each educates and is educated but neither has anything delivered to them. They have acquired no new skills, not even new life skills or ones of the personal transferable kind. (The person in the novel who possesses those is the odious and shallow Wickham.) They have become better critics, better judges of the value of things, better people. Liberal education has to be more or less like this.

53

Jane Austen doesn't just tell us that Elizabeth firstly misjudges Wickham and Darcy, and then comes to judge them rightly, she shows her making her judgements, shows the judgements in the making, for us to judge. Jane Austen puts her readers and her characters on an equal footing, tests and (let's hope) educates the judgements of the one as she does those of the other. We may very well misjudge Wickham along with Elizabeth, and without her excuse. The judgements we are called on to make in reading *Pride and Prejudice* are the same sort of judgements (often the very same judgements) that the characters of the book are making, for good or ill, in their lives, and the same sort that we make in our own.

It is in the exercise of judgement, and the modification of one judgement by another, that education is seen: not of judgement in any particular professional or specialized sphere but of it in—as Carlyle calls it in *Sartor Resartus*—'the "Science of Things in General"', practised everywhere, and on matters great and small. *What party shall we vote for? Shall we get married? Whom shall we appoint? Shall I buy this newspaper? Can I be bothered with this?* It makes not for the lifelong learning we are told we must all undertake on pain of not getting a big pension, but for a lifelong growth in discrimination which is the same as development of character. Jane Austen not only puts it at the very centre of our lives, entering into and intertwined with every other aspect, even the power of love, but shows it to be a good and a value in itself.

She gives us a picture of life which a great many people, if they were consistent, would dislike and disapprove of, as irredeemably élitist. 'The unreasoned life,' said Socrates, 'is not worth living.' Jane Austen goes further: a life without judgement, her books strongly imply, would not be a human life at all. But she goes further, in the direction of the offensive, still: the more alive in judgement, she implies, simply, the more alive. The better the judge, the better the critic, the better the man or woman—the better, the more alive as a man or woman. The characters in the novel who are most alive, Darcy and Elizabeth, are those who judge best and whose judgements are most open to being educated. Jane Austen writes as if we are the sense we make and as if that sense were not only judgeable but most plainly judgeable in the way we talk and write.

It could almost be said that this is her great theme. Let us learn what we can from Elizabeth and Darcy but not overlook Emma's education under the influence of Mr Knightley, Captain Wentworth's and Miss Anne Elliot's mutual education, and not least Henry Tilney's as well as Catherine Morland's. Nor can her other ineducable monsters be safely ignored: Sir Walter Elliot, Miss Elliot and Mr William Elliot; General Tilney. We have already mentioned the Bertram girls.

*   *   *

So what an odd relation Jane Austen has to modern England: our most popular classic novelist (and, currently, perhaps, dramatist too) but in defiance of the incorrectness in our world of the 'judgemental' that is the centre of hers. Unless we can be brought to recognize that our current idea of education not only collides with hers (with that of our great writers generally and with our own common sense), there is no hope for 'education' in this country and nothing to be done about it. It is doomed to be a monstrosity and a millstone around the national neck. Unless directed by an intelligent, by an educated conception of education, all 'reform' will prove to be a process without purpose and without end, a delusion. The long sequence of reforms and improvements made from the 1960s onwards can already be seen to have about as much consistency to it as the movements of the ball on a pinball machine. The ball, of course, for all its vagaries of movement on the way, is steadily drawn to the low point on the table—but the analogy holds there too, for education may not have become better over the last 30 years or so, or even more democratic; it has undoubtedly become—along with newspapers, radio, television and public utterance of any and every kind—steadily lower. That is the significance of the Dearing Report and the Dome, Tony Blair's Cool Britannia and the People's This, That and the Other: the plebification not just of the ruling but of the educated class. Or, as we might say: for all that Britain may contain a great many educated individuals, it is now questionable whether it has an educated class.

It is a great misfortune that English literature counts for so little in English public life. Literature is, of course, in one way and another, a prominent and flourishing business. There is the Arts Council and the arts pages, the Lottery money, the Booker and the Whitbread, and the publishing and teaching industries; there is even a Minister for the Arts, with a PhD, in English literature; but none of these gives English literature any authority in English public life, not even in university departments of it.

And yet English literature, with its testimony to other possibilities, is still, triumphantly, there; and it can be—it is—still read, not just studiously but with pleasure; and while that is so, there is hope, even for our education system. For the pleasure stories and poems give us is bound up with the degree and varieties of assent they draw from us. Our pleasure depends on our assent, or, we might say, is one form it takes.

No-one, I suppose, can read *Pride and Prejudice* without taking pleasure in its happy ending. Except perhaps for some of Shakespeare's comedies (and perhaps not even those) no book has a greater power to make us share the happiness of its characters. 'Had Elizabeth been able to encounter his eye, she might have seen how well the expression of heart-felt delight, diffused over his face, became him; but, though she could not look, she could listen ... .'[70] But the happiness we feel in their happiness isn't self-indulgent or merely vicarious. It is a response to what is there in the novel. It's a kind of assent to what we have been shown, and to the judgements that belong to it. We shouldn't feel the pleasure we do if we couldn't recognize Darcy's case, for instance, as being what it is meant to be, that of a man in love, whose happiness depends on success in love. It's not only that this is how the author means us to take him—and we can see that it is—but that we actually do take him so, can't help but say, 'yes, this is what love is like.' Without that assent, the entire anxious comedy of, firstly, his tongue-tied awkwardness, then of his happiness, would fall flat.

So when we observe that the British educated classes love *Pride and Prejudice*, we are also observing that they acknowledge, even if they don't know it, the picture of education it gives them to be a true one—even though that picture is utterly irreconcilable with the way they themselves habitually talk about the matter.

Our modern educationists and politicians read Jane Austen's novel as if one thing were true, and then talk as if something not merely different but precisely opposite were. How are we to resolve that contradiction? In a way—we *want* to believe—that is to the credit of their real, underlying good sense: they know better than they think they do; they read more sincerely than they speak; they only think they think that training and education are the same and that the usefulness of education lies in the profitability of the skills it inculcates; really —though for the most part they don't know it—they think something quite different; what they really think is not gauged by what they say in their official capacities as Vice-Chancellor of This and Minister of State for That—which is very often just role-play and affectation—but by what they do as private men and women, when they are free to do as they please; and then what they do is read *Pride and Prejudice*, with pleasure and with assent.

And that is why there can be some practical point to the present book. We are not trying to change what people think, just persuade them to recognize what they know. 'Look at *Pride and Prejudice*,' we say. 'There, that's what you actually believe, isn't it? What can you find there to disagree with? Don't believe us. Believe her. Believe yourselves.'—not the selves that pretend to think the international skills league table anything but a chimera, but the selves whose pleasure in *Pride and Prejudice* is a form of assent to its author's wisdom, and a sign that they can still recognize genuine speech when they hear it.

So it isn't too much to hope, is it, that a minister of education or a prime minister (especially one who tells us he has a 'passion' for education [71]) might read a book like *Pride and Prejudice*, and learn something from it—even about education?

That's what we want to think. For the alternative is that our educated classes read our classic literature without it meaning anything to them at all. ('Hearing they hear not, neither do they understand.') And if it doesn't mean anything to them, what does?

III

THE NEW
UNIVERSITY
FOR LIFE

4 The Vision and the Mission

But I say unto you, That every idle word that men shall speak, they shall give account thereof in the day of judgement.

For by thy words thou shalt be justified, and by thy words thou shalt be condemned.[1]

MR COLLINS AS THE LEADING MODERN AUTHORITY

UNIVERSITY DONS are traditionally accused by practical men of logic-chopping and of finickiness about language. Milton as controversialist did spend too many pages attacking his opponents' grammar. But there is no way of objecting to disputes about language without also objecting to the university itself in its role of critic and former of judgement.

Jane Austen's judgements of persons are regularly expressed as judgements of their language. This does not mean that the standards she judges by are schoolma'amish or snobbish. She doesn't value correctness—social or linguistic —for its own sake. Her standards aren't narrowly intellectual or 'literary' either—ones that would necessarily find against the unintellectual or unread or those who might stumble over their words. Although no-one could be more fluent than she herself is, no-one else could think she values fluency for its own sake. Who could be less at a loss for words than her monsters, Mr Collins, Mrs Bennet, Mr Wickham, Lady Catherine de Bourgh—even, when she can fit an 'extract' to an occasion, Mary Bennet? And although she is as witty a writer as there is in the language no-one could think Jane Austen values wit for its own sake either. Mr Bennet is a clever man. He has a mind as lively as his daughter Elizabeth's and is much better read. Jane Austen makes him as witty as she is herself—in fact, his lines are even better than her own—but no-one could come away from *Pride and Prejudice* thinking wit an end in itself or that he doesn't misuse his great gifts. Mr Bennet's wit—for all the truth and justice to be found in it—has too much in common with the way he shuts himself up in his library and fails to provide for his family after his death. Being witty at his wife's and daughters' expense may be necessary for his mental health, but at the same time the wit is plainly one of the forms his irresponsibility takes.

There is no saying in advance how we ought or ought not to speak, no prescribing the best style. There are judgements to be made but no rules to follow, no skills to be exercised. Not even 'speaking well' *will* always be speaking well. Sometimes clumsiness, or silence, might be better. When Darcy first proposes to Elizabeth he 'speaks well', and is 'eloquent', but only because, it seems, he doesn't feel what he should. He doesn't yet know how much his happiness depends on success in love; and when he learns, the knowledge makes him speechless. And then his tongue-tied awkwardness says more of his love and the power love has over him than his eloquence ever did. As he says to Elizabeth when she later tells him he might have talked more, 'A man who had felt less, might.' But the instant he knows he is loved in return, love, that tied his tongue, unties it, and releases him into an articulacy that is nothing like eloquence. He doesn't speak well now, he just talks freely. He and Elizabeth 'walked on, without knowing in what direction. There was too much to be thought and felt, and said.'

Clichés similarly might be a bad sign—or not. As Jane Austen reports it, Darcy's style in his first proposal is very much a stock one. He is to be found saying the sort of thing that men like himself generally do say when called on to say such things, and he does it well—that is, ill. And yet that same style, in all its stereotypicality, is, as Jane Austen also reports it, the one in which Elizabeth accepts his second proposal; and there it is, it seems, just the thing called for, the sign that Elizabeth feels every bit what she might:

> Elizabeth, feeling all the more than common awkwardness and anxiety of his situation, now forced herself to speak; and immediately, though not very fluently, gave him to understand, that her sentiments had undergone so material a change, since the period to which he alluded, as to make her receive with gratitude and pleasure, his present assurances.[2]

The difference is that what prompts Elizabeth to have recourse to the readymade is more or less the opposite of what prompted Darcy. Whereas his stock phrases came to him easily just because of what he didn't feel, hers, as the signs of what she does feel, are the nearest way out of a crisis. We might expect that Darcy, having failed to find the right words for his first proposal, might need to find new ones for his second. But no. It wasn't different words he needed, just different feelings. His feelings having changed—he having changed—those original, wrong words have become the right ones. They are redeemed and their intended meaning reclaimed. So he doesn't need to propose afresh, only to say that he stands by what he said before: 'My affections and wishes are unchanged.'

The standards, then, by which Jane Austen judges her characters (and readers) might be those of any or all classes and sorts of person. They are to be found wherever English is found, and—translation not being an impossibility—even where it is not. They are truly the standards, that is, of the best part of the language, present—potentially so—everywhere in English life. Jane Austen writes as if language were important, all-important, but only for the life to be found in it, only for the sake of the life it makes possible (and not).

Words and the styles they combine in have no fixed values but acquire them from the life they express. They enable us to give meaning to our lives; but only to the extent that we bring their meanings to life. We have to live the meanings possible to words for words to have those meanings; if we don't, their meaningfulness is simply an illusion. The 'power of speech' *is* a power but a power to make nonsense as well as sense. Language fills the world with meanings it wouldn't otherwise have but, by the same token, it has the power to make it meaningless too. Language creates the world, our world; and can uncreate it too.

This is why Mary Bennet and Mr Collins have such fascination for Jane Austen, as people who are not really human because their language is a sort of anti-language. Never mind Samuel Beckett; here is meaninglessness, here is silence, in the midst of loquacity. Mr Collins is one of Jane Austen's—of English literature's—greatest creations. Only a very great writer could have done him. Of course, considered as a person, he could hardly have less to him and still be recognizable as one. But the significance his author discovers in him is a different matter. He may be shallow; his author's contemplation of him is anything but. He is one of her versions of Pope's dunces. A similar playfulness and inventiveness has gone into the making of him and there's a similar fascinated horror with the result. Mr Collins is no 'great Anarch', Emperor of Chaos or Goddess of Dulness; he is a country parson, proud of his wife, his garden and—most of all—his patron's permission regularly to abase himself at her dinner table. But his is the authentic 'uncreating word'. When he speaks, as when the Goddess of Dulness yawns at the end of Pope's mock-epic *The Dunciad*, Light dies, the Arts go out, Truth flees, Morality expires—''Till drown'd was Sense, and Shame, and Right, and Wrong'—not because he is a liar or immoralist but because, in his commonplace way and in his limited sphere, he makes all distinctions, all thought, all judgement, impossible.

To the creating eye of Jane Austen, as the dunces are to Pope, Mr Collins is a sort of ultimate horror, portending a world from which the possibility of meaning has been expelled, or never entered—a horror contemplated as a joke. What makes him a monster is that he is so obviously a man, and a quite harmless one, but without anything to justify his being so. He has the faculty of language (he's not Dr Frankenstein's monster) but without, apparently, anything in him—or anything but the most rudimentary egotism—to express, nothing to give meaning to the familiar words he uses. We think of the purpose of language as being to make sense; and he uses it to make nonsense, of a deep, radical but perfectly respectable kind. He is no Mrs Malaprop or Flora Finching. He speaks and writes perfectly ordinary, fluent, correct and idiomatic English (at least it isn't French). He doesn't make mistakes in grammar or spelling and he plainly uses words in the sense of their dictionary definitions. (He would probably do very well in his GCSE exam.) In every way (but one) he falls within the socially acceptable: a perfectly acceptable parson, dinner guest, master, son-in-law, husband. It's just that he has this one oddity, of using language in such a way as to destroy its capacity for making sense. Words, to him, are just counters or tokens, to be moved around and exchanged: useful but not for meaning anything.

It has been said of both Macaulay and Richard Nixon that they have styles in which it is impossible to tell the truth. But that's not much compared with Mr Collins, whose language makes no sense of any kind. He is as incapable of lying as of telling the truth. He is beyond good and evil—even if not quite as Nietzsche meant. As he is himself only going through the motions when he proposes to Elizabeth, he naturally takes her to be going through similar motions when she refuses him. She doesn't *mean* anything by it ('it' being several paragraphs of very plain speaking), it's all 'merely words of course ... the usual practice of elegant females'.[3] He is like a creature from another planet, giving a quite expert imitation of human behaviour but without having any understanding of it. He is ineducable.

*   *   *

If we say that the language in which universities now habitually conduct their affairs, and the language of public debate about education, denies the existence of the university—whatever in particular is being said about the university—we are making use of this fact that there is no separating judgement from language. It is not nit-picking to object to titles like *Management Aspects of Implementing Flexible Learning*: they are from a language which is itself the destruction of thought.

The chosen phrase comes from a document from the University of Salford.

> Consensus to a concept or vision of the desired shape and purpose of the organization not only makes the organization more effective in carrying out its mission, but also makes it more capable of dealing with future change in a positive and pro-active manner.

When Charlemagne offered the Saxons the alternative of baptism or the sword he did not add the insult of demanding 'consensus to a concept'. The smallest objection to this is that 'consensus to' is not an English idiom. This style is not only inadequate, but a kind of virus rendering blank the minds that try to use it.

We had a vacant post for a linguist with special emphasis on dialectology. The Department's practice was to ask candidates to make a short 'presentation'. One distributed a sheet of quotations (obligatory on the modern lecturer though of course the students naturally start reading the quotations instead of listening to the lecture) including this:

> ... The language question in Wales is sufficiently highly charged that some might infer that even to pay analytic attention to English in Wales, or 'Welsh English' ... represents an ideological position, perhaps even a form of capitulation, or collusion with forces threatening the Welsh language.[4]

The elementary points about English grammar ('highly charged' takes 'for' not 'that'; 'capitulation' needs a 'to', etc) are, again, just another facet of the necessary judgement that this (politically motivated) 'thinking about' language gets expressed in a kind of dissolution of language. This was offered not as a cautionary example but as modern thinking, and was successfully taken as such: the candidate was appointed and has, I believe, been thinking in the same style ever since.

Are we not, after all, rather monstrous? Our monstrosity is not quite Lady Catherine's, or Mary Bennet's. But had Mary lived now she too would have been discussing consensus to a concept.

Pope concludes *The Dunciad* with a vision of the end of the world. The world is destroyed—by the Goddess of Dulness, in a parody of the creation of the world at the beginning of Genesis—as it was made, by the word:

> Lo thy dread empire, Chaos, is restor'd;
> Light dies before thy uncreating word.

Though Chaos restored by Dulness will be, like the original, void, it will not be without form. In Pope's vision of the end of things, the physical world goes on as if nothing had happened. In ours, mankind will continue not only to be fruitful and multiply, but to speak and write in well-formed sentences, make bullet-points and spider-graphs, to pass GCSEs and meet government literacy targets (or else be subjected to procedures put in place to ensure they do next time), to be the customers who will receive, from cradle to grave, lifelong learning, duly monitored and quality assured. There is just this difference. Henceforth they will all sound like government spokespersons on education. The world ends, for Pope, not with a bang nor even a whimper, but stupefied with a yawn. It isn't comets or nuclear war or aliens that destroy it, or the Devil in any very sulphurous form. It's clichés, rubbish-talk, what Jane Austen calls 'nothing-meaning terms'. The world ends with the destruction *by* the word *of* the word. If you can't imagine this, try and read the Dearing Report.

SIR RON DEARING, SON OF COLLINS

Jane Austen always knew when to stop. After the end of her story, Charlotte *née* Lucas found that she had made an incorrigible mistake, that no establishment could compensate for Mr Collins's society. She showed herself less practical than she had imagined; she pined away and died. Mr Collins reverted to his original intention of marrying a Bennet and Mary, still available, after mature deliberation had no doubt about accepting him. More surprising, they had issue. Among their distant descendants, still keeping the breed true, is Sir Ron (as he was at the apogee of his fame) Dearing, the most influential modern example of Collins-like monstrosity.

We haven't, we confess, read all 1700 pages of Sir Ron's committee's report into higher education.[5] We made do, largely, with the 20-page summary. Strictly speaking, we can't claim to have *read* even that. But that's not our fault, for, strictly speaking, *reading* isn't something that can be done with it. The report can be down-loaded, scanned, studied, used, say, by a Government wanting to justify something-or-other, or, in its printed form, for landfill; but the one thing no-one can do with it is read it, except, like Mr Collins's letters, as symptoms. If you are exposed to the Dearing style you run—as we also see with Mr Collins's letters—a truly horrible risk: you either diagnose the disease and inoculate yourself against it by something like reading Jane Austen, or you catch it.

Sir Ron and his committee—with all its many members of a broad expertise divided into working groups—had what they call a 'vision' of Higher Education in the Third Millennium. It is a vision of a 'learning society' in which the entire population is 'learning for life'. It is a vision of high standards, rigour, search for truth, love of knowledge and understanding for their own sakes, disciplined thinking, critical analysis, culture, civilization (and cognitive skills such as an understanding of methodologies)—all things life-enriching and desirable in their own right, or whatever. Unfortunately, though Sir Ron and his Committee knew that Higher Education possessed these things, it didn't occur to them that their own Inquiry needed to. They knew they needed to travel—to France, Germany, Holland, Australia, New Zealand—but had no idea they needed to think. Or, if they had, one of the things they must have thought was that aeroplanes, trains and taxis were more use to them than the words 'university', 'thought' and 'literature' or its cognates, 'literate', 'literary' and 'literacy' (in place of the last, the more impressively technical-sounding 'communication'), for though they made extensive use of the former they found no use for the latter at all. They went into education, and came out with a report that isn't an effect of it and could only be a cause by being seen as an example of its opposite.

You might be surprised that a 1700-page report on higher education (we word-searched the full version) could find no real use for the word 'university'; you shouldn't be. A National Committee of Inquiry is a government quango and naturally looks upon the objects it inquires into—especially when they are paid for from taxes—as things subject to the powers of government. The word 'university' does occur, but usually as an adjective and never as the object of thought. But the kind of power over things that derives from paying for them is subject to rather obvious limits, even when, as in the case of a government that has got rid of constitutional checks and balances, to that power is added the power to make law. A government can do all sorts of things; what it can't do is say what those things mean. It can decide who is to get 'family allowance' but not what we are to understand by the word 'family'. It has the power to confer the legal status of 'university' upon whatever set of activities it pleases but not the power to prevent us from understanding the result as a joke. Its powers in this respect are no greater than those of the prostitute's client, who may choose what she does but not what it means to her. There, her freedom remains absolute ('the undefil'd, tho' ravish'd night and morn', as Blake puts it).

The word 'university' has a history which makes some things almost impossible to say, for example that the university should be for all, or for job-training, or to make us rich. The beauty of terms like 'higher education' and 'higher education sector', for someone with a remit, like Sir Ron, is that, denoting things that governments invent, they can be used however governments please, without fear of contradiction. The higher education sector—of the education system—doesn't exist except as a government conceives it or apart from the legislative and financial instruments that maintain it. It isn't a branch of education (which has no sectors and isn't a system), it is a branch of government. It is part not of education but of education-as-organization, 'education' as so much of *matériel* and of men and women, doing whatever they happen to be paid to do, be that what it may. Over the meaning of such things a government naturally does have power. Of an expression like 'higher education sector' Sir Ron might truly say, like Humpty Dumpty, 'When *I* use a word, it means just what I choose it to mean—neither more nor less.'

Two things ought to be noticed, though: firstly, that if Sir Ron says things about 'higher education' that can't be contradicted it's only because they are beyond the true and the false altogether. They are non-sense, for the freedom to give words what meaning we please is much like the freedom to walk, or even skate, without friction—self-contradictory. Secondly, as soon as Sir Ron starts to imagine that what he says about education-as-organization applies to education itself he ceases to talk the sort of pure non-sense which is immune from contradiction and starts talking the ordinary sort.

Doing without the word 'university', it is only natural that Sir Ron should do without 'thought' too. He does use it in his summary, once, and then in a way that is very revealing, as of something that comes in measurable, in investable, amounts, like time or 'resources': 'implementation [of the recommendation for the innovative use of the new Communications and Information Technologies to improve the quality of Higher Education] requires investment, in terms of time, thought and resources.' This is why, presumably, he speaks of the work of university teachers as if it had no definite character to it but was made up of various 'combinations' of different 'roles' or 'functions' which are 'likely to change ... at different stages of their careers'. The retort to which must be that a member of a university has just one 'role', and that is to think. He justifies himself by thought, or not at all. Thinking is to members of a university what playing is to a football team or worship to a congregation. To exchange that 'function' for some other or combination of others is to cease to *be* a member of the university, whether officially accredited by an Institute for Learning and Teaching in Higher Education (see below) or not.

'Thought' having no place in Sir Ron's vocabulary, it is again only natural that 'literature' and 'literate' should have none either. It won't have occurred to him that there could be any sense in which he was wanting in literacy himself. But what a terrible revenge the language takes on him! He has no place in his report for literature, and what he gets in its place is cant. His exemplary instances aren't Jane Austen and J. H. Newman but ... the anonymous authors of journalist cant, advertiser cant, politician cant, educator cant. What a sucker for the stuff Sir Ron is. His mind has for it the adhesiveness of fly-paper. A cliché has only to brush against it, and that's it: stuck. The Dearing Report will prove in centuries to come a sort of archaeological record of the clichés current amongst the English great and good in the summer of 1997. I have picked a whole basket of dead flies off the fly-paper (just of one species); lorry-loads remain.

The habit of metaphor is sometimes thought to be the mark of a poet. With Sir Ron, it's just a habit. Ever since Kenneth Baker (now there *was* a poet!) discovered that standards are the sort of thing that can be 'levered up' (by the National Curriculum—remember?), the literal-minded have (in Coleridge's phrase) talked of mind, and thought of bricks and mortar. So it's Sir Ron's way to use a certain range of terms in any sense but the literal (the art not so much of coining new expressions as clipping old):

quality of life [*except as something immeasurable*]; quality assurance [*of anything that can't be audited*]; mission [*but not of anything spiritual*]; vision [*ditto*]; management [*of anything but a business*]; franchise [*ditto*]; partners [*likewise*]; customers [*except of shops*]; clients [*except of solicitors and suchlike*]; delivery [*of anything but milk, coal or the post*]; provision [*but not of provisions*]; investment [*but not in the stock market*]; leading edge [*except of aeroplane wings*]; professional [*except to mean 'paid'*]; free-standing [*of anything but buildings*]; to produce [*anything but physical goods*]; drive [*anything but vehicles*]; seek continuously to improve performance of [*anything but an engine*]; generate [*anything but electricity*]; communications [*especially where no transmitters or receivers involved*]; target [*of anything but arrows*]; strategy [*except in warfare*]; mechanism [*of things immaterial*]; global market place [*for things spiritual*]; outcomes [*especially invisible*]; monitoring [*except in a schoolroom*]; etc etc.

He puts together little bits like these to make ... bigger bits. It's the verbal equivalent of meccano, lots of standardized bits put together in a few standardized ways. As with meccano, you best see what it's for *dis*assembled. A list of the report's clichés does more than convey an idea of its style, it makes the report itself superfluous. All the report's got that such a list hasn't (except a lot more of the same) is the grammatical links that join, or separate, the bits listed.

Mostly—but not always—the bits are put together grammatically, but then in sentences that might have been meant to prove the futility of grammar. The ungrammatical sentences are at least grammatically interesting, as illustrating the subtleties of usage. For Sir Ron and his Committee of Experts are not perfectly at ease amongst the subtleties of usage. Because they aren't using words to think with but are just fitting clichés together, they sometimes miss the native idiom, as in 'we received tremendous support and commitment to our task from ...' or 'we support the diversity between ...' or 'it is a strength in responding to ...' or 'to take an imaginative leap in devising ...' or (a bit of stage-French?) 'UK qualifications have standing.'

Sir Ron's cliché-aggregations are sentences in the sense that they aren't anything else. But if, as the linguists tell us, sentences make sense, they are only sentences in the way that Mr Collins's are. Mr Collins imitates sense and thereby parodies it. Sir Ron does the same. Typically Sir Ron's sentences combine a sort of windy assertiveness with banality, or something less:

> It should, therefore, be a national policy objective to be world class both in learning at all levels and in a range of research of different kinds. In higher education, this aspiration should be realised through a new compact involving institutions and their staff, students, government, employers and society in general.

> Higher Education must create a society committed to learning throughout life. That commitment will be required from individuals, the state, employers and providers of education and training.

> But over the next two decades, higher education will face challenges as well as opportunities. The effectiveness of its response will determine its future.

> The higher education sector will comprise a community of free-standing institutions dedicated to the creation of a learning society and the pursuit of excellence in their diverse missions. It will include institutions of world renown and it must be a conscious objective of national policy that the UK should continue to have such institutions.

> Higher education ... will contribute not only through ... and by ... but also by ... and ... and promoting the values that characterise higher education ... Equally ...

This is the way with words that Mr Collins and Mary Bennet have. Look what he does to the word 'compact'. What sort of compact is made between parties that not only aren't in any distinct logical relation to one another but even include one another, making up a list you could stretch out or shorten like a piece of elastic? How could you imagine these parties being separately represented? Often the weird emptiness of Sir Ron's well-constructed sentences is best brought out by trying to imagine what it is they *deny*: that it ought to be a national policy objective to be less than 'world class'? or to be 'world class' in learning but not research? or in learning at some levels not others? or in a range of research all of one kind?

Sir Ron's 'will' and 'must' are an endless tease (though no more so than his 'should'). You can't tell whether he's giving Leninist-bureaucratic orders, making predictions, making judgements or speaking in tautologies. In one passage which begins 'The future will require ...' he seems to be doing the four at once. Leaving aside the ludicrousness of the ambition to make our universities renowned (rather than just good), why *must* it be a conscious objective of national policy that they be anything at all? Is it somehow not enough just *to be* good, and to strive to be so, like Pele or Mozart or Mother Teresa? What's gained by making it, consciously, an objective—and of national policy—to be so? (Cf. some remarks below about 'goals'.) I don't suppose Sir Ron's committee made it their conscious objective to write a report that's world class, but would it have made any difference if they had? I don't suppose, either, that they had the conscious objective of being world class at having conscious objectives but world class at *that* is the one thing they undoubtedly are world class at.

Where are Sir Ron's imitation sentences going? Not—as you might think—nowhere. These cliché-agglutinations may not be the work of intelligence but they aren't the work of mere chance either, any more than those of the ancestral Collins. They have as good a reason for existing as Sir Ron himself. They are the solution to an insoluble problem: how to affirm the truth of the new master idea—that the purpose of education is to make us rich—without causing offence by denying the truth of the old—that it is to make us wise. Sir Ron is an evangelist for the new idea, and he must have seen, like other evangelists before him, that a new belief most readily supplants an old not by opposing but by merging with it. And how else could he bring wisdom to merge with riches except through the happy, distinction-annihilating power of the cliché? How else could oil and water be made to mix, chalk taste like cheese or Labour to lie down with the Tories? How else could the new idea of the university as a mass institution selling instruction in saleable skills be made compatible with the old idea of it as an élite institution giving a free and liberal education? Sir Ron does unite these opposites, but only by removing sense from both. For as we have shown there is no more genuine sense in the belief in education as investment than (from Sir Ron) in belief in the life-enhancingness of education.

In his prose all edges meet in the middle. It is the discursive equivalent of a spider-chart (see below) in that every single, distinct, plottable point on it gives directly on to every other. You don't have to *get* from A to B (or even *alpha* to *omega*) in this universe, you're already there. And it is the intelligence-defeating power of the cliché that puts you there. It is a power that makes all things possible. It makes Sir Ron to mental knots what Alexander was to string. The White Queen could believe six impossible things before breakfast. Alice should have met Sir Ron.

In Sir Ron's world there are no problems, only solutions. Lions lying down with lambs? No problem. Oil and water? No problem. Did Newman write a whole book on whether education is an end in itself or a means to an end? False problem. In Sir Ron's world (fortunate world!) it is both, simultaneously. It is life-enriching and desirable in its own right, of course, *and* a good investment (*excellent* personal investment, return averaging between 11 per cent and 14 per cent, *and* fundamental to the economic health of the nation, enabling it to compete at the cutting edge of innovation). Education and training are one and the same thing under different names. They (or it) both (or either) indifferently equip people for work *and* foster culture for its own sake. Both (or either) *both* increase knowledge and understanding for their own sakes *and* foster their application for the benefit of the economy. Things which are good in themselves are also, thank goodness, Sir Ron finds, *immensely* useful. They are even saleable. Higher education has, of course, always had the role of guarding and transmitting culture and maintaining the values which make for civilized society, but now, with the development of information technology, it faces the challenge and opportunity of selling its products, competitively, all over the world. It can now both promote, as it always has, the values which characterize itself *and also* turn them into programmes that can be marketed in the global marketplace. Good leads to goods, improving the quality of life in quantifiable and quite unmysterious ways.

Nor is there any need to fear that past, present or future expansion of the universities is incompatible with the maintenance of standards. We don't set targets but we do envisage a rise in the national average of young people participating in full-time higher education to 45 per cent, or more; we deplore the continued under-representation of socio-economic groups III to V, people with disabilities and specific ethnic minority groups; and in future we must enable *all* students, even those who have struggled to reach the threshold of higher education, to ... [better be careful here] ... to achieve beyond their expectations. But there is no need to fear that any of this will lead to lower standards because we can at the same time *make a commitment to high ones*, and thus not only have many more students, including the strugglers, but pursue quality, sustain a culture which demands disciplined thinking, and safeguard the rigour of our academic awards all at the same time.

It is just as well, of course, that the pursuit of civilization and high standards on the one hand and the pursuit of sales and expansion on the other go so conveniently together, because the need for greater investment in education-and-training to meet the international challenge and the demand, the informed demand, from all those people ready and willing to move on to higher education would drive a resumed expansion of student numbers *anyway*—that is, even if the civilization and the high standards had to (as they say in the building trade) go the journey.

The overall increase in participation in higher education (an achievement in which higher education can take justifiable pride) is to be welcomed—because it is democratic. Culture and civilization are things to approve of, and so is democracy. Never mind that some senses of 'democratic' diverge from some senses of 'cultured' and 'civilized', there's no need to choose. Get the right throb in your voice and no-one will notice. Imagine you're George Washington and you won't even notice yourself:

> higher education ... part of the conscience of society [but not any old society, *democratic* society] ...

> part of its task to accept a duty of care for the well-being of civilisation [but not any rotten old civilisation, *democratic* civilisation] ...

> a major role in shaping society [but a society that is democratic, civilised and inclusive] ...

> rights of the individual ... responsibilities of the individual ...

> respect for the individual and respect by the individual ... respect for evidence; respect for individuals and their views [respect for everything except genuine thinking] ...

> the search for truth [in a style that turns it into the blind leading the blind] ...

For Sir Ron all is possible—not just to believe, but to do. You just put in place, firstly, your national policy objective—to combine participation for all with high standards from top to bottom—and then your mechanisms for achieving it—a participation strategy, a progress monitoring mechanism and an achievement review provision, *plus* a Quality Assessment Agency with expert teams, benchmark information, a framework of qualifications and threshold standards. And Bob's-your-uncle. You've not only widened participation without lowering standards but reduced your need for an apparatus of quality assessment and audit too. You've got it all. You *can* drink simultaneously from the mouth and the source of the Nile. All you need is a long enough straw.

And Sir Ron has all sorts of straws, which he strongly recommends we suck. One (a very short one, some university members might think) is the establishment of a professional Institute for Learning and Teaching in Higher Education, whose purpose would be to establish university teaching as a profession in its own right. It would do this through its accreditation function. University teaching in the UK will never be a profession in its own right, or be world class, until it's the norm for all permanent staff with teaching responsibilities to be trained on accredited programmes. So, over the medium term, it should become the normal requirement that all new full-time academic staff with teaching responsibilities achieve at least associate membership of the Institute, for the successful completion of probation.[6]

And there we have the centrepiece of Sir Ron's vision: there at the very tip-top of the higher education tree sits Sir Ron, at the head of a Committee of his clones; immediately below, the Institute, staffed, similarly, by his clones; and below that, the universities (as it were), staffed, from top to bottom—from the medium term onwards—by virtue of the powers invested in the clones of the Institute, by no-one who is not a clone, by *accréditation*. To be a bit of Blu-tack or a bad sector on a floppy disk, yes, but to be Mary Bennet or Mr Collins, to be a clone of Ron Dearing's ... I'd rather be Dolly the Sheep.

And what will the students of the third millennium have to show for all this many-sided educational excellence? Among other things, a 'Progress File', for life. Sir Ron gives the File a paragraph to itself; and the paragraph is worth quoting in full. It is a sign of what those mysteries 'the learning society' and 'learning for life' mean:

> Young people entering higher education will increasingly come with a Progress File which records their achievements up to that point and which is intended for use throughout life. We favour the development of a national format for a transcript of achievement in higher education which students could add to their Progress Files.

And it won't end there: 'We envisage individuals building up a portfolio of achievements at a range of levels over a working lifetime,' and having them too, no doubt, conscientiously entered into their Files, as permanent measures of Progress made, and not. In this brave new world, we are to have our school reports always with us, like the *biografi* the Albanians carried under Hoxha.[7]

Sir Ron has a vision of us learning all our lives, but not just in the course of living, as we all do, like Elizabeth Bennet and Darcy, or don't, like Lydia and Wickham. His vision is not of life as a classroom, and as including criticism with breakfast, but of the classroom as life, with cant for breakfast, dinner and tea, administered by a Mr Collins or a Mary Bennet who has at least associate membership of the ILTHE, *avec accréditation*. The only alternative he can imagine is that 'individuals manage their own development and learning', which is, of course, just what Mary Bennet does, an accredited teacher with herself for her own pupil. Here is the form Big Brother is to take on our little island in the third millennium. Here's what Fate has in store for *us*. Not Hitler or Stalin or Mao (and certainly not Cromwell) but Mary Bennet, Mr Collins, Sir Ron, a Dunce and a Headmaster rolled into one and forever checking our Progress Files. A vision of a life without literature, without criticism, without thought, but *with* education—as a life sentence.

5   The New University as Training in Skills

THAT PROFESSIONAL INTERESTS are best served indirectly, Newman made the keystone of his argument for the university; and, for a hundred years, that made the keystone of many such arguments—though not the Newbolt Report's, and not Leavis's, to which ours is much indebted. Newman's dodge worked for a century, until Mrs Thatcher came along and called the bluff about the graceful versatile dentists. But where *is* the use? she asked. Where are all these graduate wealth-creators that liberal education promised to supply us with? What have we *really* to show for the expense? Useful is what you say a university is? Then let it *be* so—and *directly*.

It's simple and it's candid. And in the long run it can't be anything but healthy. Mrs Thatcher forced the university to face the questions Newman enabled it to avoid. His dodge permitted the university to flourish dishonestly, without enquiring too closely into its own nature, and to take public money on false pretences. Her challenge, if it doesn't just crush the university out of existence altogether, will force it to justify itself on more intelligent and more honest grounds.

Immediately, however, the results have been otherwise.

When it was proposed to 'break down the barrier between academic and vocational training', as *The Independent* headlined it—a 'barrier' also noticed by *The Times* and *The Daily Telegraph*[1]—there was, not for the first time in this free country, no public debate. No murmurs were heard from the universities. The journalists sang in unison.[2] The opposition parties had no need to consider. They were able to complain that the Conservatives had stolen their ideas: that is, there was all-party consensus, usually a dangerous sign in the Commons.

The nub of the White Paper's proposals was therefore to eliminate 'the distinction between polytechnics and universities' (*Telegraph*), and introduce a new 'vocational' school qualification of equal esteem with academic qualifications, handing over control of this latter sixth-form area to regional bodies dominated by businessmen. The White Paper was quoted as saying:

The title of polytechnic has never been widely understood. The British academic world realises that the polytechnics are higher education institutions achieving the same academic standards and giving the same quality of education as most universities. Many able school-leavers and their parents still tend, however, to regard the title as a reason for making them a second choice.

It was this foretaste of spin-doctoring, the emphasis on the doing away with the old academic snobbery, that allowed participants in the non-debate to avoid the awkward question whether the universities are really as useful as the polytechnics. The universities' reply to the challenge consists, in the first place, of the claim that they just are: if there is no distinction between education and training, education *is* training. The *unum necessarium*, all agree, is the supply of graduates essential to the expansion of the national economy—any graduates in anything, for the supply is offered as in itself the universities' mode of being useful.

Any suggestion that the distinction between training and education was, is, and imaginably still could be, *real*, is literally unsayable in the 'heavy' dailies, the weeklies or the Commons. Any propensity to say this ineffable is defused in advance: it would be mere *snobbery*, the snobbery of the academic looking down on the vocationally qualified mechanic. (The reverse snobbery of the practical man who looks down on the academic, like the old carpenter in *The Miller's Tale*, no longer bothers anybody.)

The then Prime Minister, John Major, led the way in breaking down the barriers and removing the distinction. 'It is a distinction well worth removing,' he said. He knew, having suffered as an outsider from the snobbery of the educated. *The Independent*, complaining that the proposed reforms were 'timid'[3] twice used the word 'snobbery' in its editorial. *The Daily Telegraph* stood out in qualifying its own support with the proviso that different things should not be confused; it didn't, however, get as far as saying what the different things are.

The proposal to allow the polytechnics to rename themselves universities naturally followed from the breaking down of the barriers and, in the absence of opposition, was enacted with remarkable speed and smoothness. The former polys devised romantic names like Northumbria (later to be judged the number one university in England[4]) or took over ones well-known already like Oxford (with an addition in small type). There was no parallel proposal to allow the universities to rename themselves polytechnics, which they have in fact been making feeble efforts to become.

The next stage after the renaming of the polys, the speed and smoothness of which was even more remarkable, was an explosion in the number of 'universities' such that the former polys themselves began to be thought of as 'old' universities. In 2000 there are more than five times as many 'universities' in the UK as there were in 1980.

With the simultaneous announcement[5] of the establishment of a University for Industry and a Life Long Learning system whereby tax reliefs would be given to workers embarking on courses (to be 'delivered' to terminals in public libraries and workplaces), any special place in the scheme of things for an institution devoted to liberal education seems finally to have vanished.

So at the turn of the millennium, on the verge of the competitive world of the twenty-first century, we had vast amounts of university education—though, of course, still not enough—all officially of equal esteem and all useful.

*   *   *

There may still be lurking doubts about whether Philosophy is as useful as Dentistry. The universities have hit on the perfect way of putting them to rest and of persuading chancellors of the exchequer to keep their cash-flow increasing, like the growth of the national economy, indefinitely. This, unfortunately, is by way of another dodge, and one, moreover, plainly descended from Newman's.

If the challenge is made to show the return on the investment in universities, the academics will give a simple and complete answer. What have we to show for all this money spent? Answer: 'skills'.

If you are a public figure and want to be taken seriously on the subject of education, you call it skills. You won't be taken seriously if you don't. It's a word that in itself obliterates the snobbish old distinction between education and training; and it makes education straightforward and definite, at one and the same time something you can 'do something about' and something worth the doing because it will increase GDP. Skills (always plural, usually adjectival) is a word that puts you in control—like Tony Blair, in control, on the *Today* programme[6] promising to do something about our shocking position in the World League Skills Table (we were forty-second). It also shows that you know that there is more to education than facts. Dickens's Gradgrind may have proceeded on the assumption that two and two make four and nothing left over, but we now know that there is something practically even more important, training in skills.

Whether training itself will do all or even most of what is expected of it is a question we need do no more than glance at, this being a work about universities not economics. 'Is training a waste of money?' is a question we would not presume to ask, though it was the title of a serious article in *The Financial Times* which even used one of our phrases,[7] and which discussed, for instance, the in-house 'universities' started by American companies, like Motorola University and 'the famous Hamburger University where Macdonald's graduates 3000 store managers a year'. 'Does training affect the bottom line? Or is it a ... PR exercise in pouring money down the drain?' It was argued that in some cases the answer may be the latter. Another article in the same financial heavyweight raised the question of the use of 'gap years'.

> 'Taking a year off between school and university can not only be made to pay,' says Simon Targett, 'it can also help your chances of landing a good job.'[8]

This is because

> The one thing that blue chip companies complain about, year in and year out, is the paucity of job skills among today's graduates. ...
>
> Such skills can be acquired in other ways . . . .

If the useful training offered by universities is actually better acquired by staying away, why go? Let us grant, however, that if, as yet another article put it, 'the courses fit a very specific business need, and ... "this morning's learning can be applied to this afternoon's job"',[9] the money spent on training may be well invested. These are precisely not the skills offered by the universities, which can keep their promise of being useful only by a drastic reinvention of the notion of 'skill'.

For the new universities' offer depends on a double slide about 'skill' much like Newman's single one about 'mind', though less defensible because dependent on a much more obvious misuse of a word.

'Skill' is not one of Wittgenstein's family-resemblance words. A skill is a teachable way of doing a particular thing. Riding a bicycle is a skill; making a spongecake calls on several skills. Some of the traditional trades like signwriting or wheelwrighting demand skills of a high order. On the other hand, skill, as Frank Palmer says, in an essay that should be classical, cannot be stretched to 'a sense of wonder' or 'to adjust to different social contexts' or 'to accept responsibility', all of which have been offered by educationists as examples of skills to be taught in schools.[10] Nor can PSE (Personal and Social Education) be thought of with any sense as a set of skills. *The Universities We Need* quotes an SCAA document—'The value of PSE was seen by some in developing interpersonal skills, including managing feelings, understanding others and learning to take responsibility for one's actions'[11]—and asks, 'What are "interpersonal skills"? Aren't interpersonal relationships more a matter of what kind of *person* you are rather than what skills you deploy? ... As for "managing feelings", there is something worrying about a person of whom you could say that he was skilled at managing his feelings.' The SCAA document includes 'the skills that enable people to make wise decisions and develop acceptable values . . . .' 'But how could morality be reduced to skills?'[12]

Are the skills that education claims to use itself any more like genuine skill? The answer to the question 'What are study skills?' given by one authority begins,

> A skill is a 'practised ability'. No doubt you will already have, or be learning, many skills—you may be able to play tennis or football well, having learned the basic skills and then practised so you get better and better at the game.[13]

Some objections could be made: not all practised abilities are skills (talking, for instance) and more goes into games than skill. But so far we would not dissent much. The question is whether education 'skills' are analogous.

There are skills which will enable you to become a good student. These skills can be learned and then practised in the same way as you learned to swim, ski or play tennis. ... This Guideline will look at developing good STUDY HABITS, improving your MEMORY, LISTENING & NOTE-TAKING, REVIEWING your work, improving your READING and ESSAY WRITING, and finally REVISION and EXAM TECHNIQUES.[14]

Are there such skills? The University of Birmingham School of Continuing Studies advertised 'two self-contained but linked half-day sessions' on 'Note-taking and Listening Skills' and 'Improving Your Essay-writing Skills'.[15] The offer was necessarily vacuous because there is no general good advice to be given about listening but 'do—if what is being said is worth listening to,' and about taking notes but 'don't if you can help it.' (People vary and some do help themselves by taking notes, though generally note-taking is a distraction from the critical attention required in a lecture audience.) In both these titles skill is redundant. Nothing is lost and, it seems to us, much gained if the word is deleted. But it couldn't possibly be, in the new university. Without skills the vacuity of the offers being made about note-taking, listening, thinking etc would be undisguisable.

The skill to end all skills was brought home by my son from a Careers lesson, supplied by the Hereford & Worcester Careers Service in 1998. 'What are key personal skills?' was a question answered, of course, in a series of multi-coloured bullet-points. For the most part they fulfilled my prediction that the genuine skills on offer are the three Rs, for they began with

- use numbers correctly
- read, write and communicate effectively

The correct use of numbers can take place in many contexts, and if you can read one document you ought to be able to read many. But after this came things that are not skills at all, like '• work as part of a team' and '• show enthusiasm and interest.' The latter may really be a skill (that is, *fake* an interest) but if so is undesirable. The one that took my fancy, though, was in the middle:

- learn new skills

Now there's a skill for you. Learn the skill of learning skills and what else do you need? In fact it makes redundant even the more advanced skills also listed: '• problem solve [*sic*] ... • action plan [*sic*] ... • speak different languages.' Why worry if you have the skill of learning new skills? Wait until you need to action plan or to problem solve, or to use new languages, then use your universal skill of acquiring skills as required. (The putting into practice of the '• speak different languages' skill was first recorded on the Day of Pentecost, but was then rightly regarded as miraculous.) There is not, and in the nature of genuine skill could not be, such a skill.

The following year, even glossier and with even more colours, the equivalent brochure listed 'employability skills' that included 'interest in the job' and 'experience of the job' which would also have to be miraculous (though not a skill) to someone trying to get their first job.

In this age of the marriage of the entrepreneur with education, a number of businesses have naturally been marketing the sale of educational skills. The samples I have seen have much in common with Victorian marketing of patent medicines, Fenning's Fever Curer and the like, though that, being made of sulphuric acid, actually did something: if you survived the Fever Curer you were likely to have survived the fever also. The concern quoted above that offers listening as one of the key skills says in the same document what it means by listening as a skill:

> You need to be an ACTIVE LISTENER. Only 10% of what you hear or read is KEY INFORMATION. If you can learn to pick out KEY WORDS AND IDEAS from lessons, lectures, videos or books and record them in a way which is easy to review, you will greatly improve your memory skills. Your teacher may say things like:
> the main reasons/points are ...
> it is important to remember ...
> > LISTEN actively by looking for new
> > IDEAS which are shown by words which are
> > SIGNALS.
> > TAKE PART in lessons by asking questions to
> > EXPLORE the subject in greater depth and take
> > NOTES of key ideas and words [16]

How would you identify the KEY WORDS AND IDEAS? The teacher would tell you. (Key words are in any case a trap. One GCSE Biology board, I am told, gives the impression that key words are self-sufficient by docking marks if they are not used. But you do need the lock: the understanding of why the words are 'key'.) Why the teaching profession is thought to be so grossly incompetent as to waste 90 per cent of the available time we are not told.

This mind-boggling layout does seem to me actually demented. If a student wrote it in an exam, the board would call for a medical report. Which 90 per cent of *it*, by the way, is discardable noise, and what skill could tell me?

The other side of the sheet explains the same thing by an even madder 'spider plan'. This is incoherent in the sense that there is no way of knowing how or in what order the parts are supposed to be connected. 'Listening' is the spider at the middle, but whether it rushes out to bite and digest 'Ideas', 'Explore' or 'Take Part', must depend on whim. It seems to follow that if you 'Take Part' or 'Take Notes' you are probably not having 'Ideas'; which is probably true, but not helpful. Why is this imaginable as a skill (what work is being done and how?) or as having anything to do with learning except, possibly, as an inoculation against it?

Today's radio [17] reports a government 'initiative' for thinking to be taught in schools as a skill. This would certainly be a short-cut; unluckily it can't work.

The work of the university just *is* thinking, in the different modes represented by the subjects. Thinking in philosophy is just a long phrase for philosophy; to think in philosophy is just to do it, and there is no short cut to doing it by way of acquiring elsewhere the skill of thinking then applying it to philosophy. The mastery of any subject, the getting inside it, is the same as mastering its particular modes of thought. Learning at any level higher than the three Rs cannot be either a skill or a set of skills.

All the same, all this learning-skill stuff might be thought at worst harmless nonsense (though if education is devoted to making sense how can it tolerate nonsense?). But go on to the skills not needed for learning itself, and the shams may be vicious. Hereford College of Technology advertises an '8 week evening course' in 'Basic Counselling Skills'. 'So what exactly will I learn?' asked one section. Answer: 'active listening, exploring thoughts and feelings, use of language, empathy and the use of questions'. Somebody might actually need help from someone certificated in this course. Those who think empathy is a skill are unlikely to be able to share anyone's feelings. There must be human damage as a result of these shams.

But then again, the skills might be genuine and useful. On 21 October 1998 it was announced that in Sheffield, in the millennial year, would be established the University for Industry. According to Radio 4's *Today* programme, its aim was to 'promote basic literacy and numeracy skills'. 'Sounds like a good idea,' said James Naughtie, interviewing the country's first Professor of Life Long Learning. Quite possibly, though one wonders how many illiterate adults will be able to find their way to Life Long Learning. A good idea—but a *university*? If universities are there to teach you the three Rs, what are primary schools for?

*   *   *

But is not this just a peripheral muddle that leaves unscathed the basic offer of the universities to provide a trained workforce? The doubt that philosophers might not be quite as useful as dentists is answered by a different refinement of the concept of 'skill'. What the graduates have received is not skills only, but 'personal transferable skills'. How will the universities produce graduates guaranteed to increase GDP? By teaching you one useful skill in particular (like golf-course construction or tar-macadaming) but—and here is the beauty of it—a skill which will come in equally handy when you do something else. This is not quite the purely magical skill of learning skills mentioned above, though closely related, but is even more convenient. Any university degree whatever will give you 'the general (and therefore transferable) intellectual skills which lie at the heart of higher education'.[18] I first noticed the idea in one of the multi-signatured documents (a number of the signatories being philosophers) with which academics try to influence politicians:

All university Arts courses have vocational relevance in that, far more than present-day Science courses, they develop, and are recognised by employers to develop, certain skills valued over the whole range of industry, commerce, education and other services, and administration—skills such as the ability to cope with long cumbersome documents, the ability to express themselves clearly in a variety of contexts, and the ability to think on their feet.[19]

This idea appears in the *Charter* in the already quoted phrase 'students are taught transferable skills like problem-solving'; it would be impossible to justify the subsidies to Arts faculties by the *Charter*'s lights on any other assumption; and, as Blake, Smith and Standish report,

It is taken for granted [by the Green Paper on Lifelong Learning, 1998] that there is a significant corpus of skills or bodies of knowledge whose attainment facilitates performance in a range of significantly disparate activities, so that learning them makes the employee more readily switch to a different job....[20]

This, too, is why (as my fourteen-year-old son reported from a Careers lesson) all university degrees are of equal status. Whatever skill you learn will be useful in itself (if, for instance, you want to manage a Pig Enterprise, take the course in Pig Enterprise Management), but because it is compounded out of elemental skills that are the same anywhere will also enable you, when you have one of the mid-career changes we are told to expect, to switch smoothly to Floristry or the teaching of History.

This is yet another thing that doesn't sound honest and isn't.

In the nature both of genuine academic thinking and of genuine skills, the offered programme does not and cannot work. 'Transferable skills' is a contradiction in terms. Skills are not transferable. I do the washing up most days and I vacuum-clean the house most weeks. I enjoy computer chess. I have just finished writing a book with an appendix on medieval grammatical categories which, I do hope, reads lucidly, but over which I sweated blood. I have (please God) become surprisingly clear-minded about medieval grammar, but alas there has been no consequent improvement in my chess, and I wash up in just the same way that I did before I proved that the Modistae did not discover the well-formed sentence. Why should this surprise anybody? Any skills involved are so called just because they can't be transferred. Learn how to mend your car engine and you will also learn how to work out the difference between stress and beat in English sixteenth-century metrics. As one trying to do both I assure you that neither gives any assistance at all with the other.

Some work with machines or with computers resembles other work with machines or computers, but that is not because skills are transferable but because some skills extend over more than one task.

Let us hope it is true that an educated person will have some general sense of tackling new problems different from an uneducated person's, though 'problem' is so vague as to be problematic. But as Carlyle said,

Abbot Samson had no experience in governing; had served no apprenticeship to the trade of governing,—alas, only the hardest apprenticeship to that of obeying. ...But it is astonishing, continues Jocelin, how soon he learned the ways of business; and, in all sorts of affairs, became expert beyond others.[21]

This is not because lecturing in the schools, or the monastic life of poverty, chastity, obedience and prayer, formed a set of transferable skills, but because of the man Samson was after that discipline. This is one of the many places where education is in fact sharply distinct from training in skills.

Where actually, in the real world that the electronic faces are always telling us we must enter, are these transferable skills? A meeting of Birmingham tutors in continuing education was questioning the necessity always to be nagging mature students (who quite often do spare-time degree work for pure academic motives like wanting to master an academic subject) to accumulate 'credits'. The woman in charge said that testing all the time is necessary to make sure the students are acquiring the personal transferable skills to take back with them to the world of business. 'Yes, the Government says that,' I objected, 'but none of us believe it, do we?' After the obligatory apology for saying anything in favour of the then government, the reply was that she did believe in personal transferable skills. Asked for just one example, she gave her chairing of the meeting then in progress. Chair one meeting, I suppose, chair the lot. But if even chairing meetings is thought of as a skill, not an art, or not common sense, it is no wonder that so many meetings are badly run.

Another clue to what 'personal transferable skills' might be intended to refer to, beyond my guess 'reading, writing, and PC operation', was given when one of our HEFCW (Higher Education Funding Council for Wales) inspectors (see Chapter 6) pounced on a marginal comment made by one of my colleagues that cross-heads and bullet points are not appropriate to English essays. In the real world there are cross-heads and bullet points. *The Times* now obligingly saves us the trouble of reading its editorials ('long cumbersome documents'?) by giving the gist in one line at the top. This is communications skills, and if you can do it in Classics or Philosophy you can no doubt also do it in *Times* editorials. It was also intimated that our assessments were far too much based on the written word. We should be paying more attention to the skills of oral presentations (and no doubt to the eye-contacts and smiles which are so important a part of interview skills; one may smile and smile and be a villain).

Our Classics Department, similarly visited, prepared a leaflet to explain what personal transferable skills are. Some of these 'skills' are not even desirable, like 'make quick, appropriate decisions'; cf. 'the ability to think on their feet' above. An academic discipline is not the mental equivalent of speed-reading; in genuine academic thinking (as in ordinary life) it may not be possible to solve a problem against the clock. The Classics Department included things like 'show resourcefulness' and the even more immediately relevant 'withstand and deal with pressures', which would be useful if the phrases were not too vague to say anything, but also 'explain clearly' and 'give appropriate examples'. This is a version of the *Charter*'s 'problem solving' and is necessary to the whole programme. Learn how to solve problems in one context and carry over the skill to another. The reason why, as already reported, this does not work, is that what constitutes a solution of a problem in one subject will not in another. 'Explanation', as Aristotle recognized, will vary with context. Even if there were anything here properly called skill it would not be transferable. The sense of what examples are appropriate must belong within a particular discussion.

Transferable skills remain the foundation on which the new university is built, and are about to be inserted into the old. The North Commission is to impose them on Oxford, 'including computer literacy and leadership', along with '"non-examination-based" forms of assessment',[22] in order to 'meet the demands of employers'. Does it really require any penetration to see that computer skills and leadership do not belong in the same category, or even that one of these can be taught and the other can't? Whether Oxford retains its own leadership after the imposition of transferable skills remains to be seen.

If there are no such things as personal transferable skills, the consensus reason for supporting the Arts subjects collapses. We hope it need not follow that the university must be entirely abolished, but to the extent that it is supposed to be a direct preparation for wealth-acquisition that does follow. This belief in an *organon* of transferable skills may, however, go some way to explaining the sort of farce I heard of when a man with a degree in Management Consultancy turned up to run a newly-privatized power station and had no idea what to do.

Another part of the current political rhetoric about the competitive world of the next millennium flatly contradicts the part about transferable skills, for it is often recognized that skills are not transferable, that training in one process will not do anything to prepare you for other processes; we must therefore be ready and willing to retrain. (Readiness is a disposition not a skill.) Macdonald's, the worldwide fast-food chain, employs chefs who (I am told, though I have not confirmed the information) are always retrained and duly certificated by Macdonald's University as fit to cook in any Macdonald's on the face of the earth. (The training programme takes two days.) The assumption is not that they have skills which can be transferred, but that the two days will give them brand new skills.

During the general election campaign of 1997, the lecturers' union, the AUT, obtained from all the establishment parties statements of higher education policy. Unsurprisingly, they were virtually indistinguishable. Labour and the Conservatives agreed that (i) as Gillian Shephard put it, 'many will switch career more than once in their lifetime,' which demands 'flexibility' (David Blunkett's version: the demand for 'innovative and creative workforces'). On the other hand, (ii) Mrs Shephard promised to 'ensure that they are equipped with the skills … needed by the labour market of the 21st century' (Labour: 'highly skilled … workforces'). The skills are precisely what will have to be relearned if we are to have flexibility; they will serve only in the first job, after which new skills will have to be learnt. The complete self-contradictory propositions therefore ran: Conservative—'the skills and flexibility needed by the labour market' (if skills needed, flexibility not needed); Labour—'highly skilled, innovative and creative workforces' (if creative and innovative, no need to be highly skilled).

Even if personal transferable skills are a con-trick, the skills the universities teach must be genuine? Some (we have a list in Chapter 9) do look useful, though most would have been beneath the dignity of a polytechnic. If you want to sell scent and have the leisure not to learn the trade while working at it, perhaps Perfumery Business will give you some good advice. Then if you wish to branch out into mail order, Packaging will come into its own. But World Studies? Will they give you the skill to deal with the World?

The ex-universities sometimes lose *both* their own true role of providing opportunities for thought, *and* the polytechnics' true role of training in the higher reaches of useful knowledge, *and* the adult-education sorts of low-grade usefulness; for they lay on courses which, without making any pretence to thought, are not, either, at any level, useful.

Penguin sent me a catalogue called *Essential Reading for Women*.[23] This was aimed at the growing Women's Studies market. 'Women's' is surely a dative, meaning studies for women; if so it confesses in its title that it has students but neither subject nor object. University College, London was offering in the year 2000 'taster' courses for prospective students on 'Women in Mathematics', 'Women in Earth and Planetary Sciences' and 'Women in Engineering (2 days residential)'. Would any knowledge of maths be required to follow the first or of engineering for the last? Is the interest supposed to be psychological? historical? What is the aim of the 'women's studies' in terms either of thought or of usefulness?

'Women's Studies' has grossly reintroduced sex discrimination into universities by way of the repulsive and untrue principle that some academic activity is restricted to members of one sex:

> Their anthology … has no male contributors, and all its essays deal either with theoretical questions or with the work of women writers. This woman-centred approach has now become the dominant trend within Anglo-American feminist criticism.[24]

'Woman-centred' cannot but remind us of 'child-centred' (though it has not yet become the dominant trend that children's books are written by children), and with that gives the even more repulsive hint that women are the more imbecile sex. The other sex can sometimes, however, be admitted on a kind of honorary-imbecile basis.[25]

It is hardly to be pretended, is it, that Tourism is a subject calling for the disinterested pursuit of truth for its own sake? It does not follow, however, from the non-academic nature of the activity that anything useful is going on. Can Tourism even be made to sound as if it is of any use to the local boarding-house keepers (who in fact mock it)?

If only a few students are sitting an exam it is labour-saving to amalgamate several groups into one exam hall, which can become a sort of microcosm of the new university. In one such, the handful of English students who had opted to read some Chaucer (unread by the rest) were alongside a few students writing on French Modernist Poetry, and more than a dozen on Language and Reality, no doubt discussing Plato, Rorty and so on; but the bulk, 80 or 90, drawn from the Faculties of Engineering, Science and Arts, and pursuing courses in 'Business Studies, Management Science, European Business Studies, European Management Science, American Management Studies, Modern Languages with Business Studies [and/or the still catch-all subject], Geography', were sitting a three-hour paper called Tourism Studies.[26]

A misdistribution of papers to confront the Language and Reality philosophers with this one might have led to interesting academic results. The answers that could have been made, in a sort of way, to some of the questions, could only have been Arts-faculty kinds: opinion based on impressions or experience, or refined common sense. This was evidently not what the setters had in mind; the questions were all invitations to be pseudo-scientific:

1 Explain briefly what is meant by each of the following:
   (a) Tourism destination segmentation
   (b) Sustainable tourism development
   (c) Carrying capacity (in relation to tourism development)
   (Each part of the question carries one third of the marks.)

2 Enumerate and discuss the dimensions of the tourism industry and their interrelationships with each other.

The dimensions: as if of a warplane. They must really be arbitrarily decided by the experts in Tourism. Tourism is to be defined as what is discussed in the Department of Tourism. Arbitrary definition naturally leads to pseudo-scientific treatment of very vague matters. 'With positive host–guest interaction and, therefore, socio-cultural impacts, can tourism become a worthy effort towards fostering world peace? Cite examples to support your answer.' The one-word answer to that is 'No'; otherwise it is the kind of 'question' that would actually be better treated in a primary school, where the debates may be at their own level quite sensible and unmarred by academic cant and pomposity.

This examination couldn't in any way provoke to thought. Really to do academic work in this examination would be to reject the questions. If I were recruiting for a tourist agency I would consider a completed course in Tourism a positive drawback. It would certificate something worse than a simple waste of time, namely that the graduate had successfully 'taken on board' a lot of pretentious waffle, with the likely upshot of enhanced self-importance and salary expectations.

Tourism may be thought to be a sitting duck (though it's worth insisting that the mansion-house of the goodly family of the Sciences should not breed sitting ducks), but what about Business Management? Is not that directly useful?

'Management', though it pretends to be a subject teachable at university level, is actually one of the great bluffs of the age, along with its first cousin skills. The two together, management-skills, is a double-whammy that few of the recipient 'customers' can resist. But where is the definable content or method that makes Management a subject? And how can it avoid the gross fallaciousness of supposing that the organization of human beings is a collection of general skills that can be taught on courses?

Management magazines being amongst the ephemera discarded on railway trains, I have sampled a few, and am still surprised that they bear out so consistently my prediction that they *must* be childish. Pick up examples on any inter-city. If we must have one quoted:

> As part of the National Health Service drive to implement Opportunity 2000—the Business in the Community initiative to get more women into management posts— senior NHS women have been given the chance to learn vital management skills.
>
> The women, a mixture of clinicians and managers, spent three days exploring The Industrial Society's unique five way management model. This looks at managing not only those who report to us, but also managing ourselves, our colleagues, those above us and the strategic picture.[27]

Perhaps this should be recommended to the Church of England, which seems to be having some difficulty managing 'ourselves' (some of its members), and even more in managing 'those above us' (God). The uniqueness claimed for The Industrial Society's 'model', I regret to report, does not consist in its absolute meaningless. That is something it shares with the rest.

Meanwhile, in the 'real world' of commerce, which does effectively confirm or contradict the judgements of investors by way of share prices, 'BTR was built by one man—Sir Owen Green—on a single premise: that management was a generic skill, and that good managers could manage anything. In the end, this proved false ... .'[28] Cf. 'The idea that a good manager can manage any business has been largely discredited.'[29] If so, what is taught at management schools?[30]

And what about a Centre for European Business Studies? Well, business studies of any sort—and what is added to them by 'European': is European Business somehow academically different from American Business? When I asked in the College *Newsletter* nobody told me. (The members of the Centre maintain a large output of what they call 'double-blind-refereed papers',[31] which one takes to be publications adjudicated by experts blind in both eyes.) 'Fatuous non-university subjects' was a phrase in a letter the *Newsletter* did print from a much-respected professor of Geology, whose subject has been got rid of in the college, about Tourism and Business Studies.[32] Nobody tried to refute him.

Again, we may be thought to be picking off the unhealthy stragglers on the periphery of the useful herd. But everything we have said of Football Management or the poor little European Business School at Swansea applies *a fortiori* to the Oxford Business School, the development of which made a long-running story in *The Financial Times*. 'Oxford University wants a leading MBA course but academics oppose the £40m project.' At last, I thought, a genuine debate. They will surely not let Oxford down to the level of Harvard. At Oxford they still know that there is no intellectual substance in business schools? This, however, was not to be the subject of the debate. The building proposed is to be 'on a greenfield site in the heart of the city'. It was an environment issue, not an academic one. That sharp journal was not on the *qui vive* for signs of academic nervousness from the business school. They were there, however. The same issue carried a letter from the Chairman of the Council of the School of Management Studies, University of Oxford, in which he declared his hope

> that as Oxford, and even Cambridge, wholeheartedly develop their business schools, more of our brightest students will perceive a career in business as a respectable intellectual challenge, and thereby increase the quality of our national management resource.

(Though if, as he also hoped, the students come from across the world, we shall also be increasing the quality of the management resource of our competitors.) There is room for improvement, then, and not all the brightest students manage to notice the respectable intellectual challenge?

The following week, the dons voted no. 'Some dons fear that academic freedom would be restricted by the foundation.'[33] This, however, was because the benefactor whose millions were to endow the school had prudently allotted to himself 'controlling influence on the foundation', not because nothing calling itself a Business School can possibly have any academic standards—a remark no doubt too ungentlemanly for Oxford. The following year the dons relented and the prestigious development is to go ahead by which the great university dangerously recognizes as belonging to it a set of activities which are neither inductions to thought nor to useful skills.

If Oxford goes, can Cambridge be far behind? 'The course is particularly attractive to overseas students', at £17,500 a year.[34] Is the idea then that our national economy gets the £17,500 and is then further advantaged by the sending back to Asia, the USA etc of competitors crippled by the management course?

In our less ambitious way at Swansea we offered 'Evening Programmes for Management Development'[35] about things like 'Project structures and features', 'Planning of projects: estimating costs and duration' and 'Computers in project management'—which might all be common sense or, more likely, common sense adulterated by jargon—for which the fee for ten consecutive Thursday evenings was a more modest £220.

The one sure thing about the relation to wealth creation of both expensive Cambridge and downmarket Swansea is that sums of money make their way from individuals and/or their employers to the universities and their employees. If any useful skill is involved it is in the extraction of £17,500 and £220 respectively.

For though many university departments can have nothing to do with either thought or usefulness they do have a function, and an economic one at that: to increase the size of universities by getting more money from government, students and students' parents. This is the one and only genuine bit of economic growth inspired by the new university. Sometimes this is said with surprising frankness. 'On the question of research, this College has been in the forefront of expansion with the express purpose of providing additional funds with which we could bring in active new staff.'[36] The universities do contribute to the local economies by employing labour, but in much the same way (though without the justification of meeting human needs) as old folks' homes and prisons.

The very worst thing in the post-university—and that is saying something—is the appropriation to and by universities of the styles of 'marketing'. They 'market' their own courses; they lay on courses in Marketing. Put the university prospectuses in the same folder as the holiday brochures and see if you can tell the difference.

The corruption of language naturally comes to a head in the departments that create themselves out of it.

> The College is pleased to announce the establishment of the British Rail Chair of Marketing in the Department of Management Science and Statistics. Welcoming the announcement the Principal said 'Both the College and British Rail view this appointment as the next vital step in the development of Business and Management research and teaching activities at Swansea.'
>
> The new professor will provide a full undergraduate option in marketing for business students ....[37]

Marketing is persuading people to buy goods and services. Sometimes, coincidentally, this may be done by pointing out some truths about the goods and services, but the persuasion is the defining factor. A genuine university could not conceivably find room for such a chair, supposedly the final mark of recognized academic status: it would have to be called British Rail Professor of Lying.

It may seem unduly heavy to invoke Socrates again, but let us bear in mind that the institutions we are considering were quite recently supposed to take to their limits and beyond the serious thought of which the human race is capable. Socrates was put to death for making the worse appear the better reason, and for corrupting youth. History has vindicated the judgement of his friends that Socrates was not guilty, and that on the contrary he had been following reason as far as he could and wherever it led. But had he pleaded guilty, he would not have thought the punishment unduly severe.

A bad style will make the worse appear the better reason, and if this happens in 'the education service' the result cannot but be the corruption of youth. The marketer, interested in persuasion not truth, exactly fits the bad name that Socrates tried to give rhetoricians and sophists. The effort to persuade regardless of truth is by definition an enemy of that pursuit of truth which has always been the inspiration of the university. It again does not follow that the aim has been achieved. Not everybody who wants to be a professional liar succeeds—not even when the skill is dignified by the name of 'spin doctoring'.

*   *   *

So ... we have achieved Newman's ideal, and allowed Pig Enterprise Management and Wine Studies to sprout as new shoots of the one tree of knowledge. Contemplated by the human mind they form part of the one large system. There are no natural or real limits between part and part; Lighting Design is ever running into Knitwear Studies, and both into Sanskrit.

In the bad old days, the Newbolt Report quotes a witness as saying, 'education was purely utilitarian; its object was limited to giving children the instrument for earning a living.'[38] The compulsive 'modern' in new educational policy only falls short of indicating a return to the bad old days because then what was taught was genuinely useful. The 'modern' points to something worse, because the modern utilitarianism only makes a promise that cannot be kept.

A degree in a non-subject will not qualify anybody to do anything, not even to become a successful con-man. The more likely result is demoralization. It is almost equally untrue that a degree even in a genuine subject will do as much to prepare anyone for running a company or a factory as experience of the relevant concern.

What happened was not that the polys became universities but that both polytechnics and universities went on using a name the significance of which had evaporated even in the act of immense proliferation. Are there 261 universities in this country, or two, or none?

6   How to Run a New University in Seven Easy Lessons

> Idleness is a disease which must be combated; but I would not advise a rigid adherence to a particular plan of study. I myself have never persisted in any plan for two days together.
>
> Dr Johnson[1]

HAVING ATTAINED THE FIRST, overriding objective, and got funding, management's challenge is to run the new university so as to get it well up the league tables while satisfying the highest international standards, and the customers.

The word 'customer' appears three times in the short Introduction to the *Charter* signed by the then Secretary of State, and recurs throughout. Not long since, at the doctor's you were a patient, on the train a passenger, at the solicitor's a client, and at a university an undergraduate or student. Now everybody is a customer, everywhere, even on the trains. This may seem common sense. If the relations are basically the same in all these cases why not use the same word? (Has the usage extended yet to penitents in the confessional or prisoners?) But *are* they basically the same?

To customers are supposed to be delivered goods or services, in this case education. Education is obviously not goods, but must it follow that it is a service? So the Minister thought: 'Universities and colleges are more and more aware of the need to deliver high-quality services, responding to the needs and demands of customers.'

Service itself, which may cover quite an area, has a core idea that something is done for somebody in return for a fee: a case argued, an illness treated, hair cut, a meal served, possibly, even, a skilled trade taught to an apprentice. University education does not do anything for anybody. We know in advance what we expect from a service. No student knows except in the most embryonic way what is going to happen to him as a result of education.

What happens in the real thing is that students join in a community of scholars, by practising a style of thinking which they demonstrate in examinations. How is that a service? Where a service is being offered, the university has ceased to function, because nobody is being inducted into thought, and the real university is replaced by the sham. In the sham, the customers are to be satisfied: as follows.

(i) TEACH

> Instruction, that mysterious communing of Wisdom with Ignorance, is no longer an indefinable tentative process ... but a secure, universal, straightforward business, to be conducted in the gross, by proper mechanism, with such intellect as comes to hand.[2]

The service universities promise to provide to the customers can only be the delivery of knowledge and skills, which can only be done by teaching, as Lady Catherine's 'regular instruction' is now called. A way of downgrading a university is to turn it into a 'teaching only' institution, that is, with no research going on: so 'teaching' must be the irreducible basic university activity, to which 'research' adds a touch of upmarket class.

'Teaching', unluckily, though the word is universally used without qualms, is not what happens in the real university. 'I see the word "teaching" in inverted commas,' wrote Leavis; 'I don't like it, because of the suggestion it carries of telling—authoritative telling.'[3] This perhaps derives from Quiller-Couch's pointed quotation of the terms on which he had been appointed professor, 'But I ask you to note the phrase "to promote, so far as may be in his power, the study"—not, you will observe, "to teach"....'.[4] Rush Rhees 'wrestled with philosophical problems before the class as if for the first time.'[5] That is university work, but 'teaching'?

There are times when 'authoritative telling' does properly come in. Characteristically it is introductory work. I am permanently grateful to my colleague and friend David Parry for teaching me some Old Norse and for enormously improving my Old English. That certainly involved a great deal of 'teaching', the well-judged authoritative imparting of information and correction of mistakes. The sign of the success was that towards the end of the Old Norse course I began to be able to form an opinion and join in a discussion. But as soon as I was capable of making any kind of judgement of the difference between the *Vǫlsunga* and *Laxdæla* sagas, teaching in the primary sense was at an end, the introductory phase was over and—I want to say—the real university work was starting. I am not now the equal of David Parry on Old Norse and never shall be, but I can talk to him about it with some common basis in knowledge, and it is this talk, if anything, that is going to get me further in the subject—as well, possibly, as him. There is no positive good, and an open invitation to confusion, if we stretch the word 'teaching' to cover this kind of discussion.

Tutorials (now abolished) were a central part of my work over the years. A small group, a tutor and perhaps only one student or perhaps as many as four, meets often enough to get to know one another and discuss, often on the basis of a student essay, some question connected with English literature (and in my experience the smaller the scope for one tutorial the better). I have had some of my best and some of my worst university experiences in tutorials. I used to forbid notebooks in tutorial because the usual meaning of the appearance of the notebook is to turn the conversation of the tutorial into a teaching hour. In goes the transferred information or, worse, the transferred opinions.

I know what it means to teach French, also to teach pupils, but what does it mean to teach *Macbeth* or *The Rainbow* (suchlike phrases being commonly heard in the new university), if not to give students a, or even the, correct way of taking a book? And what is that but, one way or another, the replacement of thought by indoctrination? or of something yet lower down the intellectual scale, the mere repetition of a tutor's notes?

The quality of teaching in my department was assessed by a team led by a management consultant (an ex-chemist) sent down from HEFCW. We were all told as soon as we heard of this visitation that we could give up all hope of any academic work for the next six months, preparing for it, and some of my hardest-working colleagues duly spent their long vacation manufacturing minutes, mission statements and the like for the perusal of the Assessors. The latter told us what to expect. 'The assessment is concerned with the reception and conveyance of material by and to the students.'[6] The customers will have material conveyed to them and will convey it back to us by way of assessed essays or examination scripts. This two-way shifting of information is to be expected if we are teachers and they taught. Simultaneously a number of us were concerned about the previous summer's Shakespeare scripts, which had been doing exactly that and were in consequence at once eccentric and deadly dull. One of the worst things that happens when marking exam scripts is to have one's not-very-inspired thoughts conveyed back to one in script after script. Did I really say that? Oh! I probably *did*! There is all the difference in the world between that and the still exhilarating experience of reading a script which shows that a student has really listened and made something of what one was driving at. The usual sign is either some taking further of a lecturer's line of thought or some disagreement. The ordinary word for this activity is discussion, and it cannot be subsumed in 'teaching'.

During my final session in the University of Wales I was asked seriously, by two students on separate occasions, whether they were allowed to use the first person singular in essays. Their tutors in the first year had recommended the third-person (Mary-Bennet-style) appeal to those popular authorities 'many critics', whom they were to repeat uninspected. The essays that year were the worst I have ever seen, being full of indiscriminate quotation of second-rate criticism as authoritative, and showing no sign of thinking (thought is individual). The university that tries to reduce thought to teaching actually stifles thought.

In universities, undergraduates read for degrees, with what help they can get from the senior members. (Some of the best students virtually ignore the senior members without being visibly the worse for it.) The mark of progress is for the students to be able to continue the intellectual activity that constitutes their subject beyond anything they are taught. Different ways of offering help are appropriate in different subjects. Sometimes this goes well, sometimes badly, and it is never possible to predict good years or bad years in advance, until the university is degraded to a mechanism for conveying information and has ceased to be a university.

What I wanted to say about 'teaching' came to me one somnolent afternoon when I was training to be an 'appraiser' (what *that* is is something we can be spared); as phrases about 'performance' and 'system' and 'management' floated around, and as I shut off and looked through the window at the warm May mist over Swansea Bay, a sort of catch came into my mind:

> Thought
> can't be taught.

(Elizabeth Bennet would not have put it like that, but I hope she would agree.) If so, 'teaching' cannot be the central, defining activity of the university. Or, as Newman put it, 'Gentlemen ... you have come, not merely to be taught, but to learn.'[7]

(ii) IN COURSES

If our customers are, like the Bertram girls, to be professionally instructed, how is it to be done? What can be taught? The answer, obviously, is *courses*. Anything called a course can be planned as to content and method, and then delivered by way of teaching. At the end of the ideal course you will ideally know and be tested on just what the course has taught you, no more and no less. So it is a full answer, in the twenty-first century, to any objection that a graduate is lacking in knowledge of some part of his subject (Shakespeare, let's say, in the case of an English graduate) for the graduate to say, 'It wasn't on the course.' Courses also have the great advantage of being inspectable (see section v). The quality of a course can be assured whether or not the course has anything to do with education.

This contradicts an older fashion, when we used to be told that learning should be 'heuristic', but then, you can't have everything. I was subjected to some pressure (not, to be fair to my former colleagues, much) because I always refused to publish a contents list of my Chaucer option. We used to spend the first few weeks sampling the poet's very various kinds of poetry. Then I asked the students to go on sampling while we discussed the dream poems. At the end of the first term I then asked them what they would like to discuss next. Occasionally we had to resort to votes. This seemed to me a good way, and one in the spirit of university study, of conducting the class; but it couldn't be called a 'course'.

The whole conception of a statable course belongs to the useful, instrumental knowledge which we deny to be the province of the university. Machine maintenance is rightly taught in courses. The knowledge aimed at can be described in advance, and the aim is simply to attain it. University knowledge is not structurable in the kind of way demanded. Leavis's seminars had no structure whatever: they were determined by the relative urgency of what he was trying to think about.[8]

I was glad to see at the Cambridge Music Faculty open day that even in a subject where a fairly well-defined body of material is to be covered, titles of series of lectures were such as 'European Counterpoint 1580–1750', which does give scope for different emphases and treatments.

The new university, however, can operate only in courses of a different and more modern kind.

(iii) WITH AIMS, OBJECTIVES AND GOALS

According to the *Charter*, 'Your university or college should explain the aims and structure of your course.'[9] This in fact applies at all levels of education, from the demands made by national testing of seven-year-olds up through GCSE and A-level to honours degrees. If information is to be conveyed to and from the students, *what* information must be precisely specified. (The New A-level schemes have dropped the old name 'syllabus' and are called 'specifications'.) So the statable aim is to convey such-and-such information.

Examining boards therefore go into detail about what their aims are, at GCSE or degree level. University prospectuses now state the aims and objectives and goals both of the whole institution and of particular courses. The style for formulating such aims shows, unfortunately, that whatever the paraphrasable content, the real aim is to make nonsense. There used to be an organization called PICKUP 'on campus'. Ours exhorted us to 'Make sure your college's strategic and tactical aims include improved performance goals, more flexible procedures and more creative thinking....'[10] To the small extent that this means anything at all it just means 'do better', but nobody with any advice on how to do better could possibly put it like this.

To make us take 'Goals' with proper seriousness a refinement of vocabulary was needed. Aims, for instance, have to be distinguished from objectives. One official document told me on the authority of HEFCW that aims are 'what the institution wishes to become or achieve in measurable terms' while objectives are 'the means and methods by which these aims are realised'.[11] In English an objective cannot mean a method. It is always a bad sign when bureaucrats resort to the redefinition of common words. In common speech aims and objectives are not far off synonymous.

If a subject is well studied a department has no further aim, and any general statements about what 'well studied' means are vapid without the actuality of the study itself.

In extreme cases the effort to state an academic aim becomes a self-contradiction. If the aims could be clearly stated, the course would already have finished. 'What do you say in your new book?' I once heard one academic ask another after a meeting of the Arts Faculty. 'You will have to read it,' was the inevitable reply.

Practical questions are of course important. Is most of the work done in tutorials or lectures? What is the library like? But it is logically impossible for the student to understand the 'structure of the course' in advance of reading; the structure is internally related to the subject. On the other hand it is quite possible for a student to make his own coherence within a subject. Oddly enough this can hardly be said in the age of infinite student choice.

The 'mission statement' that accompanied Dr R. S. Thomas's letter set out the aims (not the objectives) of University College, Swansea. They included, as well as the already quoted 'to facilitate regional economic growth and national wealth creation' a final one (of only three) even more splendid: 'to contribute towards meeting the needs of society as a whole.'[12] Imagine this even in the next manifesto of New Labour: 'to meet the needs of society as a whole.' Like what? Breakfast, dinner, lunch and tea/Are all the human frame requires? or do we also need the National Lottery? Turn it into a party game: give an answer to the question what it could possibly mean to meet the needs of society as a whole.

Must there not be something wrong with an institution devoted to thought which announces as its aim something that anyone without the benefits of higher education can see at a glance is quite vacuous? But any statement of 'goals' will necessarily be either vacuous or tautologous or just plain wrong.

It is better to avoid phrases like 'the goal of a university', as a road liable to subsidence. The aim, the objective and the goal of the university is just to be a university; the aims of the departments are to pursue their respective subjects as best they can. Improvement should always be striven for, but just as part of the ordinary well-being of the university, not as a goal. A goal can be scored, but there is no point at which the university can pass a resolution to the effect that its goal has been attained, and that the effort to improve is no longer necessary. On the other hand there is a real possibility of a university's losing its nature, even as part of its aiming at goals, if the goal is facilitating regional economic growth and the like.

Many human institutions are like this. The goals defined are either platitudinous or false. A nation has no goal as a nation except to go on realizing its character. If a nation confuses this with reforms or improvements or party politics and says the nation must be democratic (or whatever) the goal is false; if the goal is something like making the national life better and more wholesome the use of 'goal' just leads to tautology. It is even possible for an unlucky academic politician to be both platitudinous and false at the same time, as when it is said that the goal of the university is to aid the national economy. (The word-processor keeps trying to make me write 'gaol'.)

To these conceptual objections to 'goals' I have to add a theological one. 'First define your goal, then set about achieving it,' an engineer exhorted us; he naturally joined 'goals' and 'customers':

> 'Quality' is defined as 'fitness for purpose', the customers indicating the purpose, the educators providing the fitness. Put more precisely, this amounts to 'the specifying of worthwhile educational goals and enabling students to achieve them'.[13]

'Worthwhile' is a slide: there is no more need for these customers *qua* customers to keep to the worthwhile than the customers of Woolworths, nor is there any indication of how they are to recognize what is worthwhile. But let us stick to 'goals'. The once-hackneyed tag from Burns about the best-laid schemes of mice and men is relevant. Even in the Soviet Union the aims of five-year plans were not always attained. And, 'The good that I would, I do not, but the evil which I would not, that I do.' Giving the universities' intentions the benefit of all the doubts, we know what road good intentions proverbially pave. 'To this project ... it can only be objected, that, like many projects, it is, if not generally impracticable, yet evidently hopeless, as it supposes more zeal, concord and perseverance, than a view of mankind gives reason for expecting.'[14] The talk about goals and objectives has too little sense of the necessary chanciness of education. One can do one's best to prepare a lecture and still give a bad one. Sometimes, even, it seems afterwards that what made the lecture bad was the effort at preparation or the need to keep to aims and objectives. Conversely, to be at one's best at one's least premeditated is a very common experience, and not just in universities.[15]

What staff might look to be doing in universities is some thinking ourselves, if we can manage it, and some discussion and conversation (that is, thinking in groups) with our students. That's all, but it will be impossible if we also have to set ourselves the goals of achieving well-defined course objectives and of customer satisfaction. But what a difference it would make to the world if the universities were allowed to pursue the goal of going on being universities!

(iv) IN MODULES

If, however, universities are there to teach the magical personal transferable skills by way of imparting information through courses with well-defined aims, it probably follows, as declared by a Swansea document, that 'The quality of teaching provision may be enhanced if modular degree programmes are introduced.'[16] A 'module' does indeed sound like a manageable, goal-directed, teachable object.

> DEFINITION OF MODULARITY
> ... reduced to its basic form, it may be described as:
> division of a degree scheme into individual components, each with its own learning goal;
> assessment of student performance in each component during or as soon as possible after the completion of teaching associated with it;
> frequent feedback to students on their academic performance.[17]

Degrees in the future will consist of a certain number, usually 36 (yes, 36), of modules, added up.

I have never met an academic who believed that modularization will improve the university academically, that is, in its nature, and no academic advantages were mentioned in the list of pros and cons given by the Swansea *Report of the Teaching Committee on Modularisation and Semesterisation*.[18] In fact that ten-page document nowhere mentioned principles at all. My own Dean of the Swansea Arts Faculty (who steamrollered modularization through the Faculty in gross defiance of the Faculty's majority opinion and was rewarded with a Vice-Principalship) remarked that 'there are no convincing academic arguments in favour of [modularization],' and that 'On a purely academic basis ... I have not seen any argument which leads me to believe that modularity has any intrinsic academic superiority.' Though he is an Egyptologist not a logician, it is still remarkable that he thought that this follows: 'Therefore, for me, the issue has to be decided on the basis of practical considerations.' The possibility that modularization might academically be a change for the worse did not enter his head, though he heard that opinion repeatedly argued, and though in one of the discussions the practicalities resolved themselves, for him, into damage limitation.

Comments were invited on the question, sent top-down, as to what progress we could make with modularization. (We were never asked what we thought of it in principle.) My own comment in a letter to the same Dean was:

> Amongst the possible objections to modularity [mentioned in a circulated document] is:
>
> [Modularity] may lead to a lack of coherence in a student's scheme of study.

This is seriously understated. It follows a definition of modularity as 'division of a degree scheme into individual components, each with its own learning goal'.

If a degree scheme can be so divided, no questions of coherence can arise. If a degree scheme cannot be so divided without loss of coherence, lack of coherence is not something that modularity may (or may not) 'lead to', but is part of the definition of modularity. Modularity *per se* is, in these circumstances, incoherence.

Item 5 on the same agenda, also from the Academic Board, a report on the 'New Procedures for the Approval of Degree Schemes', told us that 'In putting into effect any arrangements for the approval of schemes of study to be introduced in October 1992 or thereafter' the first principle that has to be 'addressed' is 'The need to preserve and enhance academic standards'.

If this is meant seriously it automatically rules out modularity in the subjects I know anything about, the degree schemes of which do aim at coherence, because modularity by definition renders them incoherent.

(Dear non-academic Reader: guess which if any of the quoted phrases about academic standards and modularity were meant to be taken seriously.) This communication having received no attention, we expand it a little.

I am told that one of the explanations of the old fact that some doctors 'do men to dyen through their drinkes · ere destinee it wolde' is that medical degrees are traditionally constructed on modular lines: one set of memorizings (information conveyed to and from the medic) for first MB, another for second MB and never the twain shall meet. Learn the brain and then forget it and learn the lungs and giblets and forget *them*. My only experience of this kind of thing was learning Linotype typesetting, which indeed was a course divided into parts (keyboard, casting, distribution etc); but all the time it was necessary to keep in mind what the parts were doing in the whole machine. Nobody would have thought of doing one bit without the rest, and if they had they certainly wouldn't have learnt Linotype operation and maintenance. Nor would the Linotype course have been turned into a degree scheme by the introduction of a bit of Greek tragedy or midwifery.

By the quoted definition of modularity, university studies must be divisible into discrete units, each with its own definable goal, teachable in 12-week courses some of which may be taken at different institutions, and which in principle can be mixed. This is a simple contradiction of the idea of a university subject. The mastering of a genuine subject does include some pondering and frequenting. The belief, for example, that one bit of a literature can be studied at degree level satisfactorily in 12 weeks, without a context of other such studies, is a nonsense. Nor is the nonsense confined to the Arts Faculty. In the top-of-the-league-table University of Northumbria the word 'unitization' is employed for the same thing, defined by a member of the Chemistry Department as 'the destruction of academic subjects'.

Even if modular degrees are awarded in genuine subjects rather than in indisciplined mixtures, the modular principle is vicious. It is obvious, for instance, that there is no sense in learning one bit of the grammar of a language in the hope that it will be self-sufficient. But hardly anything academically worth doing, *possibly* excluding mathematics and the mastery of musical techniques, can be reduced to discrete parts and then built up step by step, and even in these examples the steps have to be taken in order. In philosophy, you don't progress from the simpler problems to the more difficult. As soon as you ask questions in a certain way you are doing philosophy, however primitively. Progress consists of asking them more intelligently or more insistently or from a base in a more thorough knowledge of philosophizing. And although different areas of the subject can conveniently be examined separately (aesthetics, moral philosophy, epistemology, logic), I don't believe that the parts can be done properly in isolation, without the kind of analogies, comparisons, glimpses from one bit to another that make the subject a whole. 'For him, philosophy was one subject, not a collection of specialisms.'[19]

Modularity, anyway, is supported not as a way of studying the academic subjects, but by the offer of infinite mixture. I read an American student's cv after noticing that her contributions to class discussion were at once strange and uninteresting. She was majoring in Health Care Studies but had also done a bit of mathematics somewhere and also, unless my memory is playing tricks, the ancient civilization of the Aegean islands. Now she was completing the all-roundness of her degree by studying women in medieval English literature. I only saw the last bit, but having read the print-out it didn't surprise me that she wasn't making much of the medieval women.

It may be that some bits of one subject can be used in another, including the study of a fragment of a literature; but in that case it still needs a different whole to belong to. Notoriously, in my subject, Chaucer and Langland used to be used (before they were judged too difficult) as sources for social history. Fair enough, as long as we know what is going on and as long as the sources are read with reasonable sensitivity. But studied in themselves (this is quite possible, despite the defeatist schools of critics who deny it), works of literature take time to sink in, they have to be compared with others, and with many other matters, in the formation of educated judgement. This is one reason why some 'taught MAs' are shallower than undergraduate work: they deal, hastily, with one bit of something. Educated judgement is simply not analysable into discrete fragments.

Take the case of Classics. This consists of the study of Latin and Greek, in particular the literatures, but with a good deal of history, some philosophy, and since the great generation of Jane Harrison, much anthropology. The point of the study is to put these things together, to see, for instance, that the study of the Latin language acquires a new sense if it is part of the study of Classics.

But still, everything does have to start somewhere. Perhaps a bit of philosophy or a bit of Latin is better than none? *Soit*, especially at school, where beginnings are made—or, in the case of the University of Wales, Swansea, Part One, with its excellent Greek, Latin, Welsh, Italian for beginners, and an introduction to philosophy that presupposes no previous acquaintance with the subject.

Universities, however, are for taking things further. Graduation is a certificate that a student may now go all lengths of research if he wishes, not that he has made three dozen starts.

Modules are generally designed to last 12 weeks with, in unsemesterized universities, a vacation coming during the 12; the teaching will normally occupy two hours a week or less. Modules belong with 'teaching' because each of the starts will have to be in a course that has been intensively taught. What can be done in 24 hours spread over 12 weeks? Crash courses, introductions for students totally ignorant—computer programming, grammar of Old English or whatever. What can be reliably expected in subjects taught in modules that do not lend themselves to crash-introductions is short bursts of jargon. It is easy enough to pick up an academic jargon in 12 weeks without taking in with it any hint of the possibly serious thought of which the jargon is a deformity.

The great attraction of modularity is said to be the freedom of choice it gives students (and consequently the pressure on course tutors to be popular). Even if modular courses are in some sense chosen, regimentation in the following of courses is a *sine qua non* of modularization, for it is only the following of a course, as against demonstration of thinking about a subject, that can constitute completion of a module. The awarding of a print-out of details of courses completed, with grades, instead of the old-fashioned overall class of degree, is already held in check in this country only by employers' distrust of it. A departmental power-broker to the committee that is his special creation, on the effect of modularization on the presently permitted transfers from one subject to another during the first month of the university year: 'That degree of freedom's gonna disappear.' [20]

The *Charter* exhorts students to attend lectures, which is more than I ever did. (My advice to students to ask themselves whether the lectures were as much use as the same time spent reading or talking once or twice got me into hot water.) But an ordinary lecture series is often by different people with various points of view, and will look to an examination which can be approached in various ways. Students will be able to pursue different interests and emphases on, say, Victorian Poetry, while showing knowledge of and intelligent interest in the subject. What happens when Victorian Poetry is treated as an option (an embryo module) with one Tutor offering one 'correct' point of view we shall see below.

Modularity may nonetheless look like a healthy step away from specialism. Subject boundaries are not rigid. Before we know where we are we find ourselves doing a bit of philosophy or history or even theology when we thought it was literary criticism. If the tree of knowledge is one, the more of it we climb the better. Plato and Aristotle must remain the ideals, and imagine either of them as a one-subject specialist! And what about Oxford Greats or Mods, combinations of subjects, or the Cambridge Tripos system, which is an open invitation to undergraduates to change subjects midway? Are they not proto-modules? The differences are that a tripos consists of two big bites at possibly different cherries, and that its aim is at putting the two together, for which the system presupposes sufficient general culture in the undergraduate. In the provinces, before general degrees were renamed joint honours, the joint honours degree was thought harder than single honours, and only the ablest students were permitted to sit for one.

Newman thought that the tree of knowledge is one, and the subjects are the branches. Modularity gives us a bunch of twigs but no tree.

Each Module, said the 'Minutes', 'attracts [*sic*] a *credit* which is related to its weight within the scheme' and 'can be a free-standing piece of work, or may have *pre-requisites* or *co-requisites* according to the particular scheme.' This is the attempt to disarm the objections I have been making. A judicious set of regulations will ensure that the modules will not be free-standing if their free-standingness would damage the coherence of the degree-scheme. Directors of studies will be appointed to guide the customers along paths which will often enough coincide with the old degree subjects. Damage-limitation will take some such forms, undertaken in the new names of counselling, guidelines and suchlike exercises of power without responsibility.

If my (commonly held) fears are alarmist, if the subjects are to be allowed to retain some coherence, would it not be better to say so and drop the modularity jargon? If the choices are not after all going to be free, why had we to go through the trauma?

But I just don't believe that modularity can be transformed into something coherent. It is beyond even the ingenuity of academic politicians to turn round so cleanly a system whose first principle is that the units are 'freestanding'. The first reason for modularization we were offered was: 'Students will have greater freedom to construct their own degree courses out of a wide range of elements.' As one academic put it,

> In the end though, the question is whether you are prepared to trust students (most of them, most of the time) to make sensible decisions in a relatively free intellectual environment. Most of the time they do, I'm glad to say—and since they're legally adults, it's only right that they should have the chance.[21]

By definition, though, undergraduate students are not mature enough to make their own syllabuses or to examine themselves. If they were they would not need a university. Sensible decisions presuppose an experience which by definition the students have not yet had. I also notice that *we* know what is sensible. Nothing can be done, however, if the decisions are not sensible. 'The integrating principle in other words is their interest rather than any presupposition on our part on what should be covered.'[22] This does to my certain knowledge cover the student of English literature uninterested in English poetry or Shakespeare or both. But why is this university equivalent of child-centred learning thought to have an integrating principle at all?

Modularity is obviously intended to make university subjects student-centred not subject-centred. The extreme example is the graduate in 'Independent Studies', i.e. a degree put together by the student, who designs projects and coursework to suit his interests, in order to emerge with a degree which makes no formal claim to coherence. Of course these are degrees without finals examinations.

> John Wakeford, director of the school of independent studies set up at the University of Lancaster in the early 1970s, argues that a reason for establishing it was to 'isolate people with wild ideas in one school and let them get on with it.' [His words not mine.]
> Modularisation of courses will bring many mainstream courses more in line with the Lancaster model as students compile unique degrees.[23]

The same article reports that 70 per cent of students completing these degrees at Lancaster get a first or an upper second. How such a degree can be meaningfully classified is a nice question which can only possibly be answered if we allow that to graduate is not to have mastered a coherent discipline. A practical question more in tune with the post-university is to inquire whether these degrees impress prospective employers, and if so why.

Choices of modules within subjects are usually made in ignorance. If a student has enough glimmerings and hints to be able to make an intelligent choice of subject, that is as much as can be hoped. As a medievalist I know what it is for the university to suffer from bogus freedom of choice: how many students, asked to choose one or two from 57 options, are going to plump for English Literature 1150–1250, the interest of which they are most unlikely to discover within the first month's work? (And it *is* very interesting. I know. So do the students who for various reasons have found themselves doing it.)

The subject has been transformed in the interests of 'freedom'. If we are free we shall decide for ourselves what to read, unhindered by élitism. It is not always realized even in universities how limited this freedom must be, just by the nature of publication and the size of libraries. Genuine freedom would be indistinguishable from chaos. In practice, students' choice is severely restricted by what academics are willing to 'teach'. Hence the Heinz-numbered modular options in the department I left. Fifty-seven is a large number of varieties but not compared with the number of possible topics.

Modularization in English in fact dictates a much more restricted 'canon' than the Cambridge English Tripos ever did (though with no guarantees against wild eccentricity) but forces the student to ignore much of it. So much you must read, but need read no more. And within each course there is no freedom whatever. The students are free to pick from Shakespeare, Crime Fiction etc, but in any of them they will be told exactly what to read and subjected to 'authoritative telling' about it.

In this way 'freedom of choice' reproduces just the circumstances which were first judged objectionable—except that the old dictation was largely imaginary (the Cambridge English Tripos has no set texts), the new very actual. The last unsurprising thing is that all the new freedom-imposers agree with each other. There are Marxist options but not fascist options, feminist courses but not anti-feminist courses, deconstruction but not reconstruction. As I write, the fashion is for New Historicism, the doctrine that old writings are never self-evidently interesting, but to be used as a mode of self-congratulation by us on our escape from previous incorrectnesses, as described by authority (see Chapter 8 for some examples). Such is the new freedom to study anything—provided it is studied in a politically correct manner and on the list. Students rapidly learn the various patters (or as a Canadian friend says, 'put in the sprinkles') but God knows what if anything they think in their hearts.

The overwhelming *practical* argument for modularization is to get into line with the majority of European universities. If we continue unmodularized we shall be out on a limb. The vaunted academic independence of our universities routinely takes this form of the dread of being out of step. Recruits, as potential customers are also known, would think of finals-oriented degrees as old-fashioned; it is unthinkable that any recruit worth having would want to go anywhere old-fashioned. Yet simultaneously it is common knowledge that Oxford and Cambridge, which just won't have modularity, still have their pick. What happens to being in line with Europe if, as seems probable, the brave new 'Europe' breaks up even before it has been formed, we are not told. It is perhaps also worth asking, though nobody of academic standing seems to be doing so in public, how this squares with the repeated assurances that the 'European Union' is not aiming at a homogenized and uniform European culture, and why our great step towards European Union has to be by way of abandoning our tradition of half a millennium.

Modularity, we are told, has been successfully used in Germany and the USA for many years. Not all that long ago we would have turned up our noses. German academic life has always been much respected in England but it has not previously been thought good to turn the respect into imitation.

What cannot be denied is that modularity in principle dissipates examinations. Courses are examined piecemeal as they run or as soon as they are completed, sometimes after only 12 weeks in the first year of the university. There is no fortnight in a student's life during which he is required to show mastery of a subject. By the outgoing finals system, whole subjects were examined.

Students please note: the belief that one degree is as good as another in 'the real world' is fanciful. That is something we really have learned from the USA. Employers please note: a degree from a modularized British university will certify (reliably or not) that on 36 occasions the graduate has been able to exhibit, during or after 12-week courses, disconnected bits of what is judged by course tutors to be skill. It will certify nothing else.

(v) TOTAL QUALITY CONTROLLED

Naturally, the performance of the new university must be properly monitored. The *Charter* promises that the universities will be subjected to proper quality control, including in their examinations. Oh, by whom? Any inspector of an educational establishment is in a position of superiority to it. The inspector possesses the standards by which to judge the performance. Schools used to be in dread of surprise visits by HMIs because of the Inspectors' powers, but their authority was also generally respected. Universities, however, recognize no superiors in the intellectual world. They could only be inspected if there were a higher level of thinking by which to judge them. The system of external examining is quite different. Until it breaks down into tolerance (you pretend my jargon is acceptable and I pretend yours is: see Chapter 8) it maintains a common standard by the presence of scholars of one intellectual community at the deliberations of another. The external examiners, however authoritative, are peers, giving advice to a board which may nevertheless in the end reject it, not superiors giving instruction about intellectual standards. In an extreme case an external examiner may veto, but so may an internal. If examiners' meetings fail to maintain standards there is no remedy within the system, as we exemplify below (see Chapter 8).

So when the universities began to be inspected, in the 1990s, the word 'inspection' was not used inside the universities, though it appeared freely enough in the press. 'All universities are now subject to inspection by the funding councils of their research and teaching programmes.'[24] Phrases like 'quality audit' were brought in, and departments were instructed to produce a 'self-assessment document' in advance of the inspectors' visit, so that the fiction could be maintained that the assessors would judge only what the departments themselves claimed to be doing.

The HEFCW-appointed Assessors were coming, we were reassured, to adjudicate our 'teaching methods', not what is 'taught', and to place us in one of three categories, unsatisfactory, satisfactory or excellent.[25] We have already seen what they understand by 'teaching'.[26]

The dust was consequently removed from the computers (acquired for about £15,000 each, a year's salary for a junior member of staff, and which are never otherwise used) by which we can get at literary databases; feeble but attractively printed poems were hung, beautifully framed, in all the corridors, and the washbasin in the gents', cracked for many years, was renewed. (During one of the later financial crises that are normally a sign of the season of mists and mellow fruitfulness in universities, the thing not to be cut was preparations for Quality Assessment. Money was still available for window-dressing.[27])

My department duly produced its 'self-assessment document'. On the document itself I forbear comment, and on the visit, which included episodes like the sitting in on a few of my classes by a grim-faced lady phonetician, so strictly in the spirit of inspecting only method that she professed herself entirely ignorant of the subject of the seminar. As I mentioned, when the great moment arrived—would we be declared excellent or only satisfactory?—we were disappointed: because we did not lay claim to be 'teaching' the 'personal transferable skills' discussed above.

Universities are not only being inspected but, despite the self-assessment fiction, judged by standards not proper to them. A self-respecting university would treat the whole thing with open contempt, but the universities take the gradings seriously, presumably because applicants for admission do too. They are thought to be part of the Quality Assurance promised by the *Charter*.

There arrived on my desk a document beginning with a preliminary sheet called, with an oddity I hope is generally perceptible, 'Mission Statement, Aims and Objectives', that went on to what ought to be an even odder title 'Total Quality Management', called afterwards in the document and here TQM.[28]

This TQM text, from 'Prof W. D. Morris, Vice Principal, and Chairman of the Teaching Committee', is not fully literate and has phrases that would be sub-edited in, say, *The Daily Telegraph* or *The Guardian*. 'Because the overall governance procedures of the College are currently under active review, the concept of fine tuning existing procedures has been felt to be the most appropriate manner to proceed.' A concept cannot be a manner to proceed and I am not sure that it can be a feeling either. 'Thus a well designed quality assurance system should obviate against the need for time-consuming "fire fighting" activities.' 'Obviate' takes a direct object. This may seem academic and pettifogging. Or, alternatively, it may not. When Air Marshal Sir Hugh Dowding received documents containing illiteracies he initialled them and returned them to the sender without further comment or action, and we won the Battle of Britain. This is, anyway, the tip of another Dearing-age iceberg of non-language.

The aim is 'the detailed development of a total quality management methodology covering all aspects of teaching, research, central administration and student welfare'. The assumption has to be that any 'quality' in a university is capable of being 'managed' in a way that makes talk of methodology appropriate, beside which the feeding of the five thousand must seem an everyday event, though regrettably lacking in the proper management procedures and not following correct guidelines. According to Prof. Morris,

> The importance of developing a corporate quality awareness must start at the highest management level in any organisation and then cascade down to all departments and employees. In the context of the UCS, this means that academic departments, administrative departments and all departments responsible for student support services and welfare *must accept and embrace a quality ethos* which is 'top down' driven.

I should no doubt have recognized 'cascade' as a term brought in from Management Science,[29] but as a mere English academic I took it at face value as a fatuous poeticality. In 1997 I participated in the last examiners' meeting of my department to discuss joint honours degrees. The following year, degrees were to be awarded by a computer into which marks had been typed. I do not know whether it is coincidence that this degree-awarding machine is called Cascade. What a shower!

The most strictly proper intellectual response to Prof. Morris is something short and offensive. 'Argument' implies that a case has been offered to criticism, which here it has not. We have already met the phenomenon. You can't argue with Mr Collins. But I will try, even with that amazing 'cascade'.

'Management' is a recent word in universities, of course brought in from industry. The College civil service, the registry staff, were traditionally quite separate from the academics. It was a surprise in 1987 to receive through the College internal mail a document about courses from the Registrar headed by a summary ending '*You must…*'. In the previous quarter of a century I had never as a member of academic staff been told by the Registrar what I 'must' do about academic matters. Naturally this will come easier to registries if they can call themselves 'management'. At my son's school the more important teachers are called 'the senior management team'. The Management of the University of Wales offered me voluntary redundancy, on condition that it was 'in the management interest'. (I made sure it was.) Real schools and universities do not have managements; they have things like deputy headteachers, Faculties, Senates, Councils, Governing Bodies, Registrars, Vice-Chancellors.

Well, it's all management isn't it, whatever name you use, just as we're all customers? As a matter of fact, no. 'Management' applies to things like estates, households, and in the present ethos, above all, limited liability companies. If all bodies are managed by managements why does not the body imposing these changes use the term of itself? But the Secretary of State for Education and Employment is not going to be renamed a Manager, nor are the officers in the Civil Service with whom he works. Her Majesty the Queen is not going to be renamed General Manager of the Realm, nor even is 'Manager' going to be brought in for the President of the European Commission.

TQM links with the 'customer' talk like this:

> Quality is about meeting 'customer needs'…. Without top level management commitment, drive and direction quality issues in an organisation will soon 'wither

on the vine'. Taking a line of least resistance by non-management involvement will leave those who operate the day to day activities of an organisation with little direction, low morale and uncompetitive. Quality has and must be managed, one cannot leave it to chance and those who think otherwise are sadly misguided.[30]

What is the sense of the clause beginning 'Taking a line ...'? 'Quality has and must be' should be 'Quality has been and must be'. Again, the ordinary sub-literacy is remarkable as a sign of something deeper, the supposition that in a university morale will be low and we shall be 'uncompetitive' if we just get on with our work.

But if quality is 'about meeting customer needs' it is not the quality we talk about in everyday life. Something is being attempted with 'quality' rather like what has been done to 'skill', and with the same purpose. As W. A. Hart says,

> In short, 'quality' in 'quality assurance' is a technical notion, only tenuously linked to 'quality' as the term is used in ordinary speech. It is quality in the sense of 'fit for a purpose' (and crucially also within a certain price range) rather than quality in the sense of 'good of its kind'.[31]

We are told by Prof. Morris that 'quality assurance' is quite different from 'quality control' and demands the establishment of *'quality objectives* appropriate to our role in the higher education sector' so that we must *'establish procedures* within the College whereby these objectives may be realized'. All these phrases, anyway—and I do not pretend to be able to follow the distinction between 'quality assurance' and 'quality control'[32]—depend on an understanding of 'quality'. I was employed by 'UCS' to lecture in (not 'teach') English Language and Literature. My understanding of 'quality' is that I have to engage in the thoughts that constitute my subject to the best of my ability, with such students as will join in, and if I (or my peers) find that I cannot do it reasonably well I should resign. 'Quality' here is just the day-to-day thinking, the university subject itself. How can the Principal, whose subject I believe was acoustics, or the Council, or the Senate, tell me, top-down, what counts as quality in English Language and Literature, and hold me to it? (Any Principal might be able to, coincidentally, but in fact mine would not have made that claim.) The belief is that thinking in the university can be 'top down' driven or maintained by properly established 'managerial structures' and the 'development of employee attitudes which, when followed, results in the quality objectives being fulfilled'. It is on my authority as an experienced university lecturer that I assure the reader: these quoted words are simply and straightforwardly meaningless, and they could not have been used by anyone with any understanding of a university. Nobody who was actually acquainted with the relevant kind of quality—nobody, that is, who wasn't, by the relevant standard, unintelligent and uneducated (a Mr Collins)—could possibly use them except in contempt and parody.

They cannot even be neutral. Their actual meaning is as an attack upon thought. Thought can't be taught; it can't be managed either, and the attempt to manage thought could only damage it.

Insofar as quality ever can be assured, the university has always had procedures for assuring it: they are not managerial and bureaucratic; they are the procedures of educated conversation, debate, argument, procedures which, in the present instance, lead to the judgement that all this management-speak is self-interested claptrap. In general the present aim is to replace judgement with system. The formal exclusion of judgement culminates in the replacement of examiners' meetings by computer programmes.

That there is one uniform system controlled from the level of top management which can ensure a cascade of quality down throughout the university is not merely a harmless fallacy. It is a sign of a blankness about thinking that must lead at best to irritation with thinking. If 'quality' could be top-down driven in universities the first requirement would be that the top consisted not of managers or bureaucrats but of the best thinkers. They could not express themselves in language remotely like Prof. Morris's.

The analogy with manufacturing industry was inevitable.

> For a number of years manufacturing companies have been adopting management techniques to assure the total quality of their products. Management methodologies devised to assure total quality for manufactured artifacts and products have also been adapted for application to the service industries ... .

The attempt to see them as like industries is either stupidly or intelligently malevolent to universities (the former, I think; but I also think that in universities stupidity is the unforgiveable sin). Even if we accept for the sake of argument the huge assumption that TQM has improved quality or consistency in manufactured goods, there is no reason to suppose that it can have any bearing on quality in universities.

The one and only assurance of quality in universities is in the examinations that count towards degrees. If people of little judgement trained only in cliché are allowed to graduate with good degrees there is no quality. If they get to the top and from those cloud-capp'd towers cause these cascades of TQM (Gardeyloo!), the university is in process of committing suicide.

(vi) GIVE FIRSTS

Now that we have the whole course, with properly defined aims and objectives, taught modularly, with copper-bottomed quality guarantees, what is to prevent the performance of universities going up and up? And so we show our success by awarding more and better degrees than ever before.

At a preliminary examiners' meeting it looked as though no student was going to get a first; and though there was also only one third, and the long list had a small majority of upper seconds, we had a speech from a middle-aged senior figure telling us that it was a very bad and depressing list and will do us harm. One way or another we are going to be paid by results. If we don't publish lists containing firsts and more upper seconds, the department will be downgraded and the students disadvantaged. Other departments give more firsts and have more students going on to postgraduate work. We must not let 'antiquated' ideas of standards get in the way of producing the star-spangled class list required by government, the prosperity of the department, and the future of our graduates. That this belies the repeated talk of maintaining standards is too obvious to be worth saying, and perhaps it is not as scandalous as it sounds, merely recognizing a fact and asking us to play on the new and easier pitch. As long as nobody supposes our 2–1 means the same as before, there is no deception. 'In recent years,' as the Chairman of the Higher Education Quality Council was reported as saying, 'the upper second class degree has replaced the lower second grade as the standard honours degree.'[33] But this does overlook the way we have to think in classifications as we mark. Any experienced examiner has a good sense of what a solid 2–2 feels like, and to call it a 2–1 involves a more than mathematical exercise.

Another obvious decline has been in what we expect by way of knowledge. If a present student has read anything outside the texts prescribed for courses we treat it as gratuitous good luck. This has not always been so. It used to be known that education presupposed a level of common knowledge, including factual knowledge, but mainly (in our case) a wide enough acquaintance to make gestures towards an idea of a whole literature not just absurd. Leavis sometimes used a perfect imperative: 'Have read' so-and-so. It used to be assumed, not altogether fancifully, that we had. For instance our Shakespeare paper at Swansea was always on Shakespeare, not a list of set texts. In the years I set it, it always began with a compulsory critical-commentary question on unidentified passages. Any such paper would now be unthinkably difficult.

*   *   *

At present we have moral chaos, regimentation of 'teaching', and laxity in examining.

Moral chaos? And even if so, does it matter? Of course, the idea that the university is a semi-religious institution demanding moral commitment from its members, an institution whose 'output' if any is the clerisy, has been hibernating for a long time. It was not accidental, though, that universities originated as bodies of *clerkes* intellectually free but associated with the Church. The sceptical Chaucer gives in his Clerk a beautiful example of a student whose dedication involves a life of strict moral discipline. With recent changes in the law the senior members are no longer *in loco parentis* and no ordinary morals are enforced either on them or on the undergraduates. Counsellors have largely replaced chaplains.[34] The most blatant moral degeneracy, though, is that there is no longer any pretence that the 'customers' are being prepared for anything more onerous than earning a lot of money. There is no other connection of the modern university with virtue or the pursuit of the good. Aristotle would not have recognized it. Academic seriousness cannot long survive in these circumstances.

'Laxity of examining' may seem unjust. Examiners generally take the work seriously, even to the point of illogical agonizing over borderline cases. (Illogical because in a genuine borderline case justice is done whichever side of the border-line the student comes. That it *was* a borderline can then be stated on references. The real question is whether examiners agree about where the borders are, which, as we shall see in Chapter 8, they no longer do.) But it is not seriously disputable that students can now graduate in many Arts subjects without being able to write decent English prose and without any general culture. The knowledge required of them is that of their courses, a requirement that modularization makes the only requirement, and which is only by lucky chance knowledge as ordinarily understood, knowledge that has some home in common speech.

This topic, however, is important enough to need a separate chapter.

(vii) PUT ON THE CROWN JEWELS: RESEARCH, OR, GREAT HEAPS OF NOTHING

Having got our new university up and running, with the modularly taught getting firsts and upper seconds, it only remains to make sure we get our fair share of the crowning glory. Teaching, we saw, is the basic university activity, but to be a 'teaching only' institution is to be downmarket.

It must be reasonable to address questions about 'production' to the new universities, confident as they are of having at last got across to government the message that their products are making an essential contribution to the national economy. If you claim that we are all producing, there follows the little question *what* are we producing? What do English Literature departments produce? English Literature? As a matter of fact, they are busily engaged in denying there is any such thing.[35]

The first answer that is always given is 'graduates'—without embarrassment, although, in these early days of cloning, human beings can still produce more human beings only by way of procreation. Cloning nevertheless seems the ideal here: an ever-increasing supply of those skilled in the skill of acquiring skills etc etc. Commonplace example of the link between this possibly RUR[36] process and the wished-for prosperity: 'The College was committed to producing graduates who would make a major contribution to the future prosperity of the country....'[37] Graduates are produced by teaching.

If you ask, however, what it is that our graduates themselves might be able to produce, you get back quickly to the word 'research', research which everybody including the government expects the government to fund. Controversies rage about which universities should get what research funding, but not about whether any should get any. The permanent members of the university have to give a lead and themselves spend any time they are not 'teaching' on 'research', in accordance with the simple equation: the university = teaching + research.

There have to be questions, mysteriously overlooked by the TQM regime, about the quality of the 'research' (a word that has spread to the schools, so that on UCCA/UCAS forms I constantly saw that Julie's essays are 'well-researched'). But giving all benefits of doubts, and again admitting that in the science departments this notion that they produce research has at least some plausibility, we still have to ask what sense can it make for me in English Literature? or in Philosophy? or in Classics?

A few good books, a decreasing number (see below) of new editions, some new information, do still come out of these departments. But these products of research are hidden in a mass of published matter of a most peculiar kind.

It might be expected that 'research' would have obeyed the demands of the age, though how the productions of philosophers or historians could do so is not easy to imagine:

> In future, research will be increasingly assessed on the contribution that it will make to the national economy, and Research Council grants will go to those whose research is seen to be benefiting the economy in either the short or the long term.[38]

To be fair to the arts departments they have not tried very hard to apply this, but have understood their productivity in a very simple way. For, in this hard-nosed age, this no-nonsense age, the answer you get to the question about what we produce is another question, sometimes threatening: 'How many pages have you published last year?'; or, if you want promotion: 'Have you got a firm contract with a publisher and if so how many pages long will the book be?'

One odd consequence: the other year I was able to ensure that a publication of mine was short and competitively priced. Legible and with reasonably sized type it got into around 60 pages, paperback. With a few pushed buttons on the computer the same work would very easily and without unduly large type have made 120 pages hardback (such is printing), to be published at about eight times [*sic*] the paperback price. Through the folly of seeking readers I was only half as productive as I might have been.

After the foregoing paragraphs were written the 'models' grew more sophisticated. There is a sort of league-table in which editions are, incredibly, worth less than critical essays; with other refinements. 'Sheer quantity,' however, 'whatever the technical restrictions of the Research Assessment Exercise, carries much more weight than it ought.'[39] The refinements do not include any exercise of judgement about what work if any is of value. University departments have what is called a 'Research Rating' that depends still, for the most part, on how many pages they get out per annum. Members of staff who refrain from issuing pages drag down the department average, and departments are then in danger not only of getting considerably less money but of being assessed as 'teaching only' departments not capable of 'research'. Whether either the 'teaching' (above) or the 'research' has anything to do with thinking is the question never, never asked. In such circumstances appointment committees will tend to ask not, 'Who thinks best?' but, 'Who'll do the most for our Research Rating? Who'll bring us the most money?'

In this little island alone there are, I am told, over a thousand members of staff just in the English departments of the 'old' universities. In practice, the 'canon' of the literature consists of works by about 30 authors. Few of us (though the few do include Sir Frank Kermode) are vainglorious enough to expect to join the select number of the widely read; few indeed expect an audience outside the university. But even that is extravagant. Actually we are not read inside the university either. If the thousand conceived any hopes of being read only by the other 999, just think of the congestion. In practice, the system tacitly recognizes that our publications are not going to be read by anybody at all. Publication is to be taken as numbers of pages receivable into the library. Publications without readers does seem an extraordinary class, but it is the answer to the question what we produce.

Two new professors were to be appointed in my department: a week before the interviews the list of shortlisted names (about which the department was not consulted) was made available to us. These were, of course, academics with energetic publication records, and ones we had heard of. We sat round a table to consult about them. So and so is very impressive on paper, but such and such has done even more. Nobody had read more than a fragment here and there, and most of us hadn't read any of it. This, surprisingly, surprised nobody, nor did it prevent anyone from commenting. We really don't expect anyone to read our publications, and have no intention of reading our colleagues'.

In one case, we were told off the record, a candidate had simply declared himself to have published over two hundred articles, without bothering to list them. He seemed to have got the rationale of the system.

One thing I know for sure is that many books published by people in arts departments are literally never seen by mortal eye. You think, once more, that I am exaggerating? What evidence is there, to begin with, that they are ever read by their authors? The editor or publisher may (or may not) send the typescript to a 'referee', who may or may not read it. Or there may not be a typescript, for many publishers now prefer the book to be submitted either in the form of a camera-ready copy or floppy disk, which can be fed into a typesetting machine without anybody glancing at what it contains. Even typescript can be electronically scanned and turned into text without human intervention. Proof-reading is largely a thing of the past, 'for reasons of economy'. So, one way or another, the book gets made and sent to reviewers, and ... they read it? Don't make me laugh: I have been reviewed. When I have reviewed a book myself and read it all the way through I have more than once known for sure from the state of the printing that I am the first person to have done so. Some books are full of the kind of typographical error that could not have survived a cursory reading.

More machines produce the publisher's catalogue and other machines or human beings imitating machines scan the catalogues, make the appropriate orders, catalogue the work when it arrives at the library—and then consign it to the library stacks and the oblivion from which it has at no stage ever emerged. It may well get on reading lists, be occasionally borrowed and so keep its place in the library,[40] still without ever being read. Nobody has ever read it and nobody ever will. At length, the inevitable happens to 'that vast mass of literature which is kept with a view to being looked at some day', it

> finally drifts unread to the bourne of all waste paper, and is ground into pulp again, and rolls over the endless web again, and comes back into the world printed with more intellectual food ... .[41]

which in turn will never nourish anybody.

If on publication these books went, instead of into the stacks, straight into recycling bins, the national economy would be infinitesimally improved (production of waste-paper, savings on library administration) but there would be no other consequence whatever.

I can't give an exact figure—my research is not complete—but more than 90 per cent of university 'research' does not, strictly speaking, exist. The late Roland Barthes tried to establish a distinction between literary 'works' and 'texts'. The former are thought to be physical objects having existence on shelves, books, CD-roms, microfilms or the like; the latter exist in their active interplay with the reader. The distinction is untenable, for the object on the shelf is *only* an object, not a 'work', until read.

> In Books, not Authors, curious is my Lord;
> To all their dated Backs he turns you round,
> These Aldus printed, those Du Suëil has bound.
> Lo some are Vellom, and the rest as good
> For all his Lordship knows, but they are Wood.[42]

On the other hand, bring it into existence by reading it and the 'work' is already a 'text'. (It *is* possible to read works in a drilled way, which presumably Barthes was trying to get at.) Books exist in reading, and nowhere else. An unread book is *only* an object on a shelf, to be for instance occasionally dusted, and literally does not exist as a book.

The great effort of the Arts Faculties is being directed to the production, strictly and precisely, of NOTHING. We are straining every nerve to produce more nothing. The individuals who produce the most nothing are given chairs, and the departments that produce the greatest heaps of nothing get the best research ratings, and so, more money with which to produce more nothing. But: infinity times nothing is ... ?

The first possible answer to this riddle is 'Deconstruction'. If the demand is to look academically impressive not to make sense, output will be increased if we reduce Mr Collins to system. All works of Deconstruction are written to formula (beginning with references to Saussure, the indeterminacy of the sign etc etc.) whether by computer or living creatures. I shall quote from some Swansea examination scripts the first steps of initiation into the process.

The second possible answer seems to be 'poetry'—understood in a sense peculiar to the new university and its colonies in the literary press. One agenda item at a department meeting: whether to get some sort of honorary fellowship in the department for a Poet who works in the Department of Health Care Studies. The Department of Health Care Studies cannot list his poems under their annual publications, but we can, and they are many. We saw a publications list over a page long and the departmental mouth watered at the prospect of what this would do for our Research Rating.

In preparation for this *démarche*, the Poet had addressed a meeting of our department seminar. The address had taken the form of a new Poem, read by the Poet at the length of about 20 minutes, after which he answered questions. The answers showed him to be a well-read and intelligent man, and I could well imagine he would make a useful member of an English department. The Poem itself, I remarked at the subsequent department meeting, put me in mind of that moment of *Waiting for Godot* when Lucky (is it?) is commanded to 'think', and does so for several pages. It was as if somebody had said 'Poetize!' and out it all came. There were Images, occasionally Rhymes, recognizable Lines, mentions of Bones and Sex. Even a drift was discernible: it was about the Poet's thoughts as he looked across Swansea Bay at the smoke of Port Talbot, a theme that permitted considerable latitude. The lines, the images, the Bones went on, with occasional mentions of Swansea Bay and Port Talbot, and all much faster than a BBC newscaster would have read, and in a more monotonous voice. That it would last about 20 minutes had been announced in advance, otherwise I don't know how the end would have come. As it was we all sat it out, Poet and audience; but nothing had happened at all. I recall a Thurber story in which a pigeon is sitting on a wall, being a pigeon. Nobody in that audience could have had any perception beyond the fact that here was a Poet BEING A POET. When I said this at the department meeting nobody argued or put in a good word for the poetry. I think one of the eighteen people present had read some, but cannot vouch for that as reading was not mentioned. This Poetry was non-existent as surely as our published critical essays.

Thy No-thing of an Intended Poem, O Poet...behold it has not yet become a Thing. ... The Thing, in philosophical uncommercial language, is still a No-thing, mostly semblance and deception of the sight;—benign Oblivion incessantly gnawing at it, impatient till Chaos, to which it belongs, do reabsorb it! [43]

Carlyle's mistake was to suppose that this would matter to the Poet. Not in the least. What matters, as with any other non-existent 'publication', is the number and frequency of pages.

*   *   *

The situation does ask to be made fun of, but it means that there is a probably incurable corruption in our universities. It is an absurdity to suppose that numbers of published pages have any direct correlation with the real work of any university. During Wittgenstein's tenure of his Cambridge chair, when with a number of pupils he did the most important philosophical work since Plato, he published one review. I refrain from the complementary examples of compulsive publication of nothing. A university which doesn't know itself as the enemy of absurdity is already ceasing to be a university; all the universities that go along with this nonsense are subscribing to absurdity.

I hope that the politicians will latch on to this primary fact, that in the terms they understand the arts departments produce, literally, *nothing*. There is, according to market logic, an obvious enough conclusion, which we shall draw.

When Arts academics do have anything to publish, it really is addressed to the world: we still have to assume the possibility of common sense as embodied in the common reader. It may be that some Arts dons have a role in the world by way of addressing the common reader. We even hope this for the present work.

If the academic and bureaucratic mind could be cleared of that cant about our contribution etc, we might even get as far as regaining some understanding of what the arts faculties ought really to be doing in national life, which is very far from nothing.

IV

LEVERING UP
STANDARDS, OR,
TOP-DOWN DRIVEL

Introduction to Part IV

THE POWER GOVERNMENTS HAVE over educational 'provision' is of course great; and the richer the country and the higher the taxes, the greater the power. But the power governments have over education ... isn't power at all. The best educated government can't achieve more than the general level of culture permits. The worst can't escape the limitations of its own character. What could Mr Collins do as Prime Minister or Education Secretary? (No more than our present incumbents.) Governments might as well claim the power to make people more religious or more virtuous as better educated. (For an example, drawn from first-hand experience, of what such power amounts to in practice, see pp. 177–82.)

In 1993 (an eternity ago in 'politics'; otherwise yesterday), John Patten, as education minister, said he 'fought' for A-levels as an unashamed élitist. But you can't brag you're an élitist in clichés—can you?[1] Maybe you can in football, if you're Ron Atkinson. But in Education? If you're the Secretary of State for it? To call A-levels (they were ... they still are ...) 'the hallmark of educational quality and excellence', 'a high-quality currency' (for entry to work and the burgeoning college and university sectors), 'a jewel in the crown' (of secondary education), 'a benchmark for excellence' (not just in this country but throughout the world)—is that how an élitist talks?

Mr Patten 'fought' for A-level but not as if it were an exam—a hieroglyph that means only as much, or as little, as we can make it mean; he fought for it as if it were a historic monument—in need of a preservation order. Touch of dry rot in the Jewel Tower? Send in Rentokil. A-levels threatened? Do the same. Be in charge. Be Ministerial. Announce that you are making three important announcements. Number one: that you will augment A-level ('augment', now, that is a fine word) with a new Starred Grade which will give a real incentive to our highest flyers, as well as greatly assisting the university talent spotters; number two: that you will encourage the greater use of AS qualifications, which in the other direction can do a great deal to broaden the options (and which in fact paved the way for the subsequent government's phasing out of A-level); and number three: that you will announce the Government's Response to the Inspectors' Report (and make the levelling parties livid).

But is that how an exam standard is maintained? Bureaucratically?

Where does 'an exam standard' come from? How many or how few are the judgements—how wide or how narrow is the community—it depends on? Could exam standards be kept up by the political establishment, for instance, if the whole political establishment talked in clichés? Or worse—if it did, and the wider educated public didn't notice? Or does that (élitist?) sort of thing not belong to the defence of élitism? What counts is the will of the Secretary of State for Education, enforced through the proper procedures by Her Majesty's Inspectors of Schools? So an education minister and his *officiers* can just decide that standards be maintained? All he has to do is speak the word, and see that HMIs do the same, and it shall be so? Let there be an élite and an élite there is? Time and tide wait for no man but him?

The standard of an examination—any examination, but especially one such as A-level which, even in the sciences, has always demanded a high degree of literacy—is upheld—if it is upheld—by a wide daily life. It is the outcome of influences widely diffused and largely obscure. It is maintained or lost as the result of a multitude of people thinking a multitude of different things on a multitude of subjects in a multitude of circumstances—thoughts which act and re-act upon one another in ways that are invisible to the people thinking them. All exam marking—even in the most technical subjects with the most explicit marking schemes—depends on distinctions between what is more and less important, more and less true, better and worse sense, better and worse expression, which are themselves untechnical and inexplicit. If our hold on these general and unspecialized distinctions weakens, exam standards fall, not merely without deference to the say-so of boy secretaries of state for education but without even being recognized. 'Standards' depend, helplessly, on culture. And boy secretaries—whether of state or of stamp clubs—command that as much as they do the weather.

The impossibility of Mr Patten's doing what he announced himself as doing is proved by the style in which he announced it. We may suppose that he would have avoided clichés if he could, because, we may speculate, as an ex-don he has some inkling of what they are: not a shorthand used for convenience's sake—where we might, if we wished, have chosen something different—but a deadly automatism. We don't choose clichés, they choose us. We don't use them, they use us. They are not words that are merely unoriginal or conventional but words that, without our knowing it, have lost their meaning. Words in combinations that reveal us as—without knowing it—having lost our meaning. Words that have lost their status as words, for men who have lost their status as men. And when they get a hold on us we become updated versions of

Mr Collins or Mary Bennet. It is possible to become to clichés what Midas was to gold. It happened to John Patten when he was Education Secretary. He was able to turn to cliché words as unsuspected of it as 'Thirty years ago' or 'when I was in the sixth form'. He could turn to cliché 'already', 'some' and 'and' (as in, 'Already, some 1000 schools and colleges …').

When a politician like Mr Patten says that quite a lot of people doing General National Vocational Qualification exams means 'a richness of vocational and academic choice', the voice is the voice of Mary Bennet, and like Mr Collins he is telling neither truth nor lies. These aren't words that can be believed or disbelieved, by Mr Patten or anyone else. He isn't saying something, about something, true or false. He's croaking.

And he's got company. When a Secretary of State—in a quality newspaper— makes as many as three important announcements—including naming a new top priority—all in one go, he is not likely to be the sole author of what he says. His drivel will be other men's too. It will have been sieved and picked over, scrutinized and passed (even supplied) by the finest critical intelligences on the government's pay-roll—high flyers whose talents, like Mr Patten's own, were spotted by other high flyers with talents like Mr Patten's own. Now that 'New' Labour has displaced 'Old', it is the drivel of the entire political establishment. Mr Blair's Education, Education, Education doesn't mean, 'We will show an understanding different from the Tories.' It means even more of the same, and it sounds awfully like Mr Patten—and Mr Collins.

When a Secretary of State for Education mistakes boastful inanity for good sense forcefully expressed; when there is no-one around him in his department, the Government, the civil service, his party, his family or his friends, to supply him with the judgement he lacks himself; and when the editor of a newspaper read by two million or so of the best-educated people in the country (social classes AA and AB, all) prints the inanity, confident that his paper's readers won't know it from sense either; when inanity is current and orthodox, throughout the educated classes … how simple a matter can it be to maintain the standards of public examinations? What can Legislation and Administration do? How can anyone—any of the anyones of whom Mr Patten is an example— know whether standards are being maintained or not? Or why it matters? Mr Patten fought for A-level as an unashamed élitist. His Labour successors have decided to dilute and diversify A-level as even more unashamed anti-élitists. But where is the difference? If Mr Patten's an élitist, what's a leveller?

Policies for keeping standards up in school count for nothing unless the standards have been kept up widely outside school, in the educated class from which government members, civil servants, teachers and examiners are drawn. The sort of standard in question isn't, after all, like those guaranteed by the British Standards Institute or that metal bar kept in ideal conditions in Paris that defines how long a metre is. You can't go and look at it; it isn't an independently existing criterion; it *has* no existence aside from the acts of judgement that constitute it. It is real none the less. An exam board *can* be a good place to find it and, as we see from *Pride and Prejudice*, so can breakfast.

But it isn't something you can impose, through any variety of British, or European, Weights and Measures Act. The attempt to raise standards—'lever them up'—by a species of force is self-defeating. It can only mean that we go on for the next 20 years or so as we have for the past 20 years or so, going round in circles and multiplying cures that aggravate the disease: solving the problem of teachers doing what they like by giving them an insanely detailed National Curriculum to follow; solving the problem of them no longer having enough time for reading, writing and 'rithmetic by giving priority to National Literacy and Numeracy Hours (something teachers themselves, of course, had never ever thought of doing and never ever done). Having saved all the time infants waste in play by making school exclusively workful, we go on to solve the problem of Jack's being such a dull boy by adopting the very latest 'European' method—'learning through play'. We have just solved the problem of A-levels that are narrow and élitist by making them broad and anti-élitist. What scope this gives us for solving the problem of university entrants who are unprepared for university work!

The real problem is not a kind for which there can be an administrative solution. 'What is to be done?' asked Carlyle:

> It seems to be taken for granted ... that there is some 'thing' or handful of 'things', which could be done; some Act of Parliament, 'remedial measure' or the like, which could be passed, whereby the social malady were fairly fronted, conquered, put an end to; so that, with your remedial measure in your pocket, you could then go on triumphant, and be troubled no farther.

Instead, what was to be done—first, before anything else could be—was the doer change himself:

> ... a radical universal alteration of your regimen and way of life ... a most agonising divorce between you and your chimeras, luxuries and falsities ...
>
> ... when jargon might abate, and here and there some genuine speech begin ...
>
> If thou ask again, therefore, ... What is to be done? allow me to reply: By thee, for the present, almost nothing. Thou there, the thing for thee to do is, if possible, to cease to be a hollow sounding-shell of hearsays, egoisms, purblind dilettantisms ....[2]

Jargon, falsity, chimeras, hearsays ... they're the problem. It isn't Research Assessment Exercises or Quality Assurance Agencies or money or national curricula or concentration on literacy and numeracy skills in whole class teaching that education in this country needs. For thou there, David Blunkett, and thy Shadow, on the front bench opposite, more money to spend, for the present, will produce nothing but more money spent. More whole class teaching will produce nothing but more classes taught as wholes. The more the national curriculum, the less the reading, writing, 'rithmetic; the more the 'rithmetic, the less the music and art; the higher up the results go, the lower down the standards come; the nearer we are to England the further off from France.

We need to divorce ourselves (and some will find it agonizing) from the crippling and delusive idea that education is a service industry like dry-cleaning, identical with the material arrangements through which we seek to provide it. You might as well identify the Church that is the bride of Christ with the Church that runs a pension scheme. You might as well try to lever up the standards of love or virtue as of education. The standards successive governments strive to raise or maintain are either widely diffused throughout the educated class or else are missing even from the agencies supposed to do the raising and maintaining.

The two following chapters illustrate (with certainly not too *little* detail) how examination boards themselves are likely just to reproduce the standards of the world around them, the world from which examiners as well as candidates are recruited. What is true of one A-level and one degree level examining board has general significance for standards in the whole modern university. We are not making a wild leap from an anecdote to a world. These two examining boards are a very small part of the world, but a part of a whole; and the whole is one of those whose character can be seen in all its parts. It is little more than a bare possibility that two public examinations such as these should show such signs of collapse and the collapse not have occurred elsewhere: in these two English examinations but not others, in English but not Philosophy or History. That the rot spreads is evidence of the wholeness of the body.

7   A-level, the Jewel in the Crown

INTRODUCTORY

THE LONG but not now very thorny road to the new university probably starts officially at age seven, with the first national tests, but the first real low hurdle is GCSE. If the subject is English and if you can get an English degree unacquainted with English literature it should not be surprising that English literature is not required for GCSE English. I nevertheless was surprised. At a public school where in the first four years they have read no Shakespeare, my son followed a syllabus including a verse Anthology for which my formula is Blake + Crap. Blake is admitted, to the extent of six lyrics, as a revolutionary. Wordsworth is represented, but only by 'Daffodils' and a poem, 'Nuns Fret Not', characteristic of his elderly dull phase. Otherwise there is hardly anything capable of being read with attention. Dyer, not the *Fleece* but the sixteenth-century dullard. A very minor poem by Herbert. A section by Seamus Heaney in which his trailing after Wordsworth would be painfully apparent to anyone who knew Wordsworth. That is before you get down to the real dregs. Alice Walker (see below) is represented: the true, the unblushful E. J. Thribb, accompanied by two photographs presumably of Ms Walker, looking studiously at her pen. All poems written before 1900 are prominently labelled 'Pre-1900', just like the cigarette packets warning us of health risk. My son says: imagine applying this to music or art (he studied Van Eyck with real interest). The principle is no less absurd applied to literature. There are lots of 'poems from other cultures' (which on this showing aren't cultures at all), though not from Pre-1900 poets like Homer, and pages of stuff by the quite nice would-be poet Gillian Clarke. This is for boys and girls who for the most part are unacquainted with English poetry and have no terms of comparison. My grandmother, who went to school in the bad old days before GCSE, had to learn a lot of English poetry by heart.

Then there is GCSE fiction: one short story by Hardy and another by John (*Triffids*) Wyndham. The Hardy is deadly dull and incredible, one of the ones he couldn't be bothered with. When this is said the teacher replies, 'But look at what it says about women's rights.' Written in about 1896, this Hardy represents Pre-1900 (in the new millennium will it be Pre-2000?) to boys and girls who for the most part have never read any Dickens or Jane Austen. Then they read one scene of *The Tempest*—the one where Trinculo and Stephano discover Caliban. Why this one? Because it tells you about the class system and colonialism (New Historicism). Nowadays we treat monsters as equals?

This GCSE, from the Northern Examinations and Assessment Board, is just Aged Ignorance clipping the youthful wings. Well, perhaps GCSE has to be adapted to the capacities of the mass of children, and of teachers. But was not A-level, the final stepping-stone into the university, still so reliable ('specialist', élitist) that it had to be done away with? Is not that the reason? Politicians seem to think so.

EXAMINING THE EXAMINERS

I marked an A-level English paper in 1993,[1] and if Mr Patten had only studied that one paper, the marking scheme for it, the answers to it and the marking of those answers, he might have begun to get some idea of the difficulty of doing in fact what he thought he had done by announcement. The paper was a thoroughly bad one, bad in the most fundamental way, originating in the selection of texts and passage for comprehension.

Firstly, the distribution of answers in the 193 scripts I marked: of the eight set texts, the two classics of English literature amongst them (which were also the only texts on the paper not written in the last 30 years) received no answers at all; of the six contemporary texts, one, the most ancient (some very ordinary journalism written as long ago as, and about, the sixties) also received no answers; of the remaining five set texts, two received two or three answers each. Of the three texts preferred by almost all candidates, one (the book of the film) was answered on by every candidate.

Given the texts chosen by the examiners, this was predictable. Were *Tristram Shandy* and Pope's *Essay on Criticism* chosen deliberately as being unlikely to be read? Who is going to do Sterne when they can do Susan Hill and Alice Walker (both as much alive as they ever were, both women and one black)? If a genuine invitation was to be issued to the English literature of the eighteenth century, why not *The Dunciad*? Would the Board have been afraid of being identified? If this syllabus and examination educated anyone, it was by accident.

The Assistant Examiner who tried to raise the matter at the Co-ordination meeting was bad-temperedly and pompously silenced as having raised a question for which, 'This was not the appropriate forum.' (What other forum was there?) 'Had she written to the Board?' She had not (as the Board well knew). Collapse of female party. And warnings all round.

Two books of particular worthlessness typified the selection: Philip Howard's collection *The State of the Language* and Alice Walker's novel *The Color Purple*.

Philip Howard's own language is in such a state that he's the last person to have anything intelligent to say about anyone else's. His style (as anyone may verify from his journalism—he was the long-serving literary editor of *The Times*) is a mish-mash of mutually contending clichés. The only consistent thing about it is that it consistently betrays him. The opinions which his book are fabricated from add up to two. One is that language is always changing. The other is that style must be 'appropriate' (clichés, appropriately, he thinks may be useful, when appropriate). Both opinions he has borrowed from academic linguisticians (as journalists daily borrow and are forced to borrow from all and sundry). The second question on him in the exam paper asked the candidates what they had learned from his book. The only thing anyone could learn (owned to by one candidate) is the lesson taught by this syllabus and examination paper as a whole: don't be critical.

Answers on *The Color Purple* showed the same lesson learned. Alice Walker's book is just soap opera, but that is not how it was seen.

This selection of texts couldn't have been made by anyone with any capacity to judge books. It couldn't have been made by anyone with any taste or judgement of language at all, and it dared the candidates (and their teachers) to question the taste that had made it. None (in the 193 papers I saw) dared. All treated these books in the way they were plainly meant to, with the same undifferentiated respect they would treat any set text, any 'classic'. If the text *is* a classic no harm is done. Most eighteen-year-olds won't go far wrong taking the merits of Shakespeare and Jane Austen for granted. But Alice Walker? I read two good answers out of 193, both by candidates who had a way of speaking for her which didn't tempt you to think they were speaking for themselves. They weren't critical but they did the next best thing: they kept their distance.

And then, in the passage for 'comprehension', hostility (or just blankness) to literature gave way to hostility (or blankness) to sense itself. To get a good mark on this, the one compulsory question, the candidates had either not to understand the passage or pretend they didn't. That—of an examination that's the jewel in the crown and a benchmark for excellence—may seem far-fetched but it's the simple truth. Let me say it again, deliberately: the examination board responsible—through its question-paper, its marking scheme and its 'team leaders' who oversee the work of the assistant examiners—required that its candidates should not understand the passage it had set them for comprehension. It did not require that knowingly; it was just that none of its senior members understood the passage himself.

It was not, of course, that they had failed to understand any of the individual words or grammatical constructions, that someone had made 'slips' of a kind that could be (easily) corrected. It was much worse than that. It was that they had all failed to see what was in front of them, failed to judge it aright—both in detail and overall. They took as cogent and reasonable—and required their assistant examiners and the candidates to take as cogent and reasonable—what was in one part foolish and conceited and in another indifferent to foolishness and conceit. They had been unintelligent. And—because examination boards are excellent examples of institutions in which Quality is Top-down Driven—they saw to it that intelligence wasn't what their juniors looked for in the candidates. The initiation into a community of thinkers took the form of rewarding candidates who could prove they shared the examiners' unintelligence. Such is the crown and benchmark.

I'll look in detail at just two sets of questions and answers, on the comprehension passage and on *The Color Purple*.

The Comprehension Passage

The passage set was the theatre column from *The Independent* for 25 October, 1990. In it a group of jet-setting English theatrical celebrities are quoted, with journalistic approval, as agreeing with one another that the English (excepting their jet-setting theatrical celebrities and their journalistic hangers-on) don't understand Shakespeare as well as foreigners do—because they have the disadvantages of speaking his language and knowing his plays. Put yourself in the place of an A-level candidate faced with this:

> Amid the storm of praise that greeted Peter Brook's production of *The Mahabharata* when it came to Glasgow two years ago, there was the odd murmur of dissent. When, said some critics, were we going to see another Shakespeare from the director whose *Midsummer Night's Dream* was a landmark in British theatre? Well, Shakespeare it is that he brings to Glasgow next week, but not quite the Bard as nature intended: his long-awaited production of *The Tempest* is in French.
>
> This is not a mischievous move: the production has just opened at Les Bouffes du Nord, the theatre in Paris that Brook has made his home for twenty years. Following Yukio Ninagawa's exquisite Japanese productions, the arrival of Brook's *Tempest* in Britain prompts speculation as to what can be lost, and what can be gained, in foreign-language Shakespeare—and whether the best productions can be even more exciting than the familiar English plays. How well do texts survive the crossing?
>
> 'The plays are so dense and so rich, that even when you lose the music of Shakespeare's poetry, it's like cutting the head off a worm—a complete worm is still left,' says Brook. 'It can also be fascinating. I saw *Hamlet* once played in Azerbaijani. "To be" is "alom", and "not to be" is the same word pronounced slightly differently— "alum". To show these two total opposites you say the same word with a faintly different intonation. That's very moving, and brings a completely new meaning to it.'
>
> *La Tempête* was translated by Jean-Claude Carrière, who has done most of Brook's translations. Even a hop across the channel however, brings a different attitude to language. 'You can't have two languages more incompatible than French

and English,' according to Brook. 'In English a word is marvellous because it can have many meanings and in French a word is only marvellous if it is clear, transparent, and has only one meaning. Sometimes you have to sacrifice one phrase and then capture the feeling of it in the following phrase.'

'I shifted the alliteration for "Full fathom five", using "p" as the alliterative letter,' says Carrière. 'But occasionally you've got to be bold enough to translate directly. For "we are such stuff as dreams are made of" [*sic*] most translations use "matière" for "stuff". I used the exact translation—"étoffe"—and hidden rhymes appeared.'

Carrière has always wanted to translate *The Tempest*—he admits to having practised secretly on passages for years. 'It is the one in which Shakespeare is most free with the form—it jumps from one to another, sometimes in the middle of a line. This is very attractive for a translator ... It is fascinating to try to make your own language flexible enough to follow the secret rhythms of a writer. Of course there is something you can never quite reach.'

There may, however, be things that a translator can reveal in a Shakespeare text. 'I read and re-read the play until I can feel the words which are the most frequent,' says Carrière. 'There are always two levels; there are words which reflect the obvious themes, and words which let you know what was interesting Shakespeare at the time. In *The Tempest* the first words are "island, sea, prisoner". But the secret word, which keeps coming back, is "freedom".'

Carrière translates into modern French, and Brook points out that this can often assist the actors with comedy. Michael Bogdanov, who has directed several Shakespeares at the Hamburg Schauspielhaus, agrees: 'Because the plays are frequently re-translated for each production, they come much closer to the language of today'. Working abroad has other advantages for an English director. 'There is a much greater freedom about directing it in another language,' Bogdanov feels. 'The restrictions and taboos aren't there.'

Richard Eyre, artistic director of the National Theatre, feels finding a fresh approach can be difficult: 'Every time we do a Shakespeare play in Britain we have sitting on our shoulders this huge weight of myth.' The National recently brought over a Romanian *Hamlet* and is about to host *The Kingdom of Desire*, a Taiwanese version of *Macbeth*. 'For us,' Eyre says, '*Hamlet* is a play full of quotes—quotes of incidents as well as of language.

'When the Romanian company approached it, they didn't have that baggage. Also if it's a play about tyranny and assassination, we're not terribly in touch with that. But they've had a master-class in Eastern Europe. So they don't have to create imaginary universes ... Shakespeare has served as a great ally of dissent in Eastern Europe. In Japan he is phenomenally popular, partly because there is something about the way that he treats elemental stories that they find very attractive.'

The Romanian *Hamlet* was played with such urgency that the play seemed newly written. Audiences for Kurosawa's film *Ran*—taken from *King Lear*—or Ninagawa's stage versions of *Macbeth* and *The Tempest* often saw the plays in a new, vivid light. In a sense the language barriers may assist the audience to focus on the play differently. It could be said that the very familiarity of Shakespeare's poetry sometimes dulls our response.

'Productions from abroad can be an eye-opener,' says Bogdanov, adding that directors have far more time to work on a play in almost every country outside Britain. 'So much of the good work on Shakespeare is going on in other countries. In Britain we tend to skate along on the surface and think it is the poetry of the language that is most important. People try and seduce with the language rather than the ideas.'

Bringing a different culture to the plays, as did Ninagawa, can unlock new meanings. Peter Brook is using actors from different theatrical traditions for Shakespeare's most elusive, magical play—Sotigui Kouyaté, who plays Prospero, and Bakary Sangaré (Ariel) are both from Mali. 'It seemed to me that actors whose culture means they have no problem with believing in the reality of the invisible world bring something different from actors produced by urban culture,' he explains.

'I do think that if one tries to interpret *The Tempest* in terms of master–slave relationship and so forth, one can easily miss the real qualities of the play... Reading a Shakespeare play one is touched by all manner of ambiguities, and in staging it one can easily be tempted into trying to resolve those ambiguities for the audience. But a play can't be about freedom, it can't be about power. It has to be about what's in between the fifty definitions that you can give of "pardon", the 300 things that you can say are "freedom".' Seeing Shakespeare through other eyes may help open up such possibilities, and send us back to the original refreshed. Peter Brook hopes so: 'Theatre lives on freshness. Anything that helps you discover freshness is of great value.'

Nothing much is lost in translation, after all: just the music of the poetry, the poetry of the language, the language. Without the language, you've still got the ideas. (Where, though?) You've still got the plays. It's like cutting off the head of a worm (or a theatrical jet-setter) and finding you've still got the worm complete. In fact, a worm that's more than complete. For Shakespeare's English keeps the English skating on the surface of his plays. Without it, the Romanians, Taiwanese, Azerbaijanis and Malians are free to dive in deep.

And if the foreigners don't know what to expect of a production, because they've never seen one before, so much the better. All that baggage, that huge weight of myth is removed: 'The restrictions—the taboos aren't there.' And who aren't they there for? For the foreign audience? Well, actually, no. For the jet-setting English celebrity: 'There is a much greater freedom about directing in another language.' So that's what's at the bottom of these paradoxes. The jet-setter wants to be free. The understanding of a native audience—and the expectations that understanding gives rise to—constrain him. And, very understandably, he doesn't want to be constrained. He wants to do as he likes. So the idea of the 'new and exciting' does as it likes with him; and freshness becomes another (stale) cliché.

These and other deep thoughts the journalist, Sarah Hemming, then stitches together as if they were authoritative, and as the most painless way of getting her copy. (And because the piece didn't take up enough room, someone—Sarah

herself? a copy-editor?—stuck part of Hamlet's 'to be, or not to be' speech at the
bottom of the page, in English, in French, in Welsh, in Basque and in Esperanto.
Pity about the Azerbaijani.)

And then the board presents this stuff to its candidates, not for criticism but
for 'comprehension', i.e. requiring them to treat it as if it were all the most plain
and obvious good sense. As if it could be comprehended without ridicule. As
if anyone with any interest in Shakespeare or in English or in ideas could feel
anything for it but savage contempt.

Aren't such arty-farty thought-stutterings the very worst sort of thing to put
before an average lot of eighteen-year-olds? Bullying them on the one hand,
despised by them on the other, just the thing to leave them not knowing what
to think or feel or dare to say.

The questions (especially in conjunction with the marking scheme) were of a
kind to conceal the differences between the better and the worse candidates. It
would take a very unusual eighteen-year-old to express contempt for a passage
set for comprehension in an exam but, given the right questions, one might
reasonably expect the better candidates to wonder whether there was not something suspect about the relation between 'language' and 'ideas', 'poetry' and 'the
play' proposed by Monsignors Brook, Bogdanov and Eyre. An intelligent,
well-taught eighteen-year-old who liked Shakespeare ought to be capable of
discussing whether Shakespeare's 'ideas' exist apart from his language, whether his
poetry is just a distracting 'music', whether it is an entirely unqualified advantage
to come to a play (or symphony or football match) without expectations—
because without knowledge—and whether (though no-one wants plays any
more than bread to be stale) 'freshness' is quite the all-valuable quality Brook
and his colleagues think it. A clever eighteen-year-old might even want to ask
how someone who was seeing Shakespeare performed for the first time could
know whether the performance was fresh or not.

The questions asked were of a kind to make any real comprehension of the
passage a maddening distraction, for example:

> (a) Explain in your own words the different attitudes of the French and English to
> language as expressed by Brook and Carrière in paragraphs 4 and 5.
> (b) In your own words explain why Shakespeare is popular in (i) Romania and (ii)
> Japan. Use the material in paragraphs 9 to 11.

The unintelligence of the questions was then reinforced by a marking scheme
which told the examiners that what the candidates mainly had to do was locate
'the correct point'. What the examiners then had to do was tick it:

> (a) Four points are to be made, each carrying two marks. Give a tick when you are
> giving one mark and two ticks when you are giving both marks. Place the ticks in
> the body of the script at the point where you decide to award the marks. At the
> end of the answer add the ticks and place the total in the right hand margin.

The four points to be credited are:
(i)   Brook: multiple meanings for a word are ideal in English
(ii) single meanings are the goal in French
(iii) Carrière: in translation you have to achieve the same effect by different means
(iv) sometimes a literal translation brings stylistic richness.

For each point award ONE mark for the point being found and attempted and ONE extra mark for successful expression showing understanding by using own words.

(b) There are five possible points here … etc.
(i)   Romania: tyranny and assassination
(ii) don't have to create imaginary universes
(iii) Shakespeare an ally of dissent
(iv) Japan: way that he treats elemental stories
(v)   unfamiliarity with the poetry enlivens the response
For each of four points … etc.

The questions prevented the candidates judging the passage as a whole and the marking scheme prevented the examiners judging a candidate's answer as a whole. A tick for circling the point, a tick for paraphrasing it; and for writing intelligently or for glimpsing stumbling blocks where jet-setting celebrities, journalist and examining board saw only a clear, fourteen-lane highway—*nothing*. Even if the passage had been cogent and the questions made up by someone who had understood it, this kind of task—circling points (half-way to ticking boxes)—isn't a proper one for A-level English candidates; any more than ticking the points circled is a proper task for their examiners.

Ticks were used particularly stupidly in question (d), where one had to be given for the 'purpose' of the article's headlines, captions and photograph and another for their 'impact', when 'purpose' and 'impact' are one and the same thing seen from different angles. 'The purpose of all headlines is to make an impact', as you might say, or—as one candidate did say—'the purpose and impact is to attract the reader's attention'. It might do for O-level. It might do for EFL. But for A-level English Language and Literature? The jewel in the crown and benchmark of excellence? For university entrance?

A third of schoolchildren (I hear) now go on to do A-level. A lot of them—nearly a hundred thousand a year—do English. And a lot of *them* don't see or read or like Shakespeare. Robbie Williams might be part of their world, Shakespeare isn't. And it showed—in candidates who had noticed that the passage set them … well … it might be all right for *them* but it wouldn't be everyone's cup of tea. Not when it 'dropped play-names like *Hamlet*', 'appeared to assume that everybody is aware of Shakespeare is [*sic*] a prominent play writer,' 'expected its readers to have come into contact with Shakespeare's work and indeed particular plays such as *The Tempest* and also *Hamlet*' and expected even that 'the reader would understand "using 'p' as the alliterative" when a

reader may not know.' It might be 'very cultural' and 'show quite a high understanding of English' but—it had to be said—it was really for 'those with
interests in the "finer" sections of society, middle-aged and elderly members of
society whose knowledge of literature is somewhat advanced.' The truth was
that 'more than the books, appealing to most are films, plays etc. as they are not
quite as heavy going and easier to understand.'

Every A-level English paper must now be sat by lots of candidates like
that, who, when they hear *Hamlet* mentioned, reach for their Walkmans. This
question invited them to come out, unembarrassed and unashamed. And out
they came. They saw what the jet-setting celebrities thought about Shakespeare,
and that what they thought, though it was here and there offensively allusive or
used long words, wasn't all that different from what *they* thought. And they saw
that the journalist on *The Independent* approved it and that the Board didn't
mind it. So they repeated it, but more plainly. They said things that showed
they understood Peter Brook better than he understood himself:

Shakespeare's English could almost be a foreign language.

You have to contend with Shakespeare's poetry.

The poetry of the plays, which is sometimes confusing in English, and so blinds
the reader to the true meaning of the play, is often lost when translated and so the
audience can then picture the real story without hindrance.

Shakespeare is performed so often that people concentrate on the language e.g.
blank verse and rhyming cutlets [*sic*] instead of the actual acting.

In Japanese, Shakespeare's poetry is lost and therefore you have to look at the story
and what Shakespeare is actually saying and this is good.

The Japanese are seeing a new product without a stereotypical sequence of old
incidents and speeches.

The Romanians don't have a history of producing Shakespeare hanging over their
heads.

They were lucky in that they didn't have to wade through all Shakespeare's quotes
as us English do.

Shakespeare is popular in Romania as they do not have the handicap of the
English language.

These candidates really did understand the passage and deserved more ticks
than were available to give them.

But they weren't the only ones who understood it better than the examiners.
There were others who, if the questions had helped instead of hindering them,
might have been able to say what was wrong with it.

Question (a) asked the candidates to 'explain the different attitudes to
language of the French and English as expressed by Brook and Carrière'. Now,
that could mean 'find and paraphrase their (four) main points'—which is what

the examiners took it to mean. But—because it doesn't dictate what counts as 'explaining'—it permits something more (more interesting). You can see that this is so if you compare it with (b).

Whereas in (b)—'explain why Shakespeare is popular in Romania and Japan'—'explain' means 'find the cause of' and does invite answers that invite marks in the form of ticks (and crosses), in (a) 'explain' means something more like 'give a reasoned account of'. It leaves—it ought to leave—the candidate freer to answer according to his own sense of what counts as 'explaining'. Part of the point of this question (for an examiner who is himself alive to the way the word shifts its meaning) is to test what the candidates can make of 'explain'. There can't be any question of the examiners merely awarding ticks for each of 'four correct points' and ignoring everything else. Yet that was just what the marking scheme required them to do—even though not a few students showed that, put to the test, they might prove capable not just of paraphrase but of thought.

'A reasoned account' of what Brook and Carrière say about the differences between the French and the English attitude to language—an account that really did explain something—ought to go a good deal further than paraphrase, however sensible. What they say isn't obviously friendly to Brook's larger argument that Shakespeare gains from being translated. On the face of it, the differences described suggest that translations into French must be travesties. And quite a few candidates, without any help from either the question or the passage, did, in the very short space they had available (about 40 separate 'points' to be located and paraphrased in 60 minutes), tug and pick at the knot Brook had tied. They showed a capacity for thinking which the assistant examiners were forbidden to credit.

I didn't record every instance where a candidate said something deserving a tick I couldn't give but I know that I not infrequently felt indignant, sometimes sufficiently to say so in the margin of the script (putting messages in bottles and throwing them in the sea—now forbidden for fear they get back to the candidates: see p. 145). And I did record the following instances where I thought the candidate was doing something more interesting and more valuable than merely finding and paraphrasing, was making a start on criticism:

> Brook thinks that the French and English languages are incompatible because the essence of the language is so different. It is difficult then to translate one language, in which words have many meanings, into a language where the words need to be clear in meaning. He feels that both languages have very little in common.

> You can't have two languages more incompatible than French and English. By this he means that both languages are difficult to translate into the other.

> This highlights a fundamental difference in attitude to language between the English and the French, to the extent that Brook calls them the most incompatible languages. The differences are not negative though ...

This last candidate has seen what neither Brook himself, nor the journalist, nor the Board has seen, that Brook's larger argument needs rescuing. Is that worth one tick or two? or, following the marking scheme, none?

It isn't that an examiner couldn't in these cases find some plausible excuse for putting a tick or two in the margin but that he couldn't properly take into account the fact that something better was being supplied than was wanted, that he was being required to overlook exactly those qualities he should have been looking out for. It was like being told to prospect for fool's gold.

The following says exactly the opposite of what Brook says (and couldn't be given a tick by the most lenient or inconsistent examiner) but it is saying something which is not only sensible in itself but needs to be said: that for the audience of a Shakespeare play it can be an advantage to be English:

> In England we have a heritage of great Shakespeare plays and from childhood are 'brought up on' certain quotes from his plays. Shakespeare is part of a literary heritage that we are all proud of, and in some ways possessive of—in the way in which we use quotes from the plays as part of our everyday language. Other countries do not have the same background.

Now isn't this, at worst, the necessary counter-truth to Brook's own? Shouldn't Brook have thought of it for himself? Shouldn't the journalist? As they didn't, shouldn't the examiners have welcomed and rewarded it, instead of sending it away tickless?

A lot of candidates, I thought, understood the paragraphs which question (b) is based on (9 to 11) better than the examiners did. The question asks why Shakespeare is popular in Japan and Romania, but these paragraphs are only about Shakespeare's popularity where the speaker forgets what he is talking about. As pretty well all the candidates spotted (how could they miss it?), the subject of these paragraphs is the same as that of the piece as a whole: how much more foreigners make of Shakespeare than the English (unless they are jet-setting celebrities). 'Popularity' is, at most, a side issue. Many candidates seemed to me hindered by the obtuseness of the question. If they understood the passage, their answers were pulled one way; if they wanted a tick, they were pulled another.

The Color Purple

This is the book which all the candidates answered on. It is a really rubbishy, boring book—soap opera plus ishoos, the race ishoo and the sex (or rather the gender) ishoo—sentimental trash. Check this opinion if you have a few days spare: the book is very easily available. Nothing like it could ever pass as literature anywhere there was an educated class, intact as a class and confident of its taste. Only in a culture like our own, where the dominant standard is plebeian and uneducated, could such a book ever be used to prepare candidates for university entrance. Only in a culture where the contemporary standard prevailed in defiance, or ignorance, of any standard that had ever gone before could *The Color Purple* be 'studied', alongside—what shall we say?—*King Lear*, *Pride and Prejudice*, Homer? (except that of course on this A-level list the latter were unavailable).

The book is rubbish of a peculiarly American sort—something low with pretensions to the 'higher' and more 'spiritual'. The high brought horribly low by familiarity. Fake, democratic modesty, real conceit. Who needs read further than the dedication?

> To the Spirit:
> Without whose assistance
> Neither this book
> Nor I
> Would have been
> Written.

But if that sets your teeth on edge, the way Alice Walker signs off will make you wish you'd had them out:

> I thank everybody in this book for coming.
> A.W., author and medium

One of the two questions on the book could have been taken advantage of by a candidate who was inclined, and dared, to dislike it: what does it have to say about love? The other question required the candidates to think that Alice Walker has something called 'writing techniques'. (The novel is, like *Pamela*, epistolary, and presumably the different styles of the various correspondents, beginning with Celie to God, were intended.) As you couldn't possibly attribute any such thing to her, except in derision (see—as the candidates had to—the last chapter), the candidates had either to ignore that side of the question (there were several others) or to bluff their way round it. It was bluff that was wanted. (I hope that one of the things I was judged too lenient for was not penalizing its absence.)

But it was what the book prompted these young people to say about love and about life generally that interested me. All had pretty much the same thing to say—which was pretty much the same thing the book itself has to say. All the candidates, the worst and the best, seemed to understand the book equally—indistinguishably—well. As, being what it is, how could they not? The book was evidently congenial to them, they receptive to it. ('His nonsense suits their nonsense, sir.') But it was more than that. Understanding the book presented no difficulty to them because they already knew what it had to teach. It summed up what they themselves knew. They didn't read it or judge it or think about it. They merely reproduced it: that is, they innocently, candidly, expressed—produced—themselves. They and it are precipitates of the same moral chemistry, the same assumptions, the same grammar.

In reading these exam papers I felt I was being shown something much stranger and more exotic than any merely Elizabethan or medieval—or aboriginal—World Picture. I was being shown the World Picture of the present all around me, the World Picture of the young, of my own and my neighbours' children. Not the picture of the world held by the Inter City Firm on the Meadowell council estate but that held by the respectable and well-behaved, middle class, educated young of the suburban Tyne Valley. 'Great kids,' sometimes say their teachers. Great kids, all.

And I was to mark this stuff, to distinguish the better in it from the worse, in numbers out of 80. When it was all—all (all answers but two)—equally, because absolutely, worthless. To mark it, when what one felt for it (off a council estate oneself) was pure, aristocratic disdain, *desdeyn*—for what the candidates were writing; for the book they were writing about; for the Chief Examiner who not only set the book but claimed (as I was told) that the more he read it the more he saw in it; for the Team Leaders and Assistant Examiners who carried out his instructions like lackeys and footmen (Quality—Top-down Driven); for the teachers (more lackeys) who chose to 'teach' the book, as just more stuff to teach; for the parents of the candidates and the candidates themselves who would rejoice or sorrow over the marks as if they meant something, as if they were the mark of something real; and disdain, of course, for the university admissions tutors and the employers (not to mention journalists and politicians) who would treat the results as the record of real events.

The candidates' language made me feel like the residue of some extinguished nobility. Not the errors of 'SPAG' (spelling, punctuation and grammar) and idiom, common enough and bad enough though they often were. Nor the Americanized, soap opera vulgarisms like *mouthed off at, love has to be a two-way thing, can't handle relationships* (because no mum and an inattentive dad), *relationships can work* (with the components of love and mutual respect), *on a high, calling the shots*. Nor even a vocabulary full of media-words—if not home-grown then naturalized—like *lifestyle, image* and *relationship, concepts* and *factors, positive, negative, caring, supportive* and *bonding, totally, basically* and *actually* (as in *to actually do any and everyfing*). Nor the fact that no-one, not one candidate, ever tried to rise above, or sink below, plain matter-of-fact statement, that no-one liked or disliked or joked or was ironical. Nor even that everyone was more or less the same as everyone else.

All this was bad enough. I shouldn't want to pretend it didn't matter. But in the examination answers of eighteen-year-olds, mere ignorance and tastelessness, or the absence of individual character, wouldn't, on its own, seem prophetic. But something did, something which seemed to me to underlie, or surround and bind together, all these lesser failings and give them their special virulence (as AIDS can make a cold fatal). This something was a new common sense—the common sense that underlies abortion and divorce and euthanasia and privatizing prisons; pop, fashion and deodorant adverts; Alice Walker, Elizabeth Taylor, Tony Blair, Princess Diana, the 'European Union' and BS 5750; the common sense that underlies and supports the whole modern form of life—here, made candidly and unselfconsciously plain, as only youth can.

I say 'new'. In a way it's respectably old and familiar. It's certainly been a few hundred years in the making. In this country Newman called it 'liberalism' and F. R. Leavis called it 'technologico-Benthamism', in Canada George Grant called it 'technology and liberalism'. But such phrases suggest something having the character of an idea, something examinable. What these exam papers contained was something far beyond that: the idea become the underlying, unexaminable ground of any and all ideas whatsoever—unexaminable, to the holder, because comprising the language in which he conducts any conceivable examination of anything, including of the language in which he examines things. How to get far enough outside this language in order to see it? Impossible, except by learning another language. Shakespeare's would do. What could be more commonsensical than such assumptions as these: that what is real is material-mechanical, and can be manipulated and measured; that all values are relative; that there is no judgement ... that doesn't infringe some-one's freedom; that if there is any final good it is that freedom, and equality in freedom; that there are no ends ... that aren't means to other ends (not even that end of all ends, happiness). This isn't new in itself, of course, but the frank brutality with which these respectable eighteen-year-olds say it, without apparently being aware that they are saying anything at all—that's new.

What are these truths which they hold to be self-evident, and which Alice Walker helps them state? They're the good ol' American truths—life, liberty and the pursuit of happiness, rights to—after 200 years of development and a new land-fall in the Old World. They're our own chickens, come home to roost—as crows, with sentiment. I quote the candidates themselves:

The important thing is to manage to sort out your life.

People can only benefit from love in the long run.

Love can help you exist happily/gain confidence/survive/get through life/carry on.

You need love to give a sense of self-worth.

We must learn to love and appreciate ourselves.

Love is about being completely content with yourself.

We must learn to accept each other for what we are and give ourselves the freedom to enjoy it.

Sexual love can transcend the borders of gender/is transferable and need not be mechanically fixed to one gender/need not be confined within its stereotypical contexts and sometimes the more unusual it is the more wounds it can heal.

Love of women for women is acceptable but love for men and women is also fine. Love is the important thing in any way you can find to suit yourself and your partner.

It doesn't matter what form it arrives in/whether of man or woman, your husband or lover/be it love for a person, love for an animal, or love for an object.

A religion that does not judge…

God no longer the white man but a thing that is everywhere/a something, a beholder of beauty instead of the white ideas of an old white man with a white beard and white hair/not a he but an it, pleased with creation. 'If people don't admire the color purple it pisses God off.'

God simply loved people to be happy and appreciate the things around them and the feelings they experienced. 'God loves everything you love' and 'God loves all them feelings. That's some of the best stuff God made' and 'me and God make love just fine.'

Love is the right of all of us.

And then there's the way these truths work themselves out in Celie's life, before and after Shug (Shug—Avery—is her Saviour and her, and her husband's, and others', lover). B[efore] S[hug], Celie

is inadequate as a woman in her own right/isolated from her own feelings;

makes no effort to discover/get in touch with her inner feelings;

has a poor self-image/no self-prestige/a lot of negativity;

has no concept of the pleasure of sex and it being a tool which can be manipulated to express love;

protects Nettie from Pa as she has no feeling of self-worth;

is timid and lacking in self-esteem and has no fighting spirit, but she does have redeeming characteristics: she knows how to survive and her sexual urges are awoken by Shug Avery. However she is no paragon;

is far too sympathetic to others and careless of herself, too considerate, but she learns, through Shug Avery, to become more aggressive and self-seeking.

Under Shug's influence, Celie becomes a paradigmatic, modern woman. Her development is multifaceted, and the facets all fit—'everything comes together for her': Her

search for herself begins;

life becomes her own/her feelings are allowed to be heard;

husband's love for Shug highlights his weakness and this is important to Celie because it shows what a woman can do to a man and how she can treat him if she tries.

She

begins to try to be her own person/becomes a person in her own right/comes to terms with who she is/recognises herself as an individual;

becomes strong enough to be her own woman/comfortable with herself/at ease with herself;

explores herself and becomes proud of what she discovers. This experience gives Celie a worth that she must also love herself;

gains the advantage of self-acceptance;

appreciates herself/can accept without being put down for feeling good about herself/makes herself feel better/is transformed to a life of self-esteem/feelings of self-love waken within her/obtains self-esteem, independence and self-love;

becomes strong/assertive/aggressive/proud/a confident assertive woman who knows what and whom she wants;

can finally live the life she wants/enjoy the lifestyle she wants;

gets control of her own life;

grows from being unhappy and unloved to someone who has gained what she wants;

becomes happy once she discovered this happiness and realized she had a right to happiness/happy to be the person she is/finally happy to be herself, and not someone's wife;

learns much in her expressions of love and anger/the love she felt let her mouth off to him, and eventually stick a fork in his hand/this is the first real anger she feels;

comes to terms with what life is all about;

realizes that life is to be enjoyed not endured;

becomes capable of living for herself, instead of through others;

develops from being self-sacrificing to someone who 'struts a bit';

so that whereas she starts off blaming herself for all the bad things that happen, in the end she blames others;

resents God because he doesn't help her in suffering/save her from bad experiences/take any notice of her. 'What God do for me?' she says;

loses her faith in God [when things go wrong], regains it [when things go right];

grows to love herself and therefore to love sex/achieves sexual liberation;

learns to relate to other women;

realizes her own and Shug's needs/realizes the concept of enjoying sex/has some flesh to direct her feelings at/utilizes her body to gain pleasure;

Sex activity enables her to gain self-confidence/the two women are naturally lovers because both are women, both have the same experiences and the same feelings;

Shug is caring and supportive/Celie and Shug are an example of the way women must support each other/the idea of sisterhood helps Celie in the area of bonding/ if women work together, they can achieve anything, can be in control/by quilting together they succeeded in creating female continuity in a world that represses female expression/Celie and her sister, Nettie, don't just love one another, like sisters. They have 'sister' love, which is an indication of the unity of women and oppression of men.

The unity of women is tried by a man (that is, by the urge for one, that is, by the wish to know that one can still get one, if one wants) but not overcome. The mature wisdom acquired in the trial brings it through:

It's important to Shug to know that she can still get a young man.

The time comes for Shug to have a fling with Grady.

Even when Shug leaves Celie for Grady, she still loves Celie, who learns that just because someone leaves you for someone else, it doesn't mean the end of love.

It does not mean that Shug loves her less but that she needs her freedom. Celie, broken hearted at first, comes to terms with that. 'Just cause I love her don't take away any of her rights.'

Love is about sharing but love is also about letting the person you love go. Celie has to learn this and she does. 'I try to teach my heart not to want what it can't have.' [*There's spiritual for you.*]

And through the unity of women—the unity of all, as women (who have taken the place of the proletariat), in the genderless society:

Celie and Albert are united by their love for Shug.

At the end when Celie's sister returns, the family is united, and Africa and America are united.

All the characters are re-united in a feminized space. Alice Walker makes all males females, all differences equal.

And what's so strange about all that then? It's no mere jargon or set of notions adopted to pass an exam with. These are the new commonplaces of—as Lawrence called it—'a newspaper-reading democracy': Christianity Benthamized, Marxized and sentimentalized. It's a new common sense (which turns the old on its head). Look at the number of different ways it offers of saying the same thing, the way the new combines with the old in it, the vulgar with the pretentious. It's not just flexible and various but organic—able to turn anything and everything it touches into a form of itself (like the vegetable from outer space in one of the Quatermass films). Here is a language capable of making sense of the world. It's a language and a common sense that draws the world together. (No wonder the French fear English.) It doesn't draw together just the Black American feminist–novelist and the (mainly) white English students writing about her. The teachers who examine the latter know a branch of the same language. Examiners need (we nod in agreement with the Chief Examiner who says so) 'sophisticated reading skills' in order to 'interact' with candidates who may not be very 'sophisticated communicators'. (Well, you wouldn't expect them to be—doing A-level English—would you?)

This new common sense joins together what used to be thought opposites. San José and Slaggyford, Christ and Jeremy Bentham, love and anger, soap opera and literature. It joins together Elizabeth Taylor—telling the audience at a pop concert for Aids sufferers to 'stay alive'—and a British Prime Minister—telling the nation he wants it to be 'at ease with itself'. All differences, as the candidate said, made equal—annulled, melted down in 'pop'. 'Love to the loveless shown that they might lovely be'... become ... 'all you need is love'.

*   *   *

What subject has been examined here as A-level 'English'? Not the one I did 38 years ago. Not the genuine subject of English at all. Something as little that as alchemy is chemistry. Wherever 'English' is a genuine subject of study—at whatever level—the standard that is appealed to, however remotely, however tacitly, is that of the literature as the best of the language. But the active standard here—throughout the paper, from the selecting of texts to the policing of marking—is that of journalism. Not the standard of the best thought and said, wherever English is spoken, over centuries, but the standard of the moment, in Wapping.

What this exam does is to make hostility to the genuine subject of English respectable and to certify proficiency in that hostility. But if so, the literature itself can still be a kind of antidote—while it can still be read. And if it could not still be read it would not need to be kept off the syllabus.

That's why this particular board, which exists to establish and preserve standards, can't allow any genuine literature into its exam. The real thing would judge the exam and the board that devised it. If only one Shakespeare play were on the same list as Alice Walker's novel, and read, the absurdity of solemnly discussing *The Color Purple* or 'comprehending' Miss Trot's 'piece' on Monsignor Block would be undisguisable. Let the students see what Jane Austen, in *Pride and Prejudice*, makes of Mr Collins, and then ask them what they have learned from Mr Howard.

INSPECTING THE INSPECTORS

How Not To Do It may have been the whole science of government in the days of the Circumlocution Office and rotten boroughs but it is hardly enough today. The science of democratic government is a bit more refined than that. It includes the art of How To Do What Can't Be Done. Nowadays when something's wrong we put initiatives in place to put it right. We want action. So action is what we get.

Somebody's dog's bit somebody's child, and you want a law against it? You've got it. Somebody's husband's dodged off and not paid up? You want him made to pay? You've got it.

You want a better education for your children? You've got it.

What hasn't been done to give you it? Parental choice, League Tables, Local Management of Schools, the National Curriculum, Quality Assurance, Baker Days, bigger sixth forms, more nurseries, more universities, bigger universities, more inspections, reform of inspections, reform of teacher training, reform of examinations, reform of the National Curriculum... more and still more reform of the National Curriculum? What has been left undone that could possibly be done?

And yet the more done, the more there seems to do.

How could that be?

Could it be that, for some things, something more—or different—is required than sheer blind activity?

Inspection—it's sometimes called monitoring—is a very important cog in the system of pulleys and levers by which educational standards are to be—as Mr Baker used to say, 'levered up'. If teachers and examiners are likely to fall below the mark—and how could they not be—what could be more sensible than to send in the inspectors to bring them back up to it and to keep them there? That's doing something, isn't it? Who can deny it?

In Circumlocution Office times, when asked, 'What is to be done?', Carlyle did once famously reply, 'By thee, for the present, almost nothing.' But that was then, and could scarcely apply now, to a body of men and women who (unlike Matthew Arnold) are all professionals—trained, interviewed and appointed, with job descriptions. A body, moreover, which has been reorganized, semi-privatized upon the most up-to-date and businesslike lines, and has a name that's an acronym, Ofsted, a logo and a colour scheme. You couldn't fairly say to them, could you, 'Thou there, the thing for thee to do is, if possible, to cease to be a hollow sounding-shell of hearsays, egoisms, purblind dilettantisms; and become, were it on the infinitely small scale, a faithful and discerning soul'? Such an old, exploded style of speech as Carlyle's couldn't apply, could it?

The same year as I marked A-level, all boards were inspected by Ofsted. The amount of work it had to do was immense: inspecting the work of seven boards examining three quarters of a million candidates writing two million scripts in eleven subjects, all over the country. Ofsted covered—that is had headings and sub-headings for—everything: every aspect of syllabuses, from principles to presentation; every aspect of exam papers, from design to marking schemes; every aspect of marking and grade awarding, from the selection and training of examiners to borderline re-marking. It covered the schools as customers too, satisfied or otherwise. No wonder it took from January to August. What an immensity of measurable activity must have been entailed: hours of listening, watching, conferring; pages of typing; miles of travelling; miles upon miles of central heating pipework and telephone and electrical cable kept employed. What organization. What a contribution to the economy—or a cost.

We can get some idea from the report it produced.[2] Did it do the job? Does it tell us whether the quality and standards of A-levels are high or not? Actually, no. Not that it has failed to. It didn't try. It judges and sets out to judge—in the ordinary sense of that common English word—nothing at all.

The 'quality and standards' Ofsted concerns itself with have nothing to do with quality and standards as ordinarily understood. Whatever the Inspectors do do with their pudding, the one thing they don't do is eat it.

An examination candidate needs not just to possess information but to make sense of it—according to the canons of his subject, according to what, within the subject and at his level, matters more and less. A student in the act of studying develops a new scale of values. Things which don't matter outside the subject and to laymen (to himself before his own initiation), within it become important. This new scale of values won't just sit alongside his old but will be incorporated into it, modifying it, modifying—if ever so slightly—him, permanently, for good or ill. As he enters more deeply into the subject, the subject enters more deeply into him.

And what is true of the candidate is true of his examiner. What qualifies the one to judge the other is not just that he knows more but that he knows better what is and isn't worth knowing in the subject. What he has more of is not only information but, as it were, the morality of the subject.

And what is true of candidates and examiners must be true of inspectors. The inspectors can no more judge the work of the examiners from a position outside the subjects being examined than, from such a position, can the examiners judge the work of the candidates, or the candidates know how to answer the examiners' questions. The work of inspection is done—if it is done—from within the subjects and within what they have in common. To inspect the 'quality and standards' of the examining boards, inspectors have to think primarily, essentially, like men and women who care—can one say?— for the honour of their subjects and of the larger order the individual subjects compose.

But not at Ofsted. Ofsted attempts the impossible—impossible not because merely very difficult but because self-contradictory: to judge the examining of the arts and sciences from a standpoint outside all art and science.

Ofsted's standpoint is, as the report itself says, 'quality assurance', 'quality control procedures', 'auditing'. The kind of 'quality' and 'standards' that is in question is that of industry, a kind that can be ascertained by rule and method, by (as an Ofsted inspector said to me in a letter) 'methodology', a kind that can be controlled (like portions), that is familiar to trading standards officers and is expressed, ideally, in quantities. We are in the world not of mere fallible judgement but of measurement and certain results. ('Never mind the quality, feel the width.') It's a world in which, if you've got 'quality', you can get a British Standards Certificate, BS 5750, to prove it.

An audit may gain in 'objectivity' over mere judgement, but only by losing sight of everything that isn't auditable, which may be—for all your audit can tell you—the most important things of all. Despite the report's sub-title, 'Quality and Standards', and its ostensible purpose, it has next to nothing to say about quality. In what it does have to say, it is like a (perfunctory) school report, handing out mere grades of approval:

Syllabuses—Appropriate

Questions—Appropriate

Demands—Appropriate

Standards—Appropriate

Quality of Papers—Sound to High

Marking—Satisfactory to Good

Overall—Immensely professional

But the report gives the reader no glimmer of an opportunity to test these verdicts, no hint of its evidence or reasoning, no hint of what makes standards appropriate or of what they might be appropriate to. It gives no hint, that is, what its own standards are. You've got to take them on trust—or not. It has no interest, really, in its own judgements. It makes them to get them out of the way and to get on with other, auditable, things. On what is ordinarily understood by the terms 'quality' and 'standards' it is practically inarticulate, as—if it's an audit—what else can it be?

The core of the report would be, you'd think, the sub-section 'Quality and Standards' within the main section 'The 1993 Examination Papers', and perhaps it is, but it consists of only one short and one longish paragraph. The short one says that quality was satisfactory to high but gives no hint what made it so. The longish one begins with a windbag's statement of the obvious, couched in an abstract jargon meant to make it seem like a discovery: 'The key criteria for effectiveness in question-papers are the appropriateness and consistency of their level of demand.'

Then it repeats what it says in the paragraph before: 'Questions were almost always judged to be pitched at an appropriate level.'

Then, without hinting what made them so, it gets on with one of the things it can talk about, the 'tighter co-ordination' required to make all demands perfectly uniform.

What the report is about is not quality and standards but 'practices and procedures', the 'examination process' as a process, a kind of industrial production line manufacturing grades. If you consider examining at a sufficiently high level of abstraction, it *will* seem to be a variety of manufacturing, and to be subject to the same quality control procedures and analyses as 'any other' manufacturing process. (Looked at from outer space, the Los Angeles smog is reportedly beautiful.)

The report notices three things and three things only about the process: how explicit all the various bits of documentation are ('Syllabuses offer a satisfactory specification of the examination requirements'); how well one section of the production line, or one input, fits in with another ('need to devise more sophisticated mechanisms for relating dissimilar components'); and how consistent practices and procedures are within and between the Boards ('variations need resolving').

The desirability of these three things—perfect explicitness of statement, harmonization of parts, uniformity of practice—the report rehearses in slightly varied phraseology over and over and over again. Look at all the ways it finds to say, in its thousand words on syllabuses, that it really does like things to be spelled out (it certainly couldn't be accused of saying one thing and doing another):

> clear indications ... satisfactory specification ... clearer statements ... specify requirements ... specific indication ... fuller account ... make clear ... say little ... guidance adequate ... less clarity ... clearly and fully ... helpful guidance ... little guidance ... how far specify ... no indication ... some guidance ... closely specifying ... clearly presented ... more clearly presented ... additional guidance ... lack clarity

But that quality assurance finds the production line to be running smoothly says nothing about the standard of the examining, the 'goods produced'. The senior examiners who selected the texts, set the paper and supervised the marking of the paper I marked didn't know good books from bad or sense from nonsense. Their examination blurred the difference between good and bad candidates. But that's nothing, to quality assurance. What matters is this:

> Some schemes were exemplary. They reflected the assessment objectives set in the syllabus very well indeed. The marks awarded corresponded with the demands of questions. Where questions required discursive answers, the marking schemes

often included criteria relating characteristics of expected answers to mark bands and, occasionally, to grades. Outstanding examples of marking schemes were those provided for English in two of the Boards [p. 20, para. 30].

Terrific: marking schemes reflect assessment objectives, marks correspond with demands, answers are related to grades by criteria—it all fits together—but *so what* if the 'objectives', the 'demands', the 'criteria' are all wrong, because the examiners are philistines? Where's the merit in their being consistently so?

Quality assurance has nothing to say about quality. Standards can't be audited. That Ofsted thinks that it has done so shows itself a collapse of standards, not among those who do badly at school, but amongst those who do so well that they go on to inspect those who examine and teach those who do best of all. The real crisis in British education is not at the bottom, amongst an underclass, but at the top, amongst those in charge. As we saw, Ofsted isn't alone in thinking that the quality of academic institutions—of thought—can be audited.

Carlyle was right: before these people can do anything they must become different people. And Nietzsche, a bit later, was right too: we need educators who are themselves educated.

There is one thing that puzzles me though: the thought that there is—there *must* be—a discrepancy between Ofsted, the organization whose logo appears on the covers of the report, and the inspectors who work for it. The latter can't be—they absolutely cannot be—as individual men and women, what they seem to be from this report, brainless philistines. They must surely be, many of them, civilized men and women. If you write to them or speak to them on the telephone, that's what they are likely to seem: nice, reasonable, thinking people. And then you look at this report they produce, and the poverty of the interests they bring to it. The contrast is bizarre. *There's* a mismatch between components for them to audit: that between themselves as living men and women and as servants of Ofsted.

What could any Minister do in the circumstances? Via the system of levers and pulleys that constitutes his mere brute power, nothing at all. As an influence perhaps a good deal, but then only with the co-operation and assent of the educated generally. The trouble is, in this country today, that many supposedly educated people aren't, and that they occupy positions for which education is necessary. The 'educated' need educating first. And what could the Minister do about that? even if he were Matthew Arnold himself?

THE NEW, MODERN A-LEVEL

English A-levels used to be very various, like university degrees. We have instanced a bad one. There were other bad ones. Examiner to Team Leader: 'You don't really believe these answers are worth the marks you are telling me to put on them, do you?' Team Leader: 'These people pay me.'

Some A-levels were very much better, quite recently; A-level did not go wobbly at a uniform pace. The Northern Ireland Board's A-levels were worth as much as some mainland degrees at a time when others, like the one we have instanced, were practically worthless. There was and is shopping around by schools to find the boards most likely to award most As and improve ALIS ratings.[3] On the other hand there are still schools that look for the genuine article, and at least for some years and in some subjects they could find it with the Oxford and Cambridge Board, in which I was an examiner in English for three years.

The Oxford and Cambridge syllabus was a good introduction to English literature (some Chaucer, at least two Shakespeare plays, poetry including Milton and Wordsworth, a classical nineteenth-century novel ...) and included a compulsory practical criticism paper.[4] At my first standardization meeting the Chief Examiner refused to give hard and fast grade outlines and emphasized that we were exercising judgement. (He was later forced to resign because our standards were said to be slack.) We formed groups of half a dozen to mark sample papers, discussing them with each other and then with the three team leaders, who once or twice modified their opinions. The spirit was of discussion, not correction. For this board I *often* marked work much better than I was accustomed to see in finals papers at Swansea, by students who were capable of writing convincingly about genuine works of literature. So there was about a decade, roughly the 1990s, when the general collapse of the universities became unmistakeable but, at least here and there, A-levels flourished.

Other cracks appeared, however, even before the millennial reorganization. Boards had to change their methods of examining quite radically in response to the demands for increasing openness and transparency. By *diktat* since 1999 students have had the right to see their marked scripts. And why not? Human judgement is a process not an event; and why should not the examined see the process and form a judgement about its justice? There is much to be said for this view. Generally speaking, though, unless there is confidence in the examiners, no procedure will save the examinations. And as human beings it is much less likely that examiners will express their true opinions on scripts if the examined are likely to see them. Some examiners were not even sure that they would be immune from legal challenge, for example libel actions. The road to other endless litigation (sexual and racial discrimination would certainly be alleged) was open.

So: from 1999 onwards candidates are permitted to see their marked scripts, but with the little drawback that henceforward there will be no comments on them. One Board's general instruction to examiners in June 1999 began, 'NO SCRIPT MAY BE ANNOTATED IN ANY WAY, with tick, cross, comment, explanation or opinion, either in pencil or in ink.' Spelling mistakes must not be corrected. Unofficially, examiners were advised to make notes for their own guidance on yellow stick-on-removable slips, or to keep notes on private sheets, but not to allow anyone else to see either. I can well imagine the resultant organizational nightmare.

By another rule every page has to have some evidence of having been read by an examiner. To get round this apparent contradiction examiners were instructed to initial every page they had read, but not in such a way that the initials could make a comment. (That any examiner should put his or her initials on an unread page is of course unthinkable.)

But though marginal and interlinear comments are strictly forbidden, customers must be satisfied and the openness of the process respected: so examiners *must* write a comment at the end of every A-level answer, even if they don't want to. This too is subject to a drawback. The comment is not permitted to be their own. They are not allowed to use their own words. A phrase has to be chosen from the 'Mark Band descriptors' (why descriptors not descriptions?) put out by boards to define what different marks mean. These are necessarily vacuous. The sense of grades is inherent in relation to the subject and the questions asked. No mark descriptor can mean more than 'Jolly good!' 'Bloody awful!' or the like. They can be actively misleading if they try to define abstractly qualities that must be present in a given grade; which is impossible in English, where there is no general form of intelligent criticism. As *The Universities We Need* puts it,

> Where checklists such as grade descriptors are drawn up, they draw from this well of experience of judgement in practice, and in their application they rely on an appropriateness of interpretation that that experience makes possible. Explicit formulation, however, can mislead us into thinking that they themselves are the authoritative source and final safeguard of standards.[5]

So the new rule that only band-descriptor phrases can be used means that no genuine individual comment will ever get back to the examinee. It also means that the comments will be virtually useless to second examiners, merely an expansion of the mark given.

Why do examiners like to write in the margins anyway? Sometimes just to let off steam. 'Rubbish!' or, less frequently, 'Yes!' But also as a record of the steps towards making a judgement—even at the elementary level of the correction of grammar and spellings, which is second nature to all teachers and cumulatively helps to form judgement. Glancing back at one's notes may concentrate the mind about a mark.

More important, examining is collaborative. I annoyed an external examiner by ignoring his instruction not to annotate scripts. His idea was that remarks by a first examiner would prejudice the 'moderator' and the external examiner, who would be second- or third-reading scripts. It would be fairer to the examined for every examiner to come to the script completely fresh and uninfluenced. I thought he had misunderstood the collaborative nature of judgement. It would be strictly on a par to say that trial by jury would be fairer if the jurymen were not allowed to hear anyone else's opinion before expressing their own. Discussion is permitted before the issue of a class list (though that too is on the way to being replaced either by computers or the disuse of classes), so why restrict it to formal meetings? It can be very helpful to see why a colleague has come to a particular judgement, particularly if the second examiner can modify the train of thought and hence the judgement. I always used to read my colleagues' remarks to see whether I could disagree—and was surprisingly often cheered up to find that I couldn't; it is encouraging that there can be standards in subjects where no opinion can be proved right or wrong.

Our new openness means that examiners are not allowed to record their judgements moment by moment, answer by answer, or on a script as a whole. And if reasonable frankness is impossible to examiners, they are certainly inhibited.

*   *   *

From now onwards good A-levels will not just be here and there; they will be impossible. I don't know whether the new system has been dubbed 'modern' or 'The People's A-level', but it is certainly what others call dumbed down, though it is still possible to imagine further steps along the same road, and it may get worse.

The old two-year A-level in three subjects examined in three-hour exams at the end of the second year is replaced by 'new modular specifications'. ('Specification' is a technical term insisted on in official literature to replace 'syllabus': guess why, and where it came from.) Students will normally take four subjects in the first year, acquire an AS (Advanced Subsidiary) level in one and continue the rest in the second year for the award of full A-level. So each full A-level 'specifies' six units arranged in two groups of three. The first three are 'free standing', completed in the first year, and can lead to the award of an AS grade. Full A-level is attained by adding the other three in the second year.

In theory it will still be possible for a whole course to be examined at the end of the second year. In practice all the schools we have heard of are embracing modularity. It is open to all the objections we made vis-à-vis degree schemes, but more so. A-level is a big step up from the fifth form. The student, though still often too much taught, has to progress in individual thinking and organize work accordingly. Progress really is often made. Then at the end of two years the mind is concentrated as the work of the whole course is drawn together for the exams. Revision can be formidable, but is worthwhile: literal revision, seeing again, and probably differently. At the end of the course the student should be much better at the subject than at the end of the first year; the whole is a fore-taste of what should happen during the reading for a degree. In the new scheme

147

the possibility of progress is recognized; the modules comprising the AS-level year are to be marked at a lower standard than those for the second.

The basic objection to modularity is that it reduces a whole to disconnected parts. To answer this objection, all new A-level specifications, unlike modular degrees, have to have a 'synoptic element'. 'This unit demands a synthesis of the knowledge and skills acquired during the course as a whole...,' says one board.[6] They sensibly make this unit practical criticism. But in the old A-level the whole examination demonstrated what is now a special requirement. The 'synoptic assessment' becomes itself another bit. Whether in general one of six bits can be made to unite the others remains to be seen, but I doubt it.

Simultaneously, the percentage of coursework marks will be increased to '30% in most subjects'.

'Key skills' becomes a compulsory component in all A-levels in all subjects. I can offer no direct report because the A-level candidates I know cut all the key skills lessons without being caught. According to the document cited, the skills looked for, bearing out my guess reported above, will be 'application of numbers', 'communication' and 'information technology'. Number has no natural application in the central Arts subjects. 'Communication' is necessary in all subjects, but is not a skill. The fallacy is the one we discussed above, the supposition that if you can communicate in Maths you can also communicate in Latin or to the postman.

The demands made on students are to be much reduced. The OCR English tells us that 'The Advanced Subsidiary GCSE specification covers, within a programme of wider reading, a minimum of four texts ....'[7] The four texts to be read include one Shakespeare play 'and at least one other pre-1900 text', which may be Mary Shelley's *Frankenstein*. The full A-level gives the opportunity, though not the requirement, to read another Shakespeare play. Though other selections from the specification can be made, a typical requirement for A-level reading over the two years would be *A* [*sic*] *Winter's Tale*, *Frankenstein*, Ivor Gurney's Selected Poems, Coleridge's Selected Poems, Ian McEwan, *The Child in Time* and L. P. Hartley, *The Go-Between*. By the board's own previous standards this is very lightweight.

The 'OCA Subject Criteria for English Literature (1999)' require that candidates meet assessment objectives including

A04 articulate independent opinions and judgements, informed by different inter-pretations of literary texts by other readers.

This in itself looks harmless; it would be satisfied by good class discussion, and the 'independent opinions and judgements' are certainly necessary. The 'other readers' requires, not superfluously, that any discussion should be based on knowledge. This applies to the discussion of published criticism as well as discussion in class. There is, though, one flaw. Unless 'interpretation' is understood as in musical performance, where the existence of the interpreted work is assumed, and 'interpretation' can be discussed like critical opinion, it is necessary to say that we read, not interpret. Interpretation is bounded by the work interpreted. 'The Lady of Shalott', for instance, is not (see Chapter 8) about Victorian industrialism. Into that possible crack, with unerring aim, is in fact being introduced the blunt instrument of compulsory 'theory'. For instance the English Association (of all people) ran a day conference on 11 March 2000 in which the assembled teachers were assured that for the future all examining boards will insist on knowledge and practice of deconstruction, defined as 'not a dismantling of the structure of a text, *but a demonstration that it has already dismantled itself.* Its apparently solid ground is no rock but thin air.' (Naturally this is just at the moment when deconstruction is fading away in the theoretical centres.)

If you happen to believe that a poem is indestructible, you are ruled out on theoretical grounds. Thin air is insisted upon. Why this is called 'theory' will be a question raised by anyone familiar with genuine theory in the arts, musical theory for instance, and it is discussed elsewhere.[8] The present point is that if the theorists have their way, and concentrate the seventeen-year-old minds on the indeterminacy of the sign, the trace, the always and only self-referentiality of language and so on, instead of encouraging them to read attentively some books worth reading, even the most serious of the young people will get bored, quite quickly. Their attention is unlikely to be revived by the other 'theoretical' demands, 'Literature and Gender'[9] and 'Literature and Psychoanalysis'.[10] The problems of English will rapidly solve themselves in the fading away of the subject.

In the new AS-level History at least one board does not require any essay writing. Imagine History tested by multiple-choice questions, bullet points or spider charts! Well, by the time you read this it will not be imaginary. It remains true that the arts subjects have no effective alternative, for the organization of thinking, to English prose. The intelligent sigh can certainly demonstrate judgement but is not examinable. Ticks from multiple-choices can no more display thought than answers on *University Challenge.* They can't even display any meaningful kind of knowledge.

The school whose report I have been using, an independent school, showed no signs of independence and was intent only on assuring parents that it was fully prepared to co-operate. There was a page about the advantages of the new system, things like 'expands horizons' (vague enough to be safe) and 'postpones decision' (a good thing?).

The latter was in support of the great claim that the new A-level will be less specialized. Why three subjects counts as undue specialization at age sixteen I don't know. In fact the student will now ordinarily pursue four (easier) subjects in the first year sixth instead of only sometimes pursuing four subjects throughout.

The pressure will be on them to mix subjects and include 'useful' ones like Business Studies.

Taken together, these changes can only mean that the sixth form will be even less of a preparation for university than at present.

So why this major change to what was so recently on all sides 'the jewel in the crown'? The A-levels of the last 40 years have been, the Minister told us, 'wrong', too narrow, too specialist, too élitist, and 'designed for a world which no longer exists'—the world, it may be, in which education had some place.[11] The old A-levels were, moreover, British. 'Blackstone ... is an enthusiast for broad-ranging European qualifications ... .'[12] Some schools, accordingly, have brought in the continental-style Baccalaureate. Have we really got to such a pass that we can no longer organize our own examinations? After all, we have been having public exams for quite a while, and only in the last decade or so has there been a real collapse. Some examiners still survive. Ampleforth has already taken the more promising route of setting its own A-level in English.

Meanwhile, any surviving university has a problem about judging the qualifications of applicants. All universities are equal but somehow there are so many applications to Oxford and Cambridge that they are effectively lottery tickets. Some colleges are unwise enough to rely on interviews; these are inherently unreliable, even setting aside the scare stories of Oxford dons who put their predilections (usually feminism or Marxism) before the search for promising intelligence. Many colleges give themselves quotas of state-educated applicants, ethnic minorities and so on, so it can help to have been to a good state school. But with the collapse of A-level, colleges have no reliable unbiased evidence on which to decide who are the strongest candidates. Some schools' references are optimistic; other schools underestimate their candidates, and yet others hardly know them. Until A-level is restored nationally, genuine universities are going to have to bring back their own entrance exams. Why ever did Oxford and Cambridge discard theirs?

8 An Examining Board in the New University

If there is no common sense: what is there?

Brian Lee[1]

I GOT A SHOCK marking a set of exam scripts; I thought them bad in a quite remarkable way. The subject was supposed to be Victorian Poetry. Here are a few passages from essays most of which ended up with 2–1 marks, and which I marked at third or lower. The quotations are *verbatim* and I observe in passing that the students' standards of ordinary literacy have certainly improved recently.

> Christina Rossetti uses an even more subtle approach in her poems, often cleverly hiding the subject of women in her poems to subvert male patriarchy cleverly from inside this culture. Her poem, By the Sea, hides women literally and symbolically; literally, because the Stanzas two and three begin respectively with the words 'Sheer' and 'Shells' both of which contain the word 'she'. Symbolically, the poem emphasizes women in many ways, and it is soon clear that it is women, not the sea, which is the subject of Rossetti's poem. Of the sea, she says 'It frets against the boundary shore' suggesting woman's attempted resistance of male dominance.

> The position of women in the patriarchal society of Victorian England was one of absolute dependence. Women were marginalised into the home, had no vote, no political or earning power. This repression and domination was so absolute that it was largely accepted by women. However, some tried to rebel, and Christina Rossetti's method was through poetry.

> Rossetti writes about the oppression of women using poetry, which was marginalised and linked to the feminine.

> The subjects [Mariana and the Lady of Shalott] are further isolated by the fact that they are women, who were repressed by Victorian patriarchy ....

> In Mariana, Tennyson also seems to point to the uprisings which were occurring in Victorian society at the time his poems were written, for example Chartism. Outside Mariana's 'grange', he tells us 'Hard by a poplar shook alway'; and we can

151

see that 'poplar' can be read as a subtle pointing to the word 'popular', and the people fighting for their 'popular' cause constantly 'shook' in their anger and attempts to change the society in which they lived.

Both the Lady and the reapers are set outside the commercial capital city of Camelot, and … indeed both maybe the victims of the industrial society—forced into labour by the exploitation of the Capitalist Society and thereby representing an alienated form of labour. [You can't win: 'marginalized' at home or exploited in industrial Camelot.]

Lancelot is very much a part of the industrial society, with 'coal black curls' and 'armour'.

Technology is shown as an intrusive force in the lady's life, in the form of Lancelot; she brings the curse upon herself by looking down on his shining armour and 'coal-black hair'; Lancelot appears as a machine.

The 'Lady' moves from her 'web' and 'loom' (perhaps suggesting the weavers moving to factories in towns—urbanisation) to 'gray', industrialised Camelot.

Orthodox religious faith during the Victorian era was thrown into chaos and confusion owing to scientific discoveries and higher criticism.

O 'Jesus quicken me,' a call for annihilation it seems because to quicken nature is to whither and die. … [She] turned into a Royal cup in an incredible inversion of traditional images in which she becomes the saviour of Christ.

The poem [Clough, 'That there are Powers'] therefore seems unsure as to the true nature of God; yet it uses as the basis of its text, the narratives of the monotheistic Christian God. This implies that faith is actually stronger than doubt, for in doubting God Clough uses the language of God himself in the form of the biblical narratives.

Whilst Arnold and Clough maybe considered to be agnostic poets, deconstructing the poems seems to reveal the potential for a greater faith to emerge from the trials of darkness of 'the darkling plane'. Whilst such readings may distort the poet's original intention, there is evidence that faith may be restated, perhaps not in its original form, but as a stronger faith, purged of previous doubts.

Clough's poem, too, inevitably speaks with the language of faith; the narratives of Christ walking on the water, his calming of the sea of Galilee and a half-reference to Noah's Ark, the 'evanescent spectrum', are powerful examples of the strength of faith and what it can perform.

Arthur Hugh Clough was also affected by industrialisation and subsequent doubt, but was eventually able to proclaim, 'That there are powers above us I admit.'

Peter took his eyes from Jesus and began to sink. Thus, it is implicit within the poem that one's faith will always let one down. … Doubt poems do assert faith but faith poems also assert doubt.

At the meeting for vetting questions, months before, I had asked to see any exam paper I would be marking, but it had not then been decided who was to mark what, and I did not see the Victorian Poetry paper. Given the chance, I would have objected to it as a whole and in its parts, and would have declined to mark the answers unless the questions were drastically altered, because (a) they were not about Victorian poetry and (b) most were grossly biased in that they invited answers only from one point of view, presumably (cf. Chapter 6) that of 'the course'. The tutor, it transpired, did think that the questions could only be answered by students who had followed the course, not students of Victorian poetry.

Not a single question addressed the matters which indisputably do belong to the study of literature—style, feeling, movement, what poetry makes of the thought and spirit of an age; and not one question allowed for the possibility that any one poem might be more interesting than any other. The questions on individual poets were without exception directed away from poetry, generally towards the class war, the industrial revolution, the subordinate position of Victorian women. 'How far and in what ways is Browning's poetry concerned with both sexual and class politics?' An ingenious student might turn that into a question about poetry, but it is much more natural to take it as a question about sexual and class politics. 'How can the voices and concerns of Chartist poetry be located in middle-class Victorian verse?' is plainly about certain opinions that may be represented in 'middle class' verse (whatever that is), not about verse.

As to bias: 'What specific strategies do Victorian women poets employ to challenge and subvert the man-made world of patriarchy?' This simply assumes that Victorian women poets did employ specific strategies etc, also that the Victorian world is properly called man-made and properly described as patri-archal. Those positions can be argued: the objection is that the question assumes them to be beyond challenge, and that no other opinion, such as that Christina Rossetti made no effort to subvert anything, is permissible. This paper, not approved by me, was quite improperly approved by an external examiner.[2]

Howbeit, I was faced simultaneously with the question-paper and the answers. So: why did I put low marks on them?

About the poems mentioned, most of the scripts—no doubt following the approved line of the seminars—made the same comments, often in the same words, and using the same quotations. My first objection was that there was hardly any independence or individuality of thought (cf. above about 'con-veyance of material' to and from students).

The scripts showed, secondly, very small acquaintance with Victorian poetry. Most Tennyson answers mentioned only 'The Lady of Shalott' and 'Mariana'; in the Christina Rossetti answers (Dante Gabriel was unmentioned) there was one lonely reference to *Goblin Market*; the answers were almost exclusively on the same three minor lyrics.

Thirdly, in obedience to the questions, the scripts were not about Victorian poetry at all. They were, if anything, a kind of history—the kind sometimes called the New Historicism—trying to use poetry to comment on Victorian power relations, though it was not history that a historian could have recognized. All these comments were risible, for instance the ones quoted about the absolute oppression of Victorian women. Tell that to the Queen, or to Mrs Oliphant, or to my grandma.

Finally, the link by which this pseudo-history was joined to Victorian poetry was consistently made by 'interpretations' that are nonsense: of a very odd kind, but certainly nonsense. Faced with the question how a text that seems to have nothing to do with Christianity is really about Christ and the Church, the medieval exegetes came up with their fourfold method of interpretation. This was made necessary by the demand that the text bear a Christian meaning. The course tutor now demands that these poems should say the correct things about the role of women, the industrial revolution and so on. The snag is that in literary criticism one is entitled to ask whether they really do. For the reader without the benefit of the course, there is no reference to industry in 'The Lady of Shalott' and Camelot bears no resemblance to Sheffield. In these scripts the problem of finding the industrial/feminist significance was again and again solved by impossible allegorical interpretations of the Lady as the oppressed weaver making her way to the grey industrialized centre of Camelot, with Lancelot as technology. Offered as a reading of the poem this is simply impossible, and as there is no external information that Tennyson is coding messages about the industrial revolution the allegorical reading is mindless, though fanciful in a way that ordinary stupidity could not be. Similarly hopeless attempts were repeatedly made to read the poplar which shook outside Mariana's window as the populace, shaking with democratic rage. It isn't, it's an ordinary poplar, never still.

These answers were based on simple misreadings, but of a fantastic kind. They are made possible by the Eagletonian contradiction[3] whereby (1) signifiers are related only to each other, i.e. words have no determinate meanings but (2) everything is really about modes of production and exchange.

Another supporting interpretative method was to pick words out from other words, more or less like the children's game of the word-square. If Christina Rossetti uses the words 'shell' and 'sheer' they are to be taken as codes for 'she' because both include 'she'. A poem about the sea chafing against the shore is therefore *really* about the Victorian female chafing against male domination. If 'It is women, not the sea, which is the subject of Rossetti's poem' what would Ms Rossetti have done had she wanted to write a poem about the sea chafing against the shore? It is just a linguistic impossibility for 'shell' to express 'she'. One might as well notice that 'shell' includes 'Hell' or that 'she' and 'her' both always include 'he'; any use, therefore, of the feminine pronouns would also always suggest the masculine. *Quod est absurdum.* The method has academic precedents, but as Johnson remarked, no precedent justifies absurdity. One critic quotes another's remark that 'the central names [of *Wuthering Heights*] are clearly (but not obviously) anagrammic.'[4] 'CATHERINE and HARETON contain HEART and EARTH' and (what can hardly be disputed) 'HEATHCLIFF... compounds HEATH and CLIFF'; so that, the critic concludes,

> the text's cryptic incorporations and inclusions compulsively enclose or contain one identity within another in an unsettling play of textual phantoms, with the result that the novel unfolds nothing less than a poetics of haunting.[5]

Wow! And all this from the names, anagrams 'in the rather loose sense', before anybody gets haunted at all, and with so much left unsaid! 'HARETON' and 'CATHERINE' both also contain 'HEAR', 'THAN', 'RAT', 'RATE', 'NEAR' and 'RATHE', so perhaps both characters are to be rated early rats ('HARETON' has the long medieval form 'RATON'). Hareton includes 'NOTE' as well as 'TONE', but Catherine's alternative is 'NOCE', hinting with 'THINE' and 'NEAR' at their long-delayed nuptials. 'THAR' (Middle English 'need') it be stated that this is a game with no rules, i.e., a bit crazy? I would have given Dr Vine a gamma, too.

That every statement includes its contradiction is untenable as a general proposition about language because if it were true it would include its own contradiction. In these scripts it was offered not as something speculative but, of all things, as unchallengeable common sense. Poems of faith are said always to *assert* doubt, and *vice versa*. NB it was not being said that the poetry of doubt has to use the language of faith, which might have led to something interesting, but that when Clough writes that our Lord is in the tomb mouldering low he *asserts* the resurrection, and when Hopkins celebrates the grandeur of God he is expressing doubt. Nonsense.

My discovery was that in the new university nonsense is no disadvantage.

When the Course Tutor saw my marks he said that there had been 'a disagreement at a high theoretical level'. His own marks often came out two classes higher than mine, and he supported them with remarks such as that there were ideas floating about. We agreed that there was no point in trying to reach agreement, and that the scripts should be referred to the external examiner —who did not want to be involved and thought that if the internal examiners had been locked up together for long enough they might have agreed marks, presumably by the exhaustion method so efficacious in the negotiation of international treaties.

I didn't agree about the high theoretical level. What I had objected to was irrationality. If there were ideas floating about it mattered to me that they were nonsensical ideas, as well as that they were all the same and belonged, it seemed, to no individual. There is nothing theoretical about the opinion that nonsense gets low marks. I know the retaliatory moves about 'sense' being ideologically conditioned, male-dominated and the like, but I am not impressed. Nonsense remains nonsense, and if nonsense does not get low marks, all marks are meaningless.

The external examiner generally ruled against my marks. He remarked, quite rightly, on the fragility of the whole system; he said that there was here an 'ideological problem'—there *was*, namely that my colleague was in the grip of an ideology—and that we had been looking for very different things. Yes indeed: I had been looking for literary criticism of Victorian poetry. Different people approach in different ways. Yes; but my first objection was to the mono-maniacal sameness of these scripts. There were arguments both ways, said the external; the scripts I had objected to had indeed been reductive, but they showed sufficient evidence of thought and knowledge. In some cases he had gone down the middle, but on the whole had gone for the more generous mark. 'Generosity' is a word often heard in these discussions; it is of an economical kind that costs the giver nothing except, perhaps, integrity.

There are only two alternatives. Either, 'interpretation' is unlimited—and we have no category of mistake or nonsense, and are unable to make a meaningful class list—or, the convening of an examining board presupposes a general consent to standards of sense. But if there is then no general agreement about what is sense and what nonsense, it is again true that no class list can be made. One or both of these is our present state, and in either case a class list using the disputed marks is unreliable.

Another script was not disputed between myself and the course tutor, but was marked down by the external examiner from the top of class 2–2 to the top of class 3. About this script I think there was general agreement: it was humane, showing a feeling for poetry, nicely written, but not rigorously argued and with a rather poor sense of relevance to questions. The rights and wrongs of this one could indeed have been argued two ways. Some might be inclined to emphasize and give credit for sensitivity and others to penalize irrelevance, though my own view was that anyone trying to write about Victorian poetry had to ignore these questions. What I will never accept is that if scripts full of outright nonsense are respectable, this one was a third. I could not avoid the inference that this candidate was being penalized for not including the required amount of nonsense, though the external examiner did explicitly deny this.

Well, perhaps it was an eccentrically bad run of scripts. Here are a few more examples, from less advanced students (again quoted *verbatim*: their grammar is not so good) examined in the same season. The topic this time is James Joyce's *Dubliners*. They were nonsensical in much the same way. The same phrases were again used time after time, phrases unconnected with reading or, often enough, with any sense at all. The mindless fancifulness was of the same *ethos* as the stuff about Victorian poetry. Here the theme is not industry or downtrodden women or faith-and-doubt but intellectual paralysis:

> The colours yellow and brown are continually used—yellow being the Symbolic colour of paralysis. [The Liberal Democrats paralytic?]

> The man [in 'An Encounter'] also questions them about which books they have read and this can be interpreted as intellectual paralysis. The picture of 'Romeo and Juliet' above the piano in 'The Dead' and 'The Two Murdered Princes in the Tower' are other examples. [Read and be paralysed? So don't risk it?]

> There is plenty to eat and drink at the party but the 'Goose' is rather symbolic being brown and cooked (preventing flight) .... [*We* eat *our* geese on the wing?]

> The snow completes this scene for us being a symbol of paralysis.

> The whole of Dublin is covered in snow, which as frozen water signifies paralysis. [Again. But do not despair: release is at hand.]

> Snow, the final paralysing image, falls 'generally all over Ireland'.... Snow, however, must melt, giving water—life-enhancing and purifying. [For those unfamiliar with Dublin slush. We must open ourselves up to this water of life but:]

> Gabriel also shows paralysis by wearing Galoshes, keeping water (a source of life out) from him.

To be fair, religion was sometimes also mentioned, though, as it seems to me, with an even wilder play of fancy:

> The boy could see no fault with the priest, when he heard that he had died, that night he had a dream of Father Flynn smiling showing his big teeth and a connection with Persia.

> After his death the sisters offer a parody of communion whilst they look into an empty fireplace.

> He has a red handkerchief which he uses to clean his clothes. This is a parody of Christ's sacrificial blood shed for the sins of mankind. It is symbolically not sufficient in this story as the priest has his hand on it.

Can these students be said in any sense to have read and understood either *Dubliners* or their own scripts? These caused no flurry, though: I was marking only one third of the paper, only a pass was required, and heavy scoring elsewhere ensured that all these students passed.

In our arts faculties there is a lot of *dis*education going on. The students come in, sometimes after A-level at a good school, interested, intelligent, ready to learn; they go out as bored but salary-expectant manufacturers of nonsense. Our graduates are *often* worse equipped to read and think about literature than our freshmen. A fairly steady decline is often observable. A-level is worth more than BA, BA is worth much more than MA,[6] MA is worth more than PhD.

Many lecturers are far from unaware of the state of affairs. One of the great developments at Cambridge in the 1920s was the secure establishment, at the heart of 'English', of 'practical criticism'. This is just the demand that a student, faced with a short English text (or preferably two, for comparison) in prose or verse, without any information about date, author or what is not contained in the text itself, should be able to say something reasonably intelligent about it. This is an essential test of the English student because it epitomizes the common judgement the whole degree is supposed to foster. If you can't make *some* initial response to a couple of short poems you have never seen before—making all allowances for the differences made by knowledge, and, more importantly, the better judgement that comes of allowing something to sink in—how are you any sort of judge of language? We were agonizing about the place of practical criticism in the new university, and I will cite at this point a paper issued by one of my younger colleagues.

I mentioned a fundamental impoverishment, both cultural and linguistic, which runs right back through the students' education and which leaves them at a loss when faced with poetry whose vocabulary, syntax and allusive range are all problematic. It seems curious that a university student having read English for a year can write of the Hardy piece 'this poem is boring and has lots of difficult words,' but it seemed only an open avowal of what the majority of candidates evidently thought but had tried to disguise. Not more than two or three demonstrated any responsiveness to poetic language. Most were anxious to write about anything but; either firing off a scatter of technical terms (onomatopoeia, alliteration, personification) in the hope of a few hits, or speculating wildly about the poem's occasion, in the 'how many children had Lady Macbeth' tradition but without any historical, literary or general knowledge to back it.

Many students appeared unused to and totally unprepared for the sort of test practical criticism sets. The increased role of coursework and the shifting of exam question approaches at A-level clearly contribute to this. I think we at least need to consider the point that such exams may be counterproductive and futile given the world our present students actually inhabit. Should we be examining them on things they can't do, or searching for those they can?

If we continue with some such exercise we need to address it in a different way; the lectures and seminars in Part One seem poorly attended in part because the students do not feel pressed to devote much attention to the subject; it allows itself to be regarded as an optional extra rather than as the centre of the year's study. This would involve a reappraisal of Part One tutorials, of course. There may well be a strong case for including some form of practical criticism, close reading or whatever we want to call it, in finals; either through a separate paper or through some variant of gobbet-type questions on many, if not perhaps all, of the current papers, if only to impress on students' minds the value we place on it—if we do.

In my naivety I may have only belatedly realised that one can no longer assume university English students will possess at least a basic command of what the close reading of literature involves. As a department we need, I think, to make a positive decision as to whether close reading is to be the centre and prerequisite of the study of English, and if so, to design and promote our teaching and examining accordingly. If not, I think we need equally to clarify what we *are* doing and what we are expecting our students to do in order to merit a degree.

The Department's response was to do away with Practical Criticism altogether, to replace it by a course on Literary Theory. There is no point, the feeling was, in trying to deal with close reading or judgement, which cannot any longer be attempted. We should concentrate on things that we (and they) *can* manage, like theory based on 'readings' of Mary Shelley's *Frankenstein*. The question what it is that we expect our English students to be able to do at the end of their courses remains unsolved, though I do not believe it is a difficult one.

The answer can only be generally the one we derived from Newman and Jane Austen: to feel one's way into something real which may go towards setting a standard of reality, and to begin to remake and judge the literature—and everything else. This, however, does assume that, as Leavis thought, English literature is 'there' as more than an academic invention, and it does mean that the subject has to be centred in attentiveness to real works of literature. If the students can't read attentively and if we can't help them, the academics are right to suppose that there is no subject of English Language and Literature: but then there isn't anything else in their departments either, except, of course, salaries.

There is no need for things to be so bad, even given the current state of the world. Simultaneously with the Victorian Poetry I was reading a set of first-year scripts about Middle English which impressed me by their knowledge (I picked up a few things) and sensitivity. They were not all saying or noticing the same thing. Also simultaneously I marked a few scripts by Spaniards to whom I had been teaching elementary Old English. The Spanish have to be told forcefully that they are allowed to utter their own opinions. More than one took to this like a duckling emerging from the nest, and after a few uncertain steps launched out on the waters of genuine literary criticism—*not* by any means always agreeing with me.

The External Examiner put the incident of the disagreement about Victorian Poetry thus in his official report (which I was not shown; I had to 'obtain' a copy, as the newspapers say of leaks):

> I was asked to adjudicate in the case of one paper where first and second markers were often three classes apart. This was in fact an ideological battle: basically the first marker disagreed violently with the thrust of the course, as reflected in several of the scripts.

So the course, not Victorian Poetry, was to be examined, and a university must 'teach' by 'courses' in which the student has to adopt the 'teacher's' 'ideology'? This is not only untrue, it is hostile to the pursuit of truth that constitutes the university. It does explain, however, why the external examiner had no qualms about judging my marks—which, I remind you, were penalizing nonsense, not any particular political opinions—unduly harsh, and thereby, on his own account, affirming one ideological position. He added that 'the whole exam system would break down if the externals' marks were regularly challenged in this way.' It already had, because there was no longer any common judgement. The unusual thing was the challenge. When common judgement goes, one sign will inevitably be that the loss is shared by the external examiners who are supposed to guarantee it.

When the external examiner ruled against me I should have demanded that no degree list be issued before an investigation by the Dean of the Arts Faculty or whatever competent body. To my shame I did not do so—because it immediately occurred to me that I would have to put my argument to the reading public, in the hope that there is still some common judgement in the world, if not in our arts faculties. So I refused to sign the class list, but did nothing more drastic to inhibit the proceedings. It is too late to prevent the graduation of these students, though I have no confidence at all in the worth of their degrees. I make my appeal instead—to common sense.

V

CONCLUSION

9 The Tree of Knowledge or a Shopping Mall?

This purifying of wit, this enritching of memory, enabling of iudgment, and enlarging of conceyt, which commonly we call learning...

Sir Philip Sidney[1]

The man we are proud to send forth from our Schools will be remarkable less for something he can take out of his wallet and exhibit for knowledge, than for *being* something, and that 'something' a man of unmistakable intellectual breeding, whose trained judgment we can trust to choose the better and reject the worse.

Sir Arthur Quiller-Couch[2]

The end of learning is to repair the ruins of our first parents by regaining to know God aright.

Milton[3]

KNOWLEDGE IS ONE, argued Newman, beautifully:

> All that exists, as contemplated by the human mind, forms one large system or complex fact, and this of course resolves itself into an indefinite number of particular facts, which, as being portions of a whole, have countless relations of every kind, one towards another. Knowledge is the apprehension of these facts, whether in themselves, or in their mutual positions and bearings. And, as all taken together form one integral object, so there are no natural or real limits between part and part; one is ever running into another; all, as viewed by the mind, are combined together, and form a correlative character one with another... .[4]

This, we think, needs an addition about the kind of value knowledge has; but when Newman sketches the alternative he is flawless. If the university is not the garden of the tree of knowledge, what is it? Newman's nightmare 'university' in which specialisms have no common ground is more alarming than it could have been in his own day, for we need only look around us to see his prophecy horribly fulfilled. The university becomes a sort of bazaar, or pantechnicon, in which wares of all kinds are heaped together for sale in stalls independent of each other ... to save the purchasers the trouble of running about from shop to shop; or an hotel or lodging house, where all professions and classes are at liberty to congregate, varying, however, according to the season, each of them strange to each, and about its own work or pleasure; whereas, if we would rightly deem of it, a University is the home, it is the mansion-house, of the goodly family of the Sciences, sisters all, and sisterly in their mutual dispositions.[5]

The difficulty for us in recognizing Jane Austen's authority on education is not that we have any doubts. We have no lurking fear that Elizabeth and Darcy's mutual education might turn out to be another rabbit-out-of-the-hat like Newman's. No, the difficulty is the move from *Pride and Prejudice* to the academy.

After all, even at best, how much of what goes on there remotely resembles the mutually correcting judgement and developing understanding of Mr Darcy and Elizabeth Bennet? And it's not just that few universities' members will resemble them in personal qualities, that most, inevitably, will resemble more closely Elizabeth's sisters or Mr Wickham; it is not just that Darcy and Elizabeth show us an ideal that not many people will be able to live up to. It is, even more, that, for perhaps the great majority of university members, the relations between Elizabeth and Darcy will only with difficulty be recognized as an ideal of university life at all.

What bearing, it might be objected, could it have on any possibility open to the student of Dentistry or Astro-physics or Marketing-with-Early-Childhood-Studies? These are subjects which test their students' technical grasp, not their personal qualities, and, in doing so, are typical of university studies. For, in the modern university the general forms of intelligence have been buried under a lumber of specialization. They are still there, but for the most part invisible, their presence a matter of inference.

Of course, distinctions between subjects aren't the invention of the modern university, and, from their antiquity and the barrenness of experiments in 'inter-disciplinarity', we might reasonably suppose them to be necessary; but the form they now take, outside the sciences, *is* an invention of the university and is regarded there—when it isn't simply taken for granted—as a proof of progress.

The modern university is a place bewitched by science, or by a sort of folk idea of science—by its practices and language, of course, but also by its organization or structure. The extreme specialization that now characterizes the organization of knowledge in the university, the proliferation of subjects and of fields within subjects and the accompanying insistence that only someone expert in a given field can speak authoritatively on its subject matter, and then only in terms of trade, does seem to resemble, or to imitate, that of science, the non-sciences modelling themselves on the sciences in the (sad) hope of reproducing their success.

One of the things science owes its success to—its practical, working success—is undoubtedly its own version of the division of labour. As science has developed, over four centuries, so its 'fields' have been constantly dividing and sub-dividing, proliferating into ever smaller sub-divisions of sub-divisions, each with the capacity to develop into a full-grown 'parent' field itself. So, notoriously, scientists in one field, even within the same 'subject', will have no more authoritative understanding of the work being done in fields distant from their own than will laymen. A working scientist need know no more of the work going on in fields other than his own than he needs in order to do his own. And yet, marvellously, this process of division and multiplication has gone ahead not only with great accuracy of distinction between the parts but without the whole falling into unintelligibility and becoming a mere chaos of bits that have no bearing on one another. It has managed to remain—despite whatever local and temporary inconsistencies may have from time to time arisen—a self-consistent whole. And it has done so because, unlikely as it might seem, common standards of what counts as good scientific work have contrived to apply right across a whole body of activities and practices of which no one person can possibly know more than a tiny fraction. Its growth has been like that of some wonderfully successful organism, continually extending itself, adapting to and colonizing new parts of its environment—a version of Newman's tree of knowledge, continuously budding and branching.

But the—it might seem, amazing—feat of creating, across centuries, a self-consistent whole from infinitely and unpredictably proliferating parts has only been accomplished because the scientific community polices itself strictly and unforgivingly. No one scientist may be able to survey all fields of science but each can survey more than just his own; all fields either overlap with other fields or are overlooked by them. There is no police force to oversee the whole and enforce common standards, but no police force is needed; for neighbours oversee neighbours and do the enforcing themselves. The continuous budding of part from part has had to be accompanied by something else, an equally continuous rejecting of parts which don't develop 'true' to the organism as a whole. To be as successful as it has been, science has had to be as intolerant of foreign bodies as it has been welcoming of new growth. If it hadn't, it would have become corrupt; ceased to be a whole; ceased to be intelligible; ceased to develop; it would have merely proliferated at random, and turned from a tree into a bunch of haphazardly fallen tent poles and blocks of dressed wood.

Which is precisely what has happened, as Newman foresaw, to the university as a whole which science is part of. The universities at large have been every bit as welcoming of new growth (that is, money) as science has, but have shown no accompanying intolerance of foreign bodies whatsoever. At any one moment the list of university 'disciplines' may be finite but it increases every year upon a principle that admits of no limit. It includes not just all the traditional Arts and Sciences—and not quite so traditional Social Sciences—and all their sub- and sub-sub-disciplines evolving into disciplines of their own—but all those vocational, quasi-vocational and pseudo-vocational courses which *all* universities, not excepting Oxford and Cambridge, now run, courses like the following:

> Arts Management; Asset Management; Beauty Science; Beauty Therapy and Sciences; Broadcasting Studies; Business Decision Analysis; Business (or Catering) Management and Sports and Exercise Sciences; Business Mathematics; Business Studies; Coaching Science; Consumer Studies; Cosmetic Sciences; Costume and Make-up; Counselling; Early Childhood Studies with Sports Science (or Marketing or Tourism with Early Childhood Studies); Embroidery; Enterprise, Entrepreneurship, Innovation; European Food Studies; Facilities Management; Fashion and Fashion Design, the Promotion of; Fine Arts Valuation; Floristry; Footwear Design; Garden Design; Global Futures; Golf Course Management; Golf Green Keeping; Golf Studies; Health and Fitness; Health Promotion; Hospitality Management; International Tourism Management; Investment; Knitware Studies; Leather Technology; Leisure Management; Lighting Design; Model Making; Packaging; Perfumery Business; Personnel; Pig Enterprise Management; Popular Music Studies; Real Estate Valuation; Sports and Exercise Sciences and Leisure Management; Sport, Recreation and Tourism; Travel and Tourism; Turf Science; Wine Studies; Women's Studies; World Studies ...

Businesses are so various and—as technologies and fashions come and go—so ephemeral that there is, literally, no limit to the number or the character of the courses that at different times might (supposedly) serve them. And each of these separated courses goes its own way without reference to any other or the standards of any other. Are the examination papers in Tourism and Leisure Management simply *rubbish* by the standards of those set in Moral Philosophy (see pp. 83–4)? Firstly, it doesn't matter if they are. The Moral Philosophers have no say in Tourism and Leisure Management. Secondly, by definition they can't be. Only those expert in Tourism and Leisure Management can say what its standards are. Or: once you're in you're in, and that's an end of it. And to get in? The funding has to be in place, that's all. The modern university can't recognize foreign bodies because it has no idea what its own tissue is. What might be part of it? Quite simply, anything. What is it then? Big.

It has imitated science in one respect—in welcoming new specialisms and all the new money and jobs and opportunities for empire-building they bring, but not in another—in vetting them for fitness to belong, for that would mean turning away new money and jobs and opportunities for empire-building. Science is good but butter is better.

We do not say that, until about 1963, the university in this country was just what it should be or that in 2000 none of it is what it should be. If the university system had been anything but very imperfect in 1963, how did it come to be the fraud it is now? For the changes it has undergone in the last 30 years weren't forced on it. We might say that it co-operated in bringing them about—except that even 'collaborate' would be too weak a word. As Hamlet said of Rosencrantz and Guildenstern, 'Why, man, they did make love to this employment.' And, the university system is now—quite apart from anything else—so big and so various that it would be strange if there weren't some good in it somewhere. There are continuities between what it was then and is now, both for good and ill. It would be astonishing if there weren't.

What we do say is: that, as big and as various as it is, the modern university system may be judged as a whole, may be summed up; that the summing up can only be that it is a fraud; that, in order to say so, we don't need to graduate in any more subjects than our own, English Literature.

This last contention will, we know, seem to many people self-evidently absurd. 'How,' they will say, 'can you possibly judge the whole university—composed of very many, very different specialisms—on evidence drawn from one alone? Pyramids stood on their tips fall over.'

This *has* force, but only the rhetorical or debating-point kind. Its force fades as soon as you ask how many (let alone which) subjects it would be necessary to judge before you had judged the university as a whole. One piece of advice we had was that four would be the minimum (mention was made of science as if it were one subject, maths, theology and law). But could the force of this objection, if real, be dissipated so cheaply? *'What?* Only *four*—from hundreds? You need at least *six/twelve/twenty-four*....' However many subjects were dealt with short of all, it might still, from this point of view, be objected that by so much had less than the whole been dealt with. And yet to offer to sum up more than a very few, close disciplines (each with its own proliferation of sub-disciplines) is, for any one man (or even two), self-evidently impossible. They wouldn't be the separate disciplines they claim to be, otherwise. And, on the other hand, the judgements of many men of many subjects cannot be amalgamated to form a single judgement, though the government does in a manner try.

So what does that mean? That the university—as a whole—*can't* be judged? We can't say whether it's any good or not? As if we couldn't know that a cat was dead without examining every last cell. This is Zeno's paradox. If the universe is divisible into parts that don't add up to a whole, the hare can't catch the tortoise, the arrow never moves and no-one knows whether cats or universities are dead or not. And yet, as we all know, arrows do fly, hares pass tortoises and men judge the health of cats not infallibly but pretty reliably all the same. Perhaps universities too.

This follows from Newman's tree of knowledge. The university (like the universe) is a whole not a sum of parts, and it is the kind of whole which—while it continues to *be* the university and not another thing masquerading under that name—may be judged (like a cake or a piece of music or a man or woman) from its parts. If it can't, then *ex hypothesi* it isn't a university at all. It's something for which we need that useful word which George Grant and Mohammed Mujeeb Rahman and others in America and Canada have coined: a 'multiversity' (our local variation must, presumably, be 'polyversity'—which has the additional benefit that it sounds as if it might have something to do with 'perversity'). It's Newman's bazaar of independent stall-holders.

It is only when we assume that the university is, properly, just such a collection of separated and diverging specialisms—i.e. that it isn't a whole—that the objection to our judging the whole from a part will be thought to have any force. The objection depends on the objector's unadmitted assumption that a bazaar of independent stall-holders is not what the university has merely happened to have become, in error and as a corruption, but just what it was always meant to be, 'in ideal perfection'. The real objection isn't to the narrowness of our range of evidence but to our (and Newman's) idea of the university. It is an unexamined expression of disbelief in the idea of liberal education itself.

Our universities are dominated by such a disbelief. University departments don't like being 'assessed'—inevitably it is more or less unpleasant—but they don't dislike the way 'assessment' recognizes their characters as independent stall-holders. The government doesn't pretend to have departments 'judged', according to how well or badly they educate their students; it has them assessed, by objective criteria, according to how well or badly they have met their own objectives. On the one hand, the University of Oxford still aims to educate its students in French and still judges the study of French literature necessary to that end; on the other, the University of Northumbria at Newcastle aims to teach its students what it once summed up as 'French for Export' and to acquaint them with the culture not of France but of Peugeot–Renault–Citroën; and above both, but not designed to register any such difference as that, is the government apparatus of assessment—whose verdict is that Modern Languages at Northumbria is worth 23 out of 24 but at Oxford only 21.

The government doesn't quail before the problem of summing up a university divided into infinite parts. It just employs enough people to cover the lot. It employs a team of people—a team of teams—to rate all courses, for both teaching and research, in all universities, numerically, on a scale (for research) of 1 to 5, according to standards appropriate to the subjects taught on them. Then—weighting for size and so forth—it takes the average for each university. And it could, of course, do what it hasn't yet got round to doing: weighting for size and so forth, take the average of all 261 or so of those averages, and thus obtain a rating for the entire British University System (of something between 1 and 5).

But that rating wouldn't be a judgement, certainly not of British universities as a whole—and not just because a score isn't a judgement, but also because, here, sameness of score doesn't mean sameness of judgement. The scores averaged together are arrived at entirely independently of one another, according to standards that are not just widely different but, in many cases, mutually hostile: as in the case of Physics and—let's say—Beauty Science; or of Philosophy and International Leisure and Tourism Management; or Art and Arts Management; or, on the one hand, let us say, Counselling and Business Studies and, on the other, Mathematics and every other branch of thought that is either carried on honestly or not at all. The scores which are averaged together as if they had a single absolutely homogeneous meaning—just like cardinal numbers—have (as the interested parties pretend not to know) wildly different meanings. Averaging these meanings as scores is perfectly rational and utterly senseless. (And there, not quite incidentally, we do get a glimpse of how you might go about coming to a judgement of the modern university: by asking the question: 'Are such exercises taken seriously in it? And by those in government educated by it?')

The very process of university 'assessment' in fact concedes the case we are making: that what we now have in this country, as an ideal not an error, is not the university at all but a mere bazaar of specialisms, the polyversity. When the Professors of Theological and Cosmetic Science or Philosophy and Tourism sit on Senate side by side, the university *has* no definite character any more, except the character of not having one.

If the universities do still make sense as a whole (if they and their place in the national life, for good and ill, can still be judged, and not just 'assessed'), then the parts will partake of the character of the whole and the whole of the parts. The character of the whole will be discernible, with greater or lesser difficulty, in the individual subjects that make it up. That Theology and Ethics are part of the whole will be discernible, for instance, in at least what does *not* go on in Anatomy and other branches of investigation into the human body. Certain experiments performed in concentration camps can't be performed in the university ... without the university taking on the character of a concentration camp. No more can the ethos and practices of advertising be introduced into it, as they have, without its taking on the character of an advertising agency, as it has.

But not even the bad imitation of good science or the good taste of best butter wholly explains the disintegration of the university into what Leavis called a 'mere collocation of specialist departments',[6] the 'bazaar, or pantechnicon,' that Newman foresaw, 'in which wares of all kinds are heaped together for sale in stalls independent of each other ... to save the purchasers the trouble of running about from shop to shop.' For that, all idea had to be extinguished of what sort of whole the non-sciences might make, of what might hold them together as one body of knowledge, seen in different lights or from different perspectives, and of where that body's centre might lie; the idea of a university as a place of liberal education had to be replaced by the idea of it as an investment in training and skills. Only then could the modern multiversity flourish.

And only some renewed understanding of liberal education will give us anything better.

The mutual correction of judgement that takes place between Elizabeth Bennet and Darcy, or Elizabeth's groping for a judgement of Mr Collins in response to her father's invitation to judge his letter, is, to our minds, a perfect example of what education is, and unless it is realistically claimed that universities offer inductions into such judgement, they had better give up. We can see from those instances that judgement is personal ('or nothing') but not private or 'subjective'. Judgements are made within traditions of judgement, in particular settings like law courts or seminar rooms or at breakfast tables. And they are formed in a world where many values are assumed, like the worth of integrity, or the hope for happiness in marriage to be based on love. Not all such values appear on syllabuses. Together they make a world.

All education is induction into the life of a world even as it renews and changes that life; academic education is just a more deliberate induction into what Leavis sometimes called 'cultural continuity'. The continuity of academic thinking with common sense is essential—but broken under the stress of extreme specialization. Academic judgement, when it has not been corrupted by specialization (as it seems to us it has been in, for example, some of what we have shown of economics), is not different in kind from common judgement, but is developed by more extensive acquaintance with 'the best that has been thought and said' and with the attendant modes of discourse and argument as embodied in the people we meet at university.

The personal influence we see at the heart of education is similar whether it be T. F. Powys educating his adoptive daughter quite unconsciously,[7] or Wittgenstein or Leavis wrestling with their angels in the company of their pupils. The difference between a university and that breakfast table at Longbourn or Powys's influence on his daughter is just that the first has to make a more formal use of knowledge and that the judgement it aims at is more public. Universities maintain common judgement (if they do) by the use they make of the knowledge we can also have in common.

Newman's one tree of knowledge is common knowledge academically developed and taken in a particular light. The educated person has to be knowledgeable, of course, and the knowledge is of what T. S. Eliot in one of his more grandiose moments called 'the mind of Europe'. The cultured person knows as much as possible of 'the best that has been thought and said in the world', by all available routes—including the low ones—though the universities award degrees in separate subjects, and efforts to amalgamate the subjects have not succeeded. The knowledge has to be of a whole, though, as it is in science, by way of different glimpses. Our view of knowledge is distorted by the present predominance of rather marginal matters (as Tolstoy called them) like the physical sciences. 'The proper study of mankind is man': in the universities, by way of history, literature, philosophy, theology.... These do all belong to the one tree; they all demand much knowledge as well as thought; they are all interrelated, though—like the sciences—separately examinable; they all depend on human judgement as well as offering to develop human judgement.

And although it is true that universities aim to develop and refine common knowledge, it is also true that those 'developments' and 'refinements' can prove shams, and that one of the necessary proofs of them is their capacity to survive outside the special atmosphere of the university in the rough and tumble of common life. It's always a bad sign if the technical terms of arts subjects wilt when introduced to common speech.

If education drifts too far from life it defeats itself. You certainly won't understand Shakespeare or the Renaissance or the Reformation if you know in your own life nothing of love, family life, politics, religion, good and evil. Shakespeare may then show you some of these things more deeply or terribly, or may provoke you to protest that life is not such as he depicts. The student's experiences will not be the same as those Shakespeare enacts, but will go towards forming the language in which human relations can have sense, and towards forming judgements of that sense, for of course not all senses are desirable. (I remember students who have said they 'identified' with Macbeth. Heaven forfend!) Formal education in schools and universities tries to take further, and in academic ways, the education that every child engages in by growing up in the human world, but if there is a discontinuity between education inside and outside school there is something wrong—with the school.

The appeal to the tree of knowledge is necessary, but to be educational, university studies have to be more than extensive reading, more than 'knowledge for its own sake' or 'pursuing the argument wherever it leads', more even than 'the disinterested pursuit of truth' and the formation of judgement under the influence of the educated. The tree is of the knowledge of good and evil. University studies have to be undertaken in a certain spirit and from a certain point of view, the spirit and the point of view embodied in Darcy and Elizabeth Bennet. Education has to be a form of the pursuit of the good.

This is the principle missing from the modern university which, if brought back into it, would rid it of its clutter of corrupt specialization and turn back a pile of twigs into a living tree again.

*   *   *

Elizabeth and Darcy are both seeking the good, though that isn't one of their phrases. It is, in one necessary way of putting it, the morality in Elizabeth Bennet that involves her in concentrated reflection and the organization of her natural gifts. Mary might claim to be pursuing the good, but can't be allowed to be so in an educated way because of her mental disqualifications which are at the same time moral. The two youngest sisters and their mother are not pursuing the good at all, but would be more educable if they were. Education, the education they administer to one another, is necessary to the kind of good Elizabeth and Darcy achieve. Let us bear in mind, on the other hand, that Darcy's education is a by-product of his love. Without love education will not get far.

Education and morality do lean on one another but are still distinguishable. There are many good but uneducated people. On the other hand education is not always undertaken in the right spirit—though when this happens we would say it does not bloom as it ought.

What should human beings be, to attain their full humanity? Aristotle thought you should be what we have to translate as 'a philosopher' (or lover of wisdom) or what we have to translate as 'a politician', by which he meant someone taking a full part in the life of the community; the very best thing was to be both at once.[8] Education should make anyone fitter to take a thoughtful part in public life, even if only the public life of the polling station, by developing common knowledge and common judgement. The benefit of university education for the individual and the state is, as Coleridge said, the formation of the clerisy, the class that judges in public.

The educated person can take up one of the roles belonging to the clerisy better than the uneducated—being a judge in the ordinary law-court sense but also teaching, preaching, writing for the newspapers, and so on. Here the commitment to the good is an obvious necessity. The journalist devoted to corrupt ideals like economic growth as a sufficient end for a community will spread corruption, and more effectively if he is a powerful and educated thinker, though the conjunction here is hard to imagine. But for instance there are notorious examples of effective MPs who are not in any sense committed to the good. Education here consists of some disciplined knowledge that enables the educated person to use knowledge, and some mature judgement of human affairs; without a simultaneous commitment to the good these powers of the educated will be at best useless and at worse vicious, but they can nevertheless be seen as the ones belonging to education that a moral but uneducated person, or a highly skilled person, may not possess.

*   *   *

Does it work? Education is not inoculation. Many students will not be educated. If Jane Austen had issued a class list (in Carlyle's 'Science of Things in General') it would by modern standards have included too large a percentage of failures, and, even worse, no upper seconds; for Kitty and Lydia must have failed outright along with the untypically bad 'mature student' their mother, Mary would be a third, Jane a lower second and Elizabeth a first. A high real failure rate does not invalidate education in the university any more than it does in the Bennet family. Contemporary universities, when they do not hide this situation by the easy route of declaring the failures successes, agonize over many failures which are not theirs. Our complaints are not about seed that fails to bring forth a hundredfold, but systemic failure that makes university education impossible. Does it work? Try asking instead whether we can do without it.

And as for that question we began with, 'What bearing could the example of Mr Darcy and Elizabeth Bennet have on the study of such technical subjects as Dentistry and Astro-physics?', we have to say, frankly, that the more genuinely technical the subject the less possible bearing the example could have on it. But, we insist on adding, what that means is, the further that subject is from the centre of the university's life. The university could afford the loss of Dentistry or Astro-physics (though we'd be sorry to see the latter go); it couldn't afford the loss of History, Philosophy, Literature ....'

But we don't admit that Jane Austen's example has no bearing on any of the subjects practised as if they were essentially technical. We have shown that it has a bearing on economics. Economics is a subject presently but not necessarily devoted to a corrupt ideal, that economic growth—never mind the form, never mind the consequences, never mind whose—is a good in itself. We *have* helped to illustrate how its unexamined devotion to that ideal helps to make the subject not only more immoral than it need be but less intelligent too. Is it really so outlandish to think that the subject would benefit from a more intelligent conception of wealth than that it presently has? or that when it offers to study the economics of education it would benefit from a more intelligent conception of education too?

And the bearing of Darcy and Elizabeth Bennet on Business Studies, and all its variants, could hardly be plainer: they should be treated by the university like the foreign bodies they are, flushed out of the system and all the money they bring into it with them.

*   *   *

Near the beginning of Chapter 5 of *Apologia pro Vita Sua*, Newman—a genuinely educated intellect if ever there was one—has some marvellous, still pertinent things to say about the self-destructiveness of the educated intellect which, rejecting all constraint, insists on its own freedom and self-sufficiency. He sees (we believe, truly) that what characterizes the modern, free-thinking intellect is that it won't accept a boundary and a foundation from outside itself and in the nature of the case cannot provide them from within. In consequence it has become randomly destructive.

Newman speaks—in fear and admiration—of 'the restless intellect', 'the wild living intellect of man', 'the immense energy of the aggressive, capricious, untrustworthy intellect', with its 'all-corroding, all dissolving scepticism', 'that universal solvent', 'the energy of human scepticism', 'that deep, plausible scepticism [which is] the development of human reason, as practically exercised by

173

the natural man' and which leads us away into 'a bottomless liberalism of thought'. He calls freedom of thought both 'one of the greatest of our natural gifts' and something that needs 'rescuing from its own suicidal excesses'.

Newman says, tentatively, modestly, that he does not think he is wrong in saying that reason tends towards 'a simple unbelief in matters of religion'. More than a century later we can be a bit bolder. Reason as understood in the modern technologico-Benthamite world tends towards a simple unbelief in *everything* —everything but the things it can make visible to itself and whose existence it can verify, 'objectively', buy and sell.

When Newman made war on liberalism he did not go as far as predicting that unbelief in religion would also appear in politics and literature (that took Carlyle). Before the twentieth century it was hard to realize that literature, civilization, the nations themselves need for their existence something very like faith. But what else but a shared unbelief makes it so easy for our liberal establishment to have Terry Eagleton in its midst? What else makes it so easy for him to be there? Well, the 'what else' is pseudo-science, 'literary theory' and the like, but its role is the legitimization of 'all-corroding, all-dissolving scepticism'.

It may still seem hard to credit that it is orthodox in university departments of English to deny the existence of 'English Literature' except as a deceit and a sham, a trick of the ruling class, serving the same purpose as the game laws but less honestly. It may seem even harder to credit that this orthodoxy is only a particular application of a more general but correspondingly less articulated one. But look around you.

Begin with the other university subjects. If there isn't a Faculty of Social Sciences, then Sociology, Psychology, Economics still belong to Arts, and dominate it. And what is their mainspring but to displace the distrusted unverifiable judgement of human things by a reliance on measurement and system? The proper study of mankind can only be allowed if done by the proper pseudo-scientific methodologies. What else do they do but teach people to distrust anything not measurable and verifiable? Latterly, when students asked me *how* to do literary criticism and I said, 'There are no methods,' they thought that was the same as admitting a fraud. What a terrible co-operation and mutual reinforcement there is between these institutionalized superstitions and the unpremeditated habits of modern correctness—all those variations on 'Be objective', 'Don't be judgemental', 'One opinion is as good as another' and the rest. Geography, which always became a ragbag the minute it diversified beyond maps, became a proper subject by quantifying itself. History, which for decades past has been frantic to get itself out of the subjective Arts Faculty, has turned itself into Sociology-of-the-Past and believes every bit of the past is as important as every other bit. (The right sort of unbelief allows you to believe anything.) Classics dissolves into Ancient History and Civilization, a particular fragment of Sociology-of-the-Past no longer boringly dependent on dead languages and their living poetry. Modern Languages are increasingly without literature, and have mechanized themselves to the point where you can graduate in French without any idea of what makes French worth knowing.

What wonder that the genuine subject English can no longer be tolerated in an academy dominated by science on the one hand and misplaced and/or pseudo-science on the other? Liberal education is an anomaly in the new university. The fault-lines between liberal education and everything around it are too pronounced. Hence the landslips which buried 'English' and threw the present writers out onto the street, luckily uninjured. We, not they, are the survivors. Where is the Arts Faculty now except amongst the redundant? (We are, however, open to offers.)

What were Chris Smith's qualifications to be Culture Secretary (and Sport at the same time)? Unlike Mr Major, he went to university and unlike Mr Collins he did more than keep terms. He made useful acquaintance, very useful. He worked; he has a doctorate; in English Literature; on the romantic poets; from Cambridge University. What more could we want? And asked by *The Spectator* whether Bob Dylan's 'poetry' is as [of course] *valid* as Keats's, Chris Smith, PhD (Cantab.) replied, 'Yes, I do believe that. The distinctions between the higher and popular arts are meaningless.'[10] Asked whether Dylan's music is as good ('valid') as Beethoven's: 'Beethoven and he are different. You can't put them in a pecking order. I wouldn't want to establish hierarchies.' We must not discriminate. That is not to say that the arts are unimportant in the only way that matters. 'The point about the popular music industry, for example, is its serious value to the economy.' *There* is the large return on a genuine investment. But how could the Arts Faculty survive for long in a nation with such a government?

Modern, 'educated', liberal-minded man can no more believe in literatures, or the nations from which they spring, than he can in God or the hierarchies of the heavenly host. Having dissolved the foundations of the religious world, secular 'reason' has made a very satisfactory start on dissolving the foundations of the secular too: if God can't be verified, can King, Noble or Gentleman? Or any of the virtues once associated with them? Can man or woman—except as a certain complexity of organs, energies and infinitely variable roles? Husbands and wives—except as partners? Manliness and womanliness? Englishness? The humanness of the unborn baby less than twenty-six weeks old? Are art and literature verifiable, 'objectively'? Good and evil? Crime and punishment? Murder—except as unlawful homicide? Quality, except in a form that may be audited, controlled and driven (top-down)? Standards, except in a form that may be levered up? Politics—as anything but climbing up or slipping down the greasy pole? Even as particular and localized a thing as the university—the idea of the university—can that be found? Can it be delivered, except as a congerie of courses? What is a university but whatever we call so? Take that complex of buildings, bodies and activities over there. Yesterday it was a polytechnic, today it is a university. It has been decreed. Who can say otherwise?

And where will it end, the march of progress into unbelief? This is a later phase than the one Carlyle found in the French Revolution, in which he saw 'the whole *demonic* nature of man ... hurled forth to rage blindly without rule or rein ... .'[11] We are well beyond the blindly raging stage. Newman's answer, in 1864, was that it could be brought to an end by the Catholic Church and Infallibility. Conrad's answer, in *Nostromo*, 40 years later, follows the logic of Newman's argument without Newman's belief in the Catholic Church: where will it end? In suicide for the 'educated', and the tyranny of 'material interests' over everybody else; the place where religion and art was shall be occupied by Alice Walker. This is the way our world ends. Well, let it—and let's hope afterwards to regain the recognition of a few realities. What educated judgement remains can see these things, and can even 'carry us through' to something better.

> If indeed these also fail us, and ... cannot vindicate themselves into clearness here and there, but at length cease even to try it,—then indeed it is all ended: national death ... well-deserved annihilation, and dismissal from God's universe, that and nothing else lies ahead for our once heroic England too. ... [but] if this small Aristocratic nucleus can hold out and work, it is in the sure case to increase and increase.[12]

It is actually the case that some people can still read English poetry. While that remains true, the university is still possible.

An Anecdote of
Institutional Life

But infinitely beautiful the wondrous work arose...

William Blake[1]

THE STATE'S OBJECTIVELY EXISTING MACHINERY of standard-raising and measurement is just a figment but, when treated as a reality, perfectly capable of doing more harm than good. When the 'education system' really is thought of as a system—a complicated arrangement of levers, pulleys and wheels—the parts put in place at the top to ensure that the parts lower down work properly may very easily make them work worse. I believe I saw this happen, on a small scale, at first hand, when I was in the Humanities Department at Newcastle Polytechnic (before it became the University of Northumbria) in the 1970s.

*　　　*　　　*

Until the mid-1970s, our students did London external general degrees. They were taught by one set of people and examined by another, and they generally got lower seconds or thirds. The meaning of the arrangement was clear and (it seemed to me when I arrived in 1972) just: 'This institution is fit to teach at degree level but not examine at it.' When we switched to the (now defunct) Council for National Academic Awards degrees, we became (like all the other polytechnics) an anomaly, something that was neither fish nor fowl, fit both to teach and examine but only under the supervision of a centralized bureaucracy.

The purpose of the CNAA was to ensure that institutions that weren't universities (I mean in fact not just in name) could do what only universities can, award degrees. Its actual function proved to be, not surprisingly, different: to provide a professional leg-up for those who joined its committees. It gave them another line on their cvs and membership of an academic equivalent of the Lions or Masons. It didn't make the polytechnics universities (that came later, and more cheaply) but it did ensure the promotion into positions of power of those who were happier in committee meetings than classrooms or libraries. It was a wonderful instance of the plasticity of things bureaucratic. Set up to serve an official purpose that was a self-contradiction, the CNAA was instantly bent to private purposes that weren't.

When we switched to the CNAA we became our students' examiners as well as their teachers, but that made no immediate difference to … well … anything: not to the way we taught, not to the way we got on (or didn't get on) with the students and with one another, not to the marks the students got. We hadn't yet twigged, that is, that henceforth *our* 'performance' was to be measured by the students' and the security of our jobs to depend on it. The continuity between London and CNAA days was, in one aspect, a very good example of quality control, assured not by machinery but something much more reliable (much cheaper too), if not conscience, quite, then the next best thing, habit.

What this meant for our students, though, was that they continued to get lower seconds and thirds (and that we didn't see why they shouldn't). What it meant for us was that the first time we applied to have our CNAA licence renewed, it was refused. Lower seconds and thirds (even if they were, now, mainly honours degrees), along with our drop-out rate, were inconsistent with our new status as an institution different from but equal to a university, and also with the typical class lists of other polytechnic Arts departments. The Visiting Panel that made the decision found other things amiss too: damaging criticisms from students, book lists that weren't up to date ('Chesterton on Dickens? *Chesterton?* In *1978?*'), a language course that was amateurish ('There is a proper discipline for the study of language—it is called linguistics. Teach your students *that*') and, as an aggravation of the rest, dislikeable manners ('Those two treated us like fools'). The Chairman of the Visiting Panel summed us up: 'There's no room in Higher Education for amateurs.'

Our jobs being in danger, we pretty quickly professionalized ourselves—or were made to, by a new Head of Department brought in from outside to save us from ourselves. We swapped our old, easygoing habits (or consciences) for something more strenuous, and our re-application the following year was successful. The key to our keeping our jobs was that our class list was sufficiently improved to promise further improvements to come. And come they did, year on year: the general degree disappeared, the thirds followed, the lower seconds became fewer and fewer, the upper seconds became common and above them began to appear an increasingly respectable sprinkling of firsts. Within two or three years our bad, old amateur ways were things of the past; we had some-body in charge who *was* in charge, and instead of a course on Language that had something to do with Literature, we had one that hadn't.

Previously, we had, probably, most of us, taught as well as we could, but we had done so, as it were, casually and with no aim in mind beyond that of being as interesting and intelligent as we could, that is, without really, in one very influential sense of the word, teaching at all. We taught without having any very definite idea of what we wanted the students to learn. And our examining showed a similar aimlessness. We marked up what we liked, marked down what we didn't, purposelessly and without thought of consequences. It was the same with the booklists we drew up and, even, with our treatment of the students (it was certainly the same with our treatment of one another). Wherever you looked, we did—you might say—as we pleased.

But not after 1978. From then on we had an aim, one that was simple, clear and measurable: to get as many students through the degree every year with as high marks as possible. We became focused and properly professional, in four ... no ... five key areas: course design, teaching, marking, student welfare and (the fifth, or the first) staff discipline.

We began, when we drew up courses, to ask ourselves, for the first time, what our courses looked like from the students' point of view. Were they adjusted to the students' interests and abilities? Would they be accessible and manageable? Was it possible for the students we got (no different from the ones we had got before) to get upper seconds in them? The other key principle we adopted for course design was that no course was to be too strongly marked by the particular interests and opinions of the person designing and teaching it. It ought to be such that any fellow professional could take it over if need be. This principle was well summed up by one of us as, 'Courses aren't like books.'

Whereas previously exams had tended to be rather an afterthought, they now became the very first thing we thought of. 'Set the exam paper and teach to it,' 'Make sure they're prepared,' 'Make sure they know what's required of them'—such became our guides. What some people deride as 'spoon feeding' we learned to think of as responsible and conscientious teaching. You knew in advance what you wanted your students to learn—that is, what to say in the exams—and you made sure you taught them it. What's wrong with that? We were encouraged to adopt a more encouraging style of class teaching too.

And we started marking differently. No-one cynically gave marks he didn't believe could be defended in public, but we did all, more or less as a matter of policy, begin giving marks at the very top end of what we thought we could defend, which had the effect, of course—not that we especially intended it to—of bringing that top end down, lower and lower. I don't say that by marking high ourselves, right across the board, we were deliberately putting pressure on external examiners to mark high too but, probably, our marking did tend to have some such effect—especially as, of course, the externals, in their own institutions, were under exactly the same pressure to mark high as we were. Internals/externals: we were all in the same boat.

We had to get our drop-out rate down too, so, as a matter of deliberate policy, we became more caring. Our way of welcoming new students to the department became much better regulated, for instance. We didn't welcome them haphazardly any longer, according to someone's individual disposition and temperament, and with other members of staff free to come along or not. We now gave them—all of us—a welcome that was official and collective. And we made sure the Polytechnic Student Welfare Officer was present too. It was a pity that, personally as well as professionally, he was a bit of a dampener, but at least he was another means for us to demonstrate our concern.

We became more conscientious as personal tutors too, requiring our students to see us at regular intervals and recording their failures to turn up. Only two of us weren't routinely conscientious; both were male; one had the gift of making the role of personal tutor a way of getting students into bed; the other could never be bothered even to learn their names. Apart from the second of these two, we all started keeping a close check on attendance and progress generally. We kept on the look-out for warning signs and when we thought we spotted them kept one another informed. If a student didn't turn up for an exam one of us would drive to his home and bring him in. We started taking student opinion seriously too. Their official representatives sat on one of the committees, and we always made a point of asking them what they thought and listening politely to whatever they said.

The key to our success was the much higher level of staff discipline imposed by the new Head. Previously we had not been used to having many meetings and had been used to going to them or not just as we pleased. Now we had a lot of meetings and were expected to attend all of them. We had also been used to treating one another very unprofessionally, in meetings even more than out. There was a general air of licence about the place. Sometimes, it is true, it could be very stimulating but it had the disadvantage of making co-operation between some members of staff more or less impossible. Even though it was a joint English/History course we were running, it was impossible, for instance, to have some members of the English staff teach jointly with some members of the History staff. If they were put together, you could never be sure how they would get on. One of the English staff in particular was very easily irritated by people who didn't think quite as he himself did. Quite small things would set him off, and then he'd insult his colleagues, openly, to their faces, in front of students, and even in front of the external examiner. And the worst of it was, you'd never know in advance what might offend him. Sometimes you didn't know afterwards either.

But all that sort of thing was put an end to. The concept (and not just the concept) of 'the actionable' was introduced into the Department. What had been a perfectly respectable argument for avoiding work, that 'if one were made to do things one didn't want to do, one would do them badly,' lost its respectability. The departmental administrative machinery was elaborated, and everybody was expected to be responsible for some part of it. We started to get into the habit of treating one another less as individuals and more as functionaries—as Admissions Officer or First Year Co-ordinator or some such.

That way, at work, foes could be friends. Our new Head himself set the example. Meetings became much more procedurally correct, with less talking out of turn and fewer personal attacks. Although, in some ways, there was less fun in the department, what there was was more equally shared. Certainly, from one point of view, the work went ahead more smoothly. The most important administrative development was the creation of the Senior Management Team, which put a real distance between those who were on it and ran things, and those who weren't and didn't. Departmental policy was no longer made (and unmade) in public dogfights but peaceably by those in positions of responsibility. This made it easier, for instance, to ensure that on the English side only those sympathetic to deconstructionist theory taught it. To have let the students see members of staff violently disagreeing with one another would have been a very retrograde step—especially as one of the likely parties to any such dispute had the habit of making professional disagreements personal. It was much better to make sure that he got nowhere near the subject. (Managers ought to manage.)

Of course, the creation of the Team might itself have become a cause of discontent, but two measures were taken to prevent it: firstly, the Team members, one by one, for a time, took to holding departmental dinner parties, to which everyone was invited and at which the new spirit of working co-operation could be reinforced; secondly, everybody was made to feel that their professional achievements were all equally valued as contributions to the department's success. Too often in the past people had felt they weren't. One of the first things the Team did was to invite people to notify it of anything they had achieved— getting a PhD, say, or an article into a refereed journal, or writing up a CNAA submission—and then it would send them a memorandum of congratulations with copies to the rest of the department. The congratulations were read out at department meetings too.

I shouldn't want to pretend, of course, that everything was now perfect. It is true that business went more smoothly and without obvious clashes. But, of course, people continued to differ from one another as much as ever; they just kept their differences hidden. Discord and friction hadn't gone away, they'd gone underground; and that, perhaps, in some ways, gave them a settled virulence they hadn't had before.

Certainly, there was something odd about the position in the department of the new Head who had been responsible for the transformation in its fortunes. He *had* saved us from ourselves, and half his reward was that on all matters and occasions of official business, including departmental dinner parties, he had our unanimous, or near unanimous, support. But the other half of his reward was, at all other times, by some instinct of mutual preference, to be solitary. With one exception (a woman, of course, with a woman's loyalty), he was never to be seen taking coffee with the members of his own department, not even his closest allies (and, as in the song of the Miller of Dee, they never took coffee with him). And it wasn't that he was unsociable by nature or boring or dis-agreeable. He was rather a clever man, literate and cultivated and (off the subject of work) with a lively sense of humour. (I remember once being brought to a stop by his saying to me, 'Maskell, when Blake said, "Opposition is true friend-ship," he meant it as a paradox.') He was no Mr Collins. We *had* a Mr Collins in the department but with him people were ordinarily sociable.

His superiors (whose backsides he had saved too) were no more grateful. When the Faculty was reorganized he didn't even get onto the subs bench. He got a new title, a bigger salary and an office somewhere out of the way, but no job. The system of official relations and officially approved judgements, which for ten years he had been treating as something real, had suddenly given way to a personal one. He made you feel uncomfortable: get him out of the way. But I expect they gave him a good reference for the job he got as an Inspector.

He did have the last laugh though—where he could—not on his superiors, on the Department. Before he left he made sure that his successor was the one of us most widely disliked by the rest.

Quite likely, our CNAA re-application of 1978 deserved to be turned down, but no more so than our original application of 1975 or any of our successful re-applications from 1979 onwards. We may not have impressed the 1978 CNAA Visiting Panel but its members were no essentially fitter, it seemed to me, than we were, merely a more concentrated essence of the managerial. Supposing they were right, and we weren't very good, what was achieved by trying to *make* us better, by their means, means themselves only dubiously good? Our results got better and better, of course, but largely because, by one means and another, we made sure they did. The students graduating in 1987 weren't better educated than their predecessors of ten years earlier, just better qualified. Departmental business was conducted with fewer public dog-fights but with correspondingly more behind-the-scenes back-biting and flank-rubbing. The improvement in results mostly meant a decline in standards; the more correctly we behaved towards one another in public, the more sincerely we disliked one another in private. There were only two unequivocal improvements, and neither had anything to do with top-down drivel or the managerial machinery it set in motion: one was that the History staff surrendered the selection of students to the English staff, and the other was that we began favouring mature students (mostly married women) over school-leavers.

An Education
Policy Document

THERE ARE SEVERE LIMITS to what even an enlightened government could do for education. No educational reform can take place in disconnection from society. How could a nation with our opinion-formers have decent universities? —or *vice versa*? At worst, it may be that if the reforms we need were possible they would not be necessary. Educational reform presupposes a certain level of existing education, whereas we are close to having to start from scratch—which would only be possible after something more like conversion than reform. There are additional difficulties in the *soi-disant* democracies of the twenty-first century. Our task, within the limits of the possible, would have been easy in the time of King Henry VIII. Simply catch the attention of the intelligent tyrant at a suitable moment. Nowadays we not only need a strong minister of education, we need 'public opinion', and the catch obviously is that the state of public opinion is part of the disease. Howbeit: we make a start. Imagine that enough of the clerisy come to see the sense in what we say: what then should be done by way of policy? We must state one assumption, as part of the hypothetical case about the clerisy. The judges, teachers, commentators and critics, clergy ... ought not to fear want, but ought not on the other hand to be very rich. Scholars are traditionally poor; which is not ideal, but it is positively a bad thing for them to become fat cats, or to expect to be courted by company boards looking for rising entrepreneurs. The educated ought to have a reasonable chance of a comfortable life in the clerisy, but not to expect a direct link between a degree and the creation of wealth.

What follows is based on our reply to an invitation to submit a policy document on education to a political party: it is free for all now; no copyright claimed for this part. The agents of the changes proposed are to be imagined to be not ourselves but a political party convinced by our book. (Of course, we are both just as open to offers of education secretaryships as to regius professorships.)

SIX PRINCIPLES

1 Education is valuable for its own sake both to the individual and to the state.

2 Because education is valuable to all, and because universal suffrage demands it, the education of the less academically able must receive as serious attention as the education of the academically more able.

3 But because there is no upper limit at which education loses its value, and because not everyone either wants or is able to pursue education as far as it can be pursued, the formation of an 'élite' must be a natural and desirable end of education.

4 Education and training are often close together in our early experience but diverge more and more the higher in education we go, and must not be confused.

5 Education is, like the armed forces and pensions, a legitimate public cost not an investment, but there can be sensible financial limits to that cost.

6 Training, on the other hand, is an investment, the cost of which should be shared by those who expect dividends from it.

The proposals that stem from these principles will at once improve the quality of both training and education, and save immense sums of public money.

* * *

Basic literacy and numeracy is already better in the schools than it was during the liberal hegemony, and we shall build on this improvement. All children will be introduced to at least the beginnings of knowledge of the best of our own form of life. English poetry will be read, and British history, and for all children there will be a sketch of European history from Greece and Rome to the present. No child will leave school ignorant of the Bible. All children will be expected to be musically literate and have some acquaintance with Western music.

A National Curriculum will be maintained, but made less dictatorial and less of a burden on teachers. The bias towards science and technology, introduced in the mistaken belief that it would help to make us rich, will be removed. As a result the smaller proportion of pupils wishing to pursue scientific subjects will be able to do so in smaller classes and with better resources. It will again be possible for a child to study to GCSE level two foreign languages and both History and Geography.

SIXTH FORMS

The attempt to create in the GNVQs a vocational 'equivalent' to A-level is badly misguided and deeply confused. The GNVQs have undermined the character and function of the old academic sixth form as preparation for university by making it too large and depriving it of its coherence; and they have done little to create a new technical sixth form in recompense. The whole apparatus of GNVQs must go. If business values the training the GNVQ subjects provide, there can be either training in the workplace or specialized technical schools.

The well-established two-year A-level in, usually, three subjects, examined at the end of the second year, will be reinstated.

Sixth forms will naturally be much reduced in size when it is realized that university entrance is not automatic and that university degrees will not necessarily lead to lucrative careers, but that preparation for university is for those of all classes and backgrounds capable of and interested in university work.

FURTHER AND CONTINUING EDUCATION

We strongly support the extramural activities of the universities, and the work of the WEA and local authorities, provided that they are genuinely educational. There is no call for the state to subsidize local classes in flower arrangement and Feng Shui, which now make up, by a very long way, most of what is 'taught' in what used to be called 'night schools'. The schools of continuing education have allowed numbers of adults who missed higher education to make contact with it. We support the principle of part-time degrees for extramural students, though we think universities should be abstemious about awarding honours after six years of part-time modular work.

One good recent development has been the recognition that not everybody is ready at age eighteen or nineteen to decide to embark on a university career. Some of the best university entrants have come in as mature students at any age from twenty-five to seventy and more, often after access courses or extramural work. This, though nobody will expect retired people to use their degrees in wealth creation, is to be strongly encouraged. For the comparatively small number of students involved there will be scholarships large enough to mitigate the hardships which three years without earned income entail for some potentially excellent but middle-aged students.

UNIVERSITIES

Educated judgement is necessary to the nation, absolutely; without it the nation loses its mind. The universities must be the seminaries of the class of opinion-formers that Coleridge called the clerisy.

During the last decade, the genuine university subjects have collapsed, often into nonsense. They have also on the one hand been adapted to the capacities of the weaker students and and on the other to the practices of some continental European and American universities which cannot be grafted on to ours.

Put together, the proliferation of useless non-subjects and the dilution of the genuine subjects mean that most of the academics at present employed in higher education, and the 'cohorts' of students they 'produce', are wasting their time. The dilution and/or nonsense in some institutions has got to the point of making genuine university work impossible to any minority still capable of pursuing it. The situation brings learning into contempt, wastes national resources, and has a demoralizing effect on the staff and students.

There will be an immediate and decisive transformation of this situation for the better with four principal measures.

1 University subjects that are neither use nor ornament will be phased out and degrees awarded in the traditional core of liberal arts subjects at every institution permitted to call itself a university.

    Genuine training courses will be transferred to other institutions. Foreign language departments that teach no literature will be classed as suppliers of training.

    A lot of universities will consequently be closed or revert to their former status, for which the name polytechnic will be reintroduced. The new poly-technics, unlike the old, will not run liberal arts courses parallelling those in the universities.

    This reform will reduce the numbers both of universities and of university students by more than three quarters, and will encourage a return to real university standards.

    We anticipate that with the re-establishment of academic standards, modular degrees will fade away.

2 Reformed universities will be adequately funded; British students' fees will normally be paid by the state and maintenance grants will be restored. Students need to concentrate their minds, and this cannot be done when they have to take paid work in the evenings, at weekends and in vacations when they should be reading. On the less inflated scale we project for the universities, the cost of this will be much more than covered by the savings we propose (as will redundancy payments). Overseas students already contribute substantially to university budgets, and we envisage that with the international reputation of our universities restored this will continue; but universities will not be permitted to reduce their intake of UK students in order to accommodate overseas students.

    There will be encouragement of genuine endowment of universities and scholarships by tax reliefs, and a promise not to tamper with endowments.

An unparsimonious level of funding will be ensured for research projects that are at once genuine and necessarily expensive, like many scientific projects with no commercial application, and like scholarly editions which will not pay for themselves.

3 Once the universities have been rescued and funded on a more realistic scale, they shall be left strictly alone. If they really are autonomous trees of knowledge without superiors they cannot be inspected. The reformed universities will return to the system of external examining by peers, not 'appraisal' and 'academic audit' by pseudo-superiors.

4 Genuine vocational training will be subjected, within reason, to market discipline.

The last is such a new proposal that quite a lot of work will be required filling in the details. The general logic is, however, clear.

If the economy must have training as investment, the resultant wealth-creation will necessarily one way or another pay for the training. It is sometimes thought that a well-trained labour-force is rather like the 'infrastructure', that the state should provide training like roads or power-lines; though many states in fact pay for roads with tolls on their users, and National Grid plc is now denationalized. The question is whether the cost of training should be borne mainly by the direct beneficiaries, or mainly by the beneficiaries of increased wealth in general, the taxpayers. We believe that the former is both fairer and quite practicable, and that the investment should be subscribed for by the investors, that is, the trained and those who use the training commercially.

It is in the interests of the state that standards of training should be reliable, and the state must have as effective an inspectorate for technical institutions as it has for schools. It does not necessarily follow that the costs of such inspection should come out of the taxes.

The state's interest in technical education will be recognized in supporting it, but not *in toto*. There are various possibilities for the mechanics of financing the new system. As a beginning, three quarters of the cost of technical tertiary education will be transferred to the fees, leaving one quarter for the exchequer, though this may vary somewhat from course to course. The national interest may possibly require some specialist training beyond what the market will support. But in general, if a business cannot do without trained personnel, three quarters of the cost will come from the business or from the trained.

A system will be introduced, along with the appropriate inspectorate for making sure that firms don't cheat, whereby firms will pay levies to the institutions whose qualified personnel they need, to a total of one quarter of the costs of such courses.

The remaining half will come from the trained. This follows from the status of their training as genuine investment. The present loan system will be much extended, with proper safeguards against any resultant hardship due to changes that make the training irrelevant, and ceilings will be fixed so that the possibility of crippling debt will not arise. Very expensive courses can have a higher proportion of fees coming from the state.

The difference between necessary skills and pseudo-academic waffle will consequently be more sharply understood. If it is really necessary to have a qualification in Leisure Studies to run a leisure centre, and if the owners of the leisure centre have to share the cost, they may well influence the qualification-granting body to make their courses more realistic. It may dawn on those running the 'tourist industry' that they don't need to employ people with qualifications in tourism. It is even possible that the new MBA schools will collapse. But that will be for the markets to decide by way of finance directors. Students who face the prospect of paying for their qualification will similarly be readier to treat the training as a genuine investment and ask whether their time and money are being well spent. This can only be good for genuine wealth-creation.

Though in the present educational fog we call this proposal new, it is little more than an adaptation to the modern world of the old ideas of apprenticeship: youths were trained partly at their own expense (by way of low pay in the years of the apprenticeship) and partly at the expense of their masters who stood to gain skilled workers. The principle continues to be sound and usable.

There are some borderline cases. Teacher training must continue to be supported by the state, as must the colleges of nursing and midwifery, though an improvement in the whole atmosphere of education will in both cases lead to a greater emphasis on experience and a reduction of theorizing. The medical schools fall halfway between true academic study and useful training, and since also their courses are longer than those for other first degrees the state will continue to support them substantially, though some considerable contribution to cost can reasonably be expected from doctors and dentists. There is no reason, however, why the supply of solicitors, so many of whom end up in the House of Commons, should make any charge on the exchequer; though as an academic subject law must be subsidized.

POSTGRADUATE STUDIES

The Conservatives insisted on universities setting up 'taught MAs', partly under the mistaken belief that these would qualify students for postgraduate work proper. By definition, graduation being the certificate that the graduate is competent to continue the study unaided, postgraduate study cannot be taught; the taught postgraduate degrees are therefore contradictions in terms, and will be phased out.

All higher degrees will be awarded by dissertation not by examination. State funding will be available for the minority of genuine postgraduate students who show themselves capable of original research and may be expected to make a career in universities.

*   *   *

As a consequence of these reforms there will be a drastic overall reduction in the size of secondary and tertiary education, releasing for productive work many middle-aged people, as well as the young who are now often wasting three of the best years of their lives on nonsense. The net direct savings anticipated from our policies will make a considerable difference to the budget. Whether they will appear as tax-reduction or be used otherwise cannot be predicted at this stage. The Liberal Democrats want to increase income tax for more education. Income tax could be reduced by at least 1 per cent within the life of one parliament and education much improved at the same time.

Can it be done? Not without another renaissance, which seems unlikely. Politics is the art of the possible, said Butler—'but we create possibility,' retorted Leavis. We think there is enough of an educated nucleus to create possibility. It is not impossible, for instance, that the present little polemic may make a stir. Let a political party once adopt something like our policies, for our reasons, and people will start to listen—and then the mainstream parties will take fright and begin to listen too. And genuine education will once more be something thinkable.

Notes on the Text

CHAPTER 1

1 *Financial Times* report of Mr Brown's first Budget speech, 3 July 1997, p. 17.
2 National Committee of Inquiry into Higher Education, *Higher Education in the Learning Society*, Stationery Office, 1997, Annexe C, para. 19.
3 Called henceforth *Charter*.
4 F. R. Leavis, *Education & the University*, 2nd edn, 1948, p. 16.
5 *The Teaching of English in England* (*The Newbolt Report*), 1921, p. 259.
6 C. P. Snow, 'Education and Sacrifice', *The New Statesman*, 17 May 1963, p. 746.
7 Advertisement in *The Financial Times* by the National Council for Vocational Qualifications, 26 January 1988.
8 David Blunkett, 'The Tough Truths of Dearing', *The Times*, 24 July 1997, p. 20.
9 Sources, *Whitaker's Almanac*, the *Blue Book*, *Education Yearbook 2000*, the *Annual Abstract of Statistics 1999*.
10 Nigel Blake, Richard Smith and Paul Standish, *The Universities We Need*, 1998, p. 51.
11 Ch. 22, para. 19.
12 Oddly, despite the present fashion for retiring at about age fifty-five, the pension advantage is not mentioned in these reports.
13 It is not stated whether the figure for average return depreciates the investment over the working life, but bear in mind that the capital invested is never seen again.
14 'Growth Theory'.
15 'Empirical Evidence'.
16 Report 7, 1.8–1.12 and Table 2.1; also Annexe A, 'Measuring the Social Rate of Return', 3, 11 and tables 1–3.
17 See Paul Ormerod, *The Death of Economics*, 1994, for a great many very similar remarks about economics.

CHAPTER 2

1 'Education of the People', *Phoenix*, 1936, pp. 594–5.
2 Department *for* Education and Employment.
3 *Newman: Prose and Poetry*, sel. Geoffrey Tillotson, 1957, p. 498. Like many eminent Victorians, Newman was always tinkering with his work, and the book generally known as *The Idea of a University* exists in a number of states. We quote the first edition as reprinted in this attractive Reynard Library volume; Newman page references are to it unless otherwise stated.
4 p. 498.
5 p. 481; cf. an equally good passage in Newman's novel *Loss and Gain*, ed. Alan G. Hill, Oxford, 1986, p. 15.
6 p. 467.
7 S. T. Coleridge, second Lay Sermon, quoted Richard Holmes, *Coleridge: Darker Reflections*, 1998, p. 448.

8   p. 462.
9   *The Curate in Charge*, 1875, repr. Gloucester, 1985, p. 203.
10 'The Function of Criticism at the Present Time', *Essays in Criticism*, first series, 1865.
11 p. 521.
12 The glance is at Professor Sir Randolph Quirk, whose doctrine as a grammarian is that he should not tell people how they ought to speak, but describe, in a spirit of scientific neutrality, how they actually do speak. It is a principle with him that from the practical point of view his profession is utterly useless. But how, as Vice-Chancellor of his university, did he justify universities to the University Grants Committee? and the public at large? By the training it gives dentists. (Cf. 'The New Battle of Britain for Our Universities', *The Times*, 2 February 1982, cited *The Gadfly*, February, 1984, pp. 5–6.)
13 Cf. the last chapter of Rush Rhees, *Without Answers*, 1969.
14 See the fuller quotations on pp. 30–31.
15 p. 465.
16 p. 503.
17 p. 505.
18 *The Idea of a University*, ed. George N. Schuster, New York, 1959, p. 183.
19 p. 497.
20 Cf. above, p. 25, from *ed. cit.*, p. 467.
21 *Ibid.*
22 William Hazlitt, 'My First Acquaintance with Poets', *The Liberal*, April, 1823, repr. *Selected Essays of William Hazlitt*, ed. Geoffrey Keynes, 1930, p. 510.
23 *The Universities We Need*, p. 82.
24 Leah Sims and Maggie Woodrow, *Franchising for Wider Access: Executive Summary*, University of North London, 1993, A1.
25 *Ibid.*, D1.
26 pp. 505–6.

CHAPTER 3

1   Ch. 43 (modern numbering), p. 276. (Chapter and page references for Jane Austen and George Eliot novels are to current Penguin editions.)
2   Ch. 14, p. 113.
3   Ch. 56, p. 368.
4   Ch. 29, p. 199.
5   Ch. 55, p. 353.
6   Ch. 2, p. 54.
7   Ch. 2, p. 56.
8   Ch. 11, p. 123.
9   Ch. 11, p. 122.
10 Ch. 36, p. 385.
11 Ch. 6, p. 68.
12 Ch. 8, p. 85.
13 Ch. 6, p. 71.
14 Ch. 5, p. 67.
15 Ch. 13, p. 108.

16 Ch. 7, p. 78.
17 Ch. 47, p. 305.
18 *Ibid.*
19 Ch. 2, p. 55.
20 Ch. 15, p. 114.
21 Ch. 22, p. 165.
22 Ch. 19, p. 146.
23 Ch. 19, p. 147.
24 Ch. 11, p. 100.
25 Ch. 19, p. 147.
26 Ch. 19, p. 148.
27 *Ibid.*
28 Ch. 4, p. 64.
29 Ch. 10, p. 93.
30 Ch. 8, p. 84.
31 Ch. 8, p. 85.
32 Ch. 9, p. 88.
33 Ch. 10, p. 93.
34 Ch. 10, p. 95.
35 Ch. 34, p. 221.
36 *Ibid.*
37 *Ibid.*
38 *Ibid.*
39 Ch. 11, pp. 102–3.
40 Ch. 58, p. 380.
41 Ch. 60, p. 388.
42 Ch. 15, p. 116.
43 Ch. 16, p. 119.
44 Ch. 16, p. 120.
45 Ch. 16, p. 121.
46 *Ibid.*
47 Ch. 16, pp. 122–3.
48 *Ibid.*
49 G. M. Hopkins, 'As Kingfishers Catch Fire'.
50 Ch. 16, p. 127.
51 Ch. 36, p. 235.
52 Ch. 16, p. 120.
53 Ch. 16, p. 122.
54 Ch. 21, p. 157.
55 Ch. 26, p. 181.
56 Ch. 36, p. 234.
57 *Ibid.*
58 *Ibid.*
59 Ch. 35, p. 227.
60 Ch. 35, p. 228.
61 Ch. 58, p. 378.
62 *Ibid.*

63 Ch. 36, p. 233.
64 Ch. 36, pp. 234–5.
65 Ch. 36, p. 236–7.
66 Ch. 36, p. 233.
67 *Ibid.*
68 Ch. 36, p. 237.
69 Ch. 36, p. 237; Ch. 37, p. 241.
70 Ch. 58, p. 375.
71 27 August 1997.

CHAPTER 4

1 Matthew, xii. 36–7.
2 Ch. 58, p. 375.
3 Ch. 19, pp. 149 and 150.
4 Attrib. Algeo 1991 and Coupland and Thomas 1989: I have lost the reference sheet.
5 Available not only in paper form (see note 2 on Ch. 1) but on the internet, the full report at www.leeds.ac.uk/educol/ncihe/natrep.htm, the summary at www.leeds.ac.uk/educol/ncihe/sumrep.htm.
6 The immediate result is that far-sighted lecturers have invested in the relevant certificates obtainable from the USA at a going rate of about $200 plus two recommendations/reports from friends. (You write mine and I'll write yours.)
7 See Lloyd Jones, *Biografi: A Traveller's Tale*, 1994.

CHAPTER 5

1 Reports of the White Paper *Higher Education: a New Framework*, 21 May 1991.
2 A partial, honourable exception was *The Daily Telegraph*.
3 'Timid Tory Plan for Training', 21 May 1991. Perhaps 'training' was suggested only by the tempting alliteration.
4 'A former polytechnic in Newcastle, now the University of Northumbria, tops the Financial Times performance indicators table …. Predictably Oxbridge scores badly … .' (*The Financial Times*, 4 December 1999).
5 25 February 1998.
6 27 November 1996.
7 27 August 1997, p. 8.
8 Subtitle-blurb for Simon Targett, 'Plug the gap—with cash and experience', *Financial Times* Weekend, 21 August 1999, p. XIII.
9 Mr Frank Nigriello, Communications Director of Unipart, quoted in Simon Targett, 'Graduates with a BAe', *The Financial Times*, 7 June 1997.
10 Cf. Frank Palmer, 'Skillsology *vs* Culture', '*My Native English*', pp. 53–60. This essay is a good example of the criticism of language that one should expect from a university. Cf. also William Hart, 'Against Skills', *The Oxford Review of Education*, vol. 4, no. 2, 1978, repr. *Our Schools/Our Selves*, September 1992, pp. 117–37; p. 117. We recommend this excellent essay.
11 p. 57.

12 p. 58.

13 *The Complete Careers and Higher Education Guidance Scheme*, Independent Schools Careers Organisation, Camberley, 1998.

14 *Ibid.*

15 25 October and 22 November 1997.

16 *The Complete Careers and Higher Education Guidance Scheme*, as above.

17 20 January 2000.

18 William Birch, 'Cloistered Against the Real World', *THES*, 2 February 1990, p. 18.

19 A letter from the Deans or other Representatives of University Faculties of Arts and Social Studies to Sir Peter Swinnerton-Dyer, Chairman, University Grants Committee, 30 March 1984.

20 *The Universities We Need*, pp. 148–9.

21 *Past and Present*, Book II, Ch. IX.

22 *Financial Times* report of the report of the North Commission, 29 January 1998, p. 8.

23 January 1997–May 1998.

24 Toril Moi, *Sexual/Textual Politics: Feminist Literary Theory*, 1985, repr. 1990, p. 51.

25 That Penguin anthology had one book by a male author (James F. McMillan, *European Women: Social History 1780–1945*). *Mother Courage* was not by Brecht but 'Letters from Mothers in Poverty at the end of the Century'.

26 Prifysgol Cymru: University of Wales Degree Examinations 1994, R/S/157/1.

27 *Briefing Plus* (The Monthly Focus on Management and Training Matters), November 1993, p. 1, published by The Industrial Society, registered charity no. 290003.

28 Tony Jackson, 'One-man Shows', *The Financial Times*, 24 November 1998, p. 25. Jackson reports that 'ostensibly, its skill was to buy ill-run companies and make them more efficient. In reality, it relied heavily on one tactic: pushing up prices.'

29 City Comment, *The Daily Telegraph*, 12 February 2000.

30 *The Times* carried a picture of 'Some of the first class of graduates from the first Football Management course, run by Liverpool University', and an accompanying article in which I could not detect any irony (15 December 1998). 'The hard-nosed message offered by the course is that football is big business. Clubs cannot afford to carry on hiring former professional players to carry out difficult, specialised jobs.' As a matter of fact, the present fashion is for businesses to focus on their 'core activities' in the hope that executives will know what they are doing. Either there is an abstract management skill, in which case it needn't specifically be football, or to run a football club demands knowledge of the game, in which case the former professional player has an advantage over the bespectacled mortar-boarded lady sitting in the middle of the front row of *The Times*'s picture. It will be interesting to see whether any football clubs take on any of these managers, and if so whether their place in the league tables improves.

31 'Some 250 delegates attended the conference and a total of eighty double-blind-refereed papers were included in the Conference Proceedings. The European Business Management School was represented by Dr A. Diamantopoulos and Professor Bodo Schlegelmilch, who presented a paper entitled "Determinants of Charity Giving: An Inter-disciplinary Review of the Literature and Suggestions for Further Research".' (*Newyddion*, 19 March 1992, p. 2).

32 *Newyddion*, 26 May 1988.

33 *The Financial Times*, 12 November 1996, front page.

34 'Cambridge has bowed to market pressures to offer a one-year MBA course' and 'Where the US lags behind', *The Financial Times*, 25 November 1996, p. 15.

35 Management Development, Advanced Professional Training, University College of Swansea, 1991.

36 Letter from the Principal of University College, Swansea, to All Members of Academic and Academically-related Staff, 10 June 1992.

37 *Newsletter*, 5 November 1987.

38 p. 253.

CHAPTER 6

1 Johnson, Boswell, Saturday 9 July 1763.

2 Carlyle, 'Signs of the Times' (1829).

3 F. R. Leavis, *English Literature in Our Time and the University*, 1967, pp. 65–6; cf. *The Human World* editorial 'Authority and Concern in the University', no. 2, 1971.

4 Sir Arthur Quiller-Couch, Inaugural, *On the Art of Writing*, Cambridge University Press, 1916, repr. 1925, p. 7.

5 *Rush Rhees on Religion and Philosophy*, ed. D. Z. Phillips, Cambridge University Press, 1997, p. xviii.

6 Minutes of a Meeting of the [University College of Swansea English] Departmental Teaching Committee with Dr Geoffrey Penzer ... 5 July 1994. There ought to be a name for the particular feeling of hopelessness inspired by this phrasing.

7 J. H. Newman, 'Discipline of Mind', repr. *The Idea of a University*, New York, 1959, p. 440.

8 Cf. Ian Robinson, 'F. R. Leavis the Cambridge Don', *The Use of English*, 43/3, 1992, pp. 244–54.

9 *Charter*, p. 3; the assumptions are pre-modular.

10 *Newsletter*, December 1987.

11 A letter from (Dr) R. S. Thomas [*non poeta*], Director of Planning and Marketing, entitled 'Strategic Plan', 5 August 1996.

12 Executive Summary of the Strategic Plan presented [by the University of Wales Swansea] to the Higher Education Funding Council for Wales, June, 1996. Whoever said that grandiloquence went out with Milton?

13 John Sparkes in *The Hire*, 5 February 1993, p. 12.

14 Johnson, *Life of Swift*.

15 Cf. Mark xiii. 11.

16 *The Approach to Total Quality Management Being Adopted at the University College of Swansea*, paper H.5536, 1994, para. 19.

17 Minutes of the First Meeting of the Academic Board Working Group on Modularisation of the University of Wales, held on 20 December 1991 ... via the Videoteaching Network (hereafter shortened to *Minutes*).

18 N.d.; ref. H.4491/HLM/LP.

19 *Rush Rhees on Religion and Philosophy*, ed. D. Z. Phillips, Cambridge University Press, 1997, Introduction, p. xi.

20 3 October 1994.

21 Colin to Jim, 8 June 1992; passed on to me by Jim.

22 *Ibid.*

23 *The Hire*, 2 July 1993, p. 4.

24 *The Times*, 27 May 1994. *The Times* thinks that this produces an 'intelligent competitiveness' that 'reflects a new and invigorating mood in British universities'.

25 The methods-only semi-fiction presumably explains why Modern Languages at Northumbria got 23 out of 24 for teaching but at Oxford only 21. Northumbria (one of whose slogans used to be—and perhaps still is—'French for Export') must teach French for business better than Oxford teaches French for education.

26 Cf. above, 'Teaching', p. 90.

27 October 1996—all departmental grant allocations reduced by 15 per cent, etc, five paragraphs of emergency cuts .... .

28 See note 16 above to p. 95.

29 Cf. 'Management control is formalised at all levels and is regulated by cascading limits of authority.' (Tesco plc Annual Accounts 1997, 'Policies and Procedures', 'Corporate Governance', p. 2.) Sell.

30 A. M. D. Armitage, letter in *The Hire*, 5 February 1993.

31 W. A. Hart, 'The Qualitymongers', *Journal of Philosophy of Education*, vol. 31, no. 2, 1997, p. 299.

32 I should no doubt have consulted the experts. 'Quality is high on the management agenda in education today' and so a specialist magazine quickly materialized, *Quality Assurance in Education*. By subscribing, 'you can keep abreast of current questions such as 'what is the relationship between Total Quality Management and quality assurance?' But you are more likely to get an answer to 'what are the costs of non-conformance?' for, as we were warned, 'Those institutions which fail to demonstrate a commitment to, and a strategy for, the management and development of quality are likely to be penalized, in a number of ways.'

33 *The Financial Times*, 4 December 1996.

34 Counsellors have to help students with private problems including the ones thrust upon them by modern life, but without any authority and without any principles. This is responsibility without power. All the counsellor has to fall back on is the aim of getting the student graduated: the functioning of the system is the only available criterion. In one institution not long ago students who wished to withdraw were routinely referred to a psychiatrist. (And, weren't there reports in the papers a year or two ago of some American research which showed that counselling did more harm than good?)

35 Cf. Ian Robinson, *The English Prophets*, 2001, Ch. 8.

36 *R.U.R.*, a play by Karel Capek about robots who destroy their human masters.

37 Principal's Address to the Court of Governors, *Newyddion* 331, 3 December 1987.

38 Circular from the Principal of University College, Swansea, 7 December 1987.

39 *The Universities We Need*, p. 165.

40 Academic libraries habitually discard books that have not been borrowed for a few years. If this had been the practice in the Middle Ages, Old English poetry would not have survived.

41 M. E. Braddon, *The Fatal Three*, 1888, repr. Stroud, 1997, p. 301.

42 Pope, 'Epistle to Burlington', pp. 134–8.

43 *Past and Present*, Book III, Ch. XII.

INTRODUCTION TO PART IV

1 'Why I'm fighting the A-level Cause', *The Daily Telegraph*, 12 November 1993.
2 *Past and Present*, Book I, Ch. IV.

CHAPTER 7

1 The basis of this account is a report I wrote to the board as the last of my duties as an assistant examiner. Though I asked for a reply I got nothing that could be called one—except that I had been inconsistent and lenient, and wouldn't be required as an examiner again.
2 GCE Advanced Supplementary and Advanced Level Examinations: Quality and Standards 1993, HMSO, £3.50.
3 These predict A-level grades from GCSE: schools take the credit for any 'value added' and may expect to be punished for any value lost, though how the schools are supposed to prevent many young people going to the bad by the age-old paths such as drink, with consequent academic effects, who knows?
4 For my reasons for thinking this a very good thing see Ian Robinson, 'UCCA to What?', *The Use of English*, 34/3, 1983.
5 p. 41.
6 OCR (Oxford and Cambridge and RSA) 'recognising achievement'. *English Literature: Approved Specifications for Teaching from September 2000*, p. 29. Should not academic authorities resist the mania for 'tab-lines'? Another board is Edexcel ('Success through qualifications'). Does it inspire confidence in their examining standards?
7 p. iv.
8 Ian Robinson, *The English Prophets*, Edgeways Books, 2001.
9 'Gender', a term in grammar, is always misused by theorists to mean 'sexuality'; but not of the kind the young folk may be expected to be interested in. The invitation will be to contemplate and disapprove of the subjection of women to men in the ages of Chaucer (e.g. the Wyf of Bath) or Queen Elizabeth or Queen Victoria.
10 If this can be done at all it is obviously postgraduate stuff for graduates well read in both literature and psychoanalysis.
11 Baroness Blackstone, Higher Education Minister and former Master of Birkbeck College, reported in *The Financial Times*, 3 October 1998.
12 *Ibid.*

CHAPTER 8

1 *'My Native English'*, eds Roger Knight and Ian Robinson, 1988, p. 157.
2 This was not the external who objected to a question of mine, 'Can one assume a consensus on what "poetic" means?' But if not what is our subject?
3 Cf. 'False Prophets' in *The English Prophets*, 2001.
4 Steven Vine, 'Crypts of Identity', *English* [the quarterly of the English Association], Autumn, 1999, p. 171. He is quoting Stevie Davies.
5 p. 172.

6 The content of at least some of these postgraduate courses is either identical with or less demanding than that of undergraduate courses, and their subject matter very elastic. In my own department, quite on Eagletonian lines, a whole literature was invented for the sake of having an MA in it, and you can become a *Magister* in this literature in twelve months flat, that is to say, three times quicker than it is possible to become a bachelor in English Language and Literature. This is 'the non-English anglophone literature of twentieth-century Wales', as the Swansea self-assessment document hopefully put it—asking us to believe in something that uses the sounds (and also, as a matter of fact, all the other features) of a particular language without being in it.

CHAPTER 9

1 *Apologie for Poetrie*, ed. Churton Collins, Oxford, 1907, repr. 1955, p. 12.
2 'Inaugural', *On the Art of Writing*, Cambridge University Press, 1916, repr. 1925, p. 10.
3 *Of Education*, p. 2; Prose Works II, facsimile edn, Menston 1968.
4 p. 402.
5 p. 441.
6 F. R. Leavis, *English Literature in Our Time and the University*, 1969, p. 3.
7 Cf. Theodora Gay Scutt, *Cuckoo in the Powys Nest*, Brynmill Press, 2000.
8 *Nicomachean Ethics.*
9 The new university naturally doesn't see it like that. Newcastle, for instance, has, for some years, felt perfectly well able to afford the loss of Philosophy.
10 Emma-Lou Montgomery, 'Bob Dylan? He's just as good as Keats', *The Daily Telegraph*, 27 March 1998. Does Charles Moore edit any of this newspaper apart from the editorial page and the one facing it?
11 *The French Revolution*, Boston, Mass., 1884, vol. I, p. 16.
12 *Shooting Niagara: and After?*, ed. cit., pp. 316, 317.

AN ANECDOTE OF INSTITUTIONAL LIFE

1 From the building of the 'Mundane Shell' in *Vala, or the Four Zoas* ('Night the Second'), William Blake: *The Complete Poems*, ed. Alicia Ostriker, 1977, p. 312.

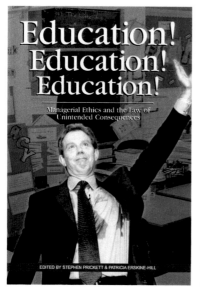

Education! Education! Education!

Managerial ethics and the law of unintended consequences

Edited by Stephen Prickett

200 pp., £14.95, 0907845 363 (pbk)

The essays in this book criticise the new positivism in education policy, whereby education is systematically reduced to those things that can be measured by so-called 'objective' tests. Curricula in primary and secondary schools have been narrowed with an emphasis on measurable results in the 3 R's and the 'quality' of university departments is now assessed by managerial exercises based on commercial audit practice. As a result, the traditional notion of liberal arts education has been replaced by utilitarian productivity indices.

Contributors include Libby Purves, Evan Harris, Archbishop Rowan Williams, Roger Scruton, Robert Grant, Bruce Charlton and Anthony Smith.
Stephen Prickett is Professor of English at Duke University.

Universities: The Recovery of an Idea

Gordon Graham

136 pp., £8.95, 0907845 371 (pbk)

Research assessment exercises, teaching quality assessment, line management, staff appraisal, student course evaluation, modularization, student fees — these are all names of innovations (and problems) — in modern British universities. How far do they reflect a more conscientious approach to the effective promotion of higher education, and how far do they constitute a significant departure from traditional academic concerns and values? Using some themes of Cardinal Newman's classic *The Idea of a University* as a springboard, this extended essay aims to address these questions.

Those who care about universities should thank Gordon Graham for doing what has needed doing so urgently (Philosophy)

Gordon Graham is Regius Professor of Moral Philosophy at the University of Aberdeen and a Fellow of the Royal Society of Edinburgh.

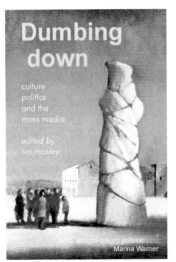

Dumbing Down: Culture, Politics and the Mass Media

Edited by Ivo Mosley

334 pp., £12.95, 0907845 657 (pbk.)

Never before in human history has so much cleverness been used to such stupid ends. The cleverness is in the creation and manipulation of markets, media and power; the stupid ends are in the destruction of community, responsibility, morality, art, religion and the natural world.

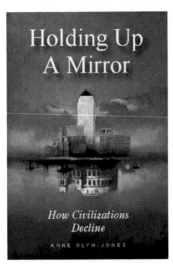

Holding Up A Mirror: How Civilizations Decline

Anne Glyn-Jones

652 pp., £14.95, 0907845 606 (pbk.)

The dynamic that promotes economic prosperity leads inexorably to the destruction of the very security and artistic achievement on which civilizations rest their claim. This book argues that the growth of prosperity is driven largely by the conviction that the material world alone constitutes true 'reality'. Yet that same dynamic undermines the authority of moral standards and leads to social and cultural disintegration.

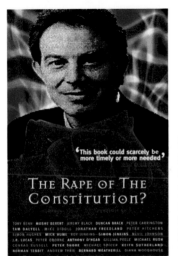

The Rape of the Constitution?

Edited by Keith Sutherland
Foreword by Michael Beloff QC

384 pp., £12.95, 0907845 703 (pbk.)

Lord Hailsham once remarked that if you removed a brick from the wall of the British Constitution, the building was likely to collapse; yet New Labour has embarked on a path of rapid constitutional change with little apparent regard for the long-term consequences. Has the steady increase in executive power turned Bagehot's 'disguised republic' into an elective dictatorship?

sample chapters, reviews & TOCs:
www.imprint-academic.com/politics